ESSAYS ON LINCOLN'S FAITH AND POLITICS

Volume IV

Hans J. Morgenthau
David Hein

Edited by

Kenneth W. Thompson

UNIVERSITY
PRESS OF
AMERICA

LANHAM • NEW YORK • LONDON

Copyright © 1983 by
Matthew Morgenthau, Susanna Morgenthau and
Kenneth W. Thompson

University Press of America,™ Inc.

4720 Boston Way
Lanham, MD 20706

3 Henrietta Street
London WC2E 8LU England

Printed in the United States of America

Library of Congress Cataloging in Publication Data

Main entry under title:

Essays on Lincoln's faith and politics.

(American values projected abroad; v. 4)
Includes bibliographical references.
Contents: The mind of Abraham Lincoln/by Hans J.
Morgenthau—Lincoln's theology and political ethics/
by David Hein
1. Lincoln, Abraham, 1809-1865—Philosophy—Ad-
dresses, essays, lectures. 2. Lincoln, Abraham, 1809-
1865—Religion—Addresses, essays, lectures. 3. Lincoln,
Abraham, 1809-1865—Personality—Addresses, essays,
lectures. I. Thompson, Kenneth W., 1921-
II. Morgenthau, Hans Joachim, 1904-   . Mind of
Abraham Lincoln, 1983. III. Hein, David . Lincoln's
theology and political ethics. 1983 , IV. Series.
JX1417.A74 1982 vol. 4   303.4'8273s   83-6494
[E457.2]   [973.7'092'4]
ISBN 0-8191-3239-X
ISBN 0-8191-3240-3 (pbk.)

AMERICAN VALUES PROJECTED ABROAD

A SERIES FUNDED BY THE EXXON EDUCATION FOUNDATION

Vol. I   Western Heritage And American Values:
Law, Theology And History
By
Alberto Coll

Vol. II   Political Traditions And Contemporary Problems
Edited by
Kenneth W. Thompson

Vol. III   Institutions for Projecting American Values Abroad
Edited by
Kenneth W. Thompson

Vol. IV   Essays on Lincoln's Faith and Politics
By
Hans J. Morgenthau and David Hein
Edited by
Kenneth W. Thompson

DEDICATED

TO

THE MEMORY OF

HANS J. MORGENTHAU

TABLE OF CONTENTS

PART ONE
THE MIND OF ABRAHAM LINCOLN
by
Hans J. Morgenthau

PART TWO
LINCOLN'S THEOLOGY AND POLITICAL ETHICS
by
David Hein

(Part 1   Lincoln's Faith)

INTRODUCTION
by
KENNETH W. THOMPSON

To exclude Abraham Lincoln from a series on American values would be inconceivable. No American President has achieved greater clarity in laying down the underlying political and moral principles on which his policies and actions were based. We look back to his political rhetoric and policy statements for the model of the leader speaking in his time and for the ages. In a day when too many of the words which go out from high places are intended to obscure or mislead more than to educate, Lincoln's simple honesty and humility is the exception. He stands alone among American Presidents who thought clearly about political ethics.

Surprisingly, the number and quality of writings about Lincoln's political ethics and religious outlook leave ample opportunity for further thought and study. While historians have traced almost every step in Lincoln's personal and political life, they have shown less concern with his political and moral ideas. Religious writers have, for the most part, sought to demonstrate either that Lincoln was religious in the traditional sense of organized religion or that he was irreligious. Efforts have been made to prove the *direct* influence of religion in Lincoln's life or the absence of such a direct influence. The vast majority of treatises on Lincoln's political ethics have been written to praise or condemn him in terms of a particular author's current view of politics, religion, and morality.

The present volume of *Essays on Lincoln's Faith and Politics* proceeds along different lines. Its two contributors are a world-renowned political scientist and a young but rising scholar of religious history. Before his death in June of 1981, Hans J. Morgenthau had completed about one-third of a substantial essay on Lincoln. (Another two-thirds consisted largely of notes and quotations.) I know from long and repeated conversations with Professor Morgenthau how much this work

ix

had come to mean in his life. I promised him I would complete his unfinished work, and in doing so I have tried to retain the style and character of his writing.

Morgenthau had been determined to have Lincoln "speak for himself" because, as he frequently declared, "no one can improve on Lincoln's words." While I have remained faithful to Morgenthau's goal and have included most of the quotations, I have also edited rather severely some of the passages from Lincoln he had included in the last two-thirds of the manuscript. My hope is that I have retained the essence of Lincoln's views as Morgenthau sought to convey them.

If Professor Morgenthau approached Lincoln's view of ethics and religion from the vantage point of the political scientist and historian, David Hein has approached the study of Lincoln's faith as a theologian and religious historian. Professor Hein, who teaches courses on religion at James Madison University and English at the Blue Ridge School, is one of the most brilliant young scholars of religion in America. He holds the Ph.D. from the Department of Religious Studies at the University of Virginia and has studied at the University of Chicago as well as other universities here and abroad. Professor Hein, who was a nationally known student leader not too many years ago and who has written with force and power on the "honor system" in universities and colleges, combines practical and professional knowledge of political science and theory with early recognition as a leading American religious historian. I feel sure Professor Morgenthau would have been pleased to be associated with Professor Hein.

It is rare that a controversial subject such as Lincoln's religious faith and its relationship to his politics can be addressed by two highly qualified authorities from different disciplines. Yet no subject is more deserving of the most careful thought of our most serious thinkers. If Lincoln's religious and political ethics represent core values in the American political tradition, they merit collaborative study by the nation's best minds whether or not they agree throughout.

The Miller Center is proud in continuing the Exxon Series on American values to publish this fourth volume, perhaps the most distinguished in the series. We applaud the importance given to moral and political values in the program of the Exxon Educational Foundation. The Council of the Miller Center shares with Exxon Trustees and Officers a sense of the priority and emphasis which should be given such subjects. We hope that in publishing the final work of a great American political theorist and the early work of a young religious historian, we are making a valuable contribution to the understanding of American values and the living ideals of its sixteenth President.

PART ONE

THE MIND OF ABRAHAM LINCOLN: A STUDY IN DETACHMENT AND PRACTICALITY

by

HANS J. MORGENTHAU

Carl Schurz in a letter to
Theodore Petrasch Oct. 1864
You are underrating the President (Lincoln). I grant he lacks higher education and his manners are not in accord with European conceptions of the dignity of a chief magistrate. He is a well-developed child of nature and is not skilled in polite phrases and poses. But he is a man of profound feelings, correct and firm principles and incorruptible honesty. His motives are unquestionable, and he possesses to a remarkable degree the characteristic, God-given trait of this people, sound common sense.

On a day Nov. 7, 1972 where a man was elected as U.S. President with a slightly different character.

M.G.L.

I. THE NATURE OF GREATNESS

My interest in this study is not primarily historic. I am not interested in writing still another biography of Lincoln, and I am particularly not interested in the controversies which have arisen among historians about the personality, the policies, and the private life of Lincoln. For instance, it makes no difference to me whether or not Lincoln was formally engaged to Ann Rutledge. Nor am I interested in his marital life and, more particularly, in the character of Mrs. Lincoln. Least of all am I concerned with the antiquarian aspects of Lincoln's life and policies.

On a higher level of historic contemplation I do not intend to sit in judgment on Lincoln's policies. I have my doubts about the soundness of some of them both before and during the Civil War. But it makes no difference to me, within the context of this study, whether he was justified in dismissing General McClellan at the time he did or whether he should have done it before or not at all. To enter into the controversies on these and other issues is not the purpose of my study. For this reason, the study draws on primary sources, especially the *Collected Works of Abraham Lincoln,* edited by Roy P. Basler, and the major biographies, rather than the interpretative and polemical works.

What I am interested in is something which perhaps cannot be done at all in a literal sense but which can only be adumbrated. That is, to take hold of the greatness of Lincoln, of the specific qualities which make Lincoln the great and unique figure which folklore celebrates and history remembers. In other words, the question I am raising is, in what does the greatness of Lincoln consist? What are its elements? And how has that greatness manifested itself in his approach to himself, to his fellow man, to the world, and to America as a particular polity? Finally, how did it reveal itself in his dealing with the two fundamental issues he had to face: the preservation of the Union and the abolition of slavery?

The question before us, then, is, first of all, what is greatness in any man and, more particularly, what is greatness in a statesman? Emerson, in the essay on the "Uses of Great Men," defines a great man as: "He is great who is what he is from nature and never reminds us of others." In that sense, Babe Ruth was a great baseball player, Escoffier a great chef, Al Capone a great racketeer, and J. Pierpont Morgan a great banker. These men were "great" because they pushed one particular human faculty—physical prowess, culinary creativity, organization of crime, acquisition of money—to the utter limits of human potentiality. They developed one human faculty to perfection. But this is a limited greatness of a functional nature: a man is called "great" because he performs a particular function to perfection. There is a difference between a "great" baseball player, a "great" chef, a "great" racketeer, a "great" financier—and a "great" man.

Emerson points to that difference when he adds to the quoted definition of a "great" man: "But he must be related to us and our life receive from him some promise of explanation." That is to say, a "great" man—in contrast to a man performing a particular function greatly—is one who at least approaches perfection in certain qualities of mind, character, and action that illuminate the very nature of man. He not only illuminates the nature of man, but he also holds up a mirror to his aspirations, he demonstrates in actual experience how far great men can go and, hence, how much farther than he thought he could a man can go who aspires to be great. Great men, to quote Emerson again, "speak to our want." As greatness is the perfection of some human potentiality that is common to all of us, so the example of greatness tends to push us to the limits of our potentialities, however much they may fall short of greatness. Thus great men not only present the awesome and exhilarating spectacle of what men are capable of when they are great, but they also give us an inkling of what can become of us if we set our eyes on greatness.

In the light of these standards of greatness, Lincoln appears indeed as a great man and even, as we shall see, a man of unique greatness, combining within himself the perfection of human potentialities, to be found in such combination in no other man known to history. More specifically, Lincoln was a great statesman and uniquely so. History knows of other great statesmen, but none achieved that combination of perfected potentialities that Lincoln did.

If one then assumes Lincoln to have been endowed, as it were, by nature with the qualities of greatness, it is irrelevant whether or not his policies were sound, whether or not they were successful. Lessing said of Raphael that he would have been a great painter even if he had been born without hands. And so I would say that Lincoln would be a great man, endowed with the qualities of a great statesman, even if he had thoroughly failed in what he undertook as a practitioner of politics.

His greatness is independent of success and failure although his ultimate success and practical achievements together with his tragic life and end have clothed his greatness with the aura of myth. In consequence, the unadorned qualities of his greatness have tended to disappear or at least to become indistinct in the mist of mythological incense and the flames of partisan rancor. Most of the writers on Lincoln have come to worship or to denigrate, not to understand. "Myth both as lie and as poetry," observes R. P. Basler in the foreword to *The Collected Works of Abraham Lincoln,* "will continue to accumulate around the symbolic figure of a great man." This study endeavors to separate myth from reality. It tries to pierce the layers of myth and lies that have obscured and distorted the true nature of Lincoln's greatness.

To try to understand wherein the greatness of Lincoln consists is in itself an important intellectual task; it is a service to historic truth. But this understanding has an important practical effect, beyond the one already mentioned of expanding the reach of human potentialities. It has nothing to do with the greatness of the object but is a function of historic understanding as such. It is a function historic knowledge has performed since the beginning of history: to teach men what it means to be a man and how to act as one. Historic knowledge in this sense is the accumulated experience of the race chronologically presented and analytically transformed. Thus Lincoln can teach us not only by dint of his greatness but also because he stood and acted in the limelight of history. He could teach us, even if he had not been great, because of his historic visibility. He can teach us doubly because of his greatness.

Because he was a great man, he can make us aware of our own potential, if not for greatness, at least for growth. Because he was a visible actor on the stage of American history, his example can instruct us about acting on that stage. Because he was a hero of a drama whose stake was the very survival of the nation as conceived by the Founders, what he was and did carries a lesson for a generation which must again face the issues which are posed not by passing circumstances but by the very nature of the American polity as originally conceived.

II. RELIGION

The issue that precedes all others both in time and importance is that of religion. When we speak here of religion we have in mind not only membership in a particular religious organization or observance of religious practices or professions of faith in a particular religious dogma. What we have in mind is primarily a religious attitude that recognizes the insufficiency of man as a finite being and seeks to orientate itself through some transcendent guidance, so that man can come to terms with himself, his fellowmen, and the universe. Religion is here conceived as a universal human attitude, with which believers, atheists, and agnostics alike approach themselves, their fellowmen, and the universe and of which the historic religions, religious organizations, and religious observances are but particular manifestations.

Lincoln expressed himself infrequently in religious terms—aside from ceremonial occasions—and when he did it was in a detached, if not negative, manner. Very early in his life, in 1837, he wrote to his fiancee, Mary Owens, "I've never been to church yet, nor probably shall not be soon. I stay away because I am conscious I should not know how to behave myself."[1]

At the very beginning of his political career, he got into trouble about religion, and it appeared that he had to take a stand. When he ran for the Illinois legislature in 1843, he received criticism from both sides, from the opponents of the High Church and from that particular religious community. As he wrote to a friend, Martin S. Morris, "It would astonish if not amuse, the older citizens of your County who twelve years ago knew me as a strange(r), friendless, uneducated, penniless boy, working on a flat boat—at ten dollars per month—to learn that I have been put down here as the candidate of pride, wealth and aristocratic family distinction. Yet so chiefly it was."[2] [He had just married into an aristocratic Southern family.] "There was too the strangest combinations of church influence against me. Baker [his opponent] is a Campbellite, and therefore as I suppose, with few exceptions got all that church. My wife has some relatives in the Presbyterian and some in the Episcopal Churches and therefore, wherever it would tell, I was set down as either the one or the other, whilst it was every where contended that no christian ought to go for me, because I belonged to no church, was suspected of being a deist, and had talked about fighting a duel."[3] This is an objective, detached and slightly amused account of the actual situation, and Lincoln obviously did not find it necessary to clarify his own position by telling his friend which of these several allegations concerning his religious identification, which cover virtually the whole spectrum, is correct. He informs his friend of the different and mutually exclusive statements people make about his religious position, but he does not tell him what his position actually is.

But three years later when Lincoln ran again for the Illinois legislature, he was compelled to take a stand on the issue. He was frontally attacked by his opponent, Rev. Cartright, an itinerant preacher, on the ground that he had openly scoffed at Christianity. Lincoln answered the attack in a "Handbill Replying to Charges of Infidelity," which was distributed in the district and printed by the newspapers. I find it a most revealing document, that reads:

> . . . That I am not a member of any Christian Church, is true; but I have never denied the truth of the Scriptures; and I have never spoken with intentional disrespect of religion in general, or of any denomination of Christians in particular. It is true that in early life I was inclined to believe in what I understand is called the 'Doctrine of Necessity'—that is, that the human mind is impelled to action, or held in rest by some power, over which the mind itself has no control; and I have sometimes (with one, two or three, but never publicly) tried to maintain this opinion in argument. The habit of arguing thus however, I have, entirely left off for more than five years. And I add here, I have always understood the same opinion to be held by several of the Christian denominations. The foregoing, is the whole truth, briefly stated, in relation to myself, upon the subject.

Lincoln continued: "I do not think I could myself, be brought to support a man for office, whom I knew to be an open enemy of, and scoffer at, religion. Leaving the higher matter of eternal consequences, between him and his Maker, I still do not think any man has the right thus to insult the feelings, and injure the morals, of the community in which he may live. If, then, I was guilty of such conduct, I should blame no man who should condemn me for it; but I do blame those, whoever they may be, who falsely put such a charge in circulation against me."[4]

It can hardly be argued that this is a particularly fervent or even convincing profession of religious belief. Its deficiencies are particularly glaring if one considers that Lincoln was running for elective office in 1846 in a rural Illinois County in which opposition to religion was tantamount to political suicide and probably still is today. This is indeed one of Lincoln's arguments. I am not so stupid, he says, to appear as an enemy of, and scoffer at, religion in a community where religious feelings predominate. But this is primarily an argument from political expediency, not from religious conviction.

As concerns religious conviction, Lincoln's argument is both negative and defensive: he does not belong to a church; he has never denied the truth of the Scriptures; he has never spoken with "intentional" disrespect of religion, which leaves the possibility open that he might have done so unintentionally. He has expressed opinions at variance at least with the mainstream of the Christian faith, but only in the presence of no more than three people and not at all during the last five years.

What Lincoln's argument really amounts to is to say that his attitude toward religion is not as bad as it has been made out to be. But this statement, so vital for his political fortunes, contains not a single positive assertion of Lincoln's belief in the tenets of the Christian faith. Thus it is a testimony both to his indifference to religious dogma and organization and to his intellectual honesty. He told the people for whose votes he competed the truth and did not deign to play the role of the true believer and religious activist in order to gain votes.

In this context it is worthy of mention that in the printed record of Lincoln's writings the name of Christ appears only once and in a completely secular context at that. Lincoln wrote, as he did from time to time, a composition for his own use, describing his impression of Niagara Falls. And there he says: "When Columbus first sought this continent—when Christ suffered on the cross—when Moses led Israel through the Red Sea—nay, even, when Adam first came from the hand of his Maker—then as now, Niagara was roaring here."[5]

It is of deeper significance that Lincoln's most explicit acknowledgment of divine intervention in human affairs is contained in a letter which I consider as one of the two morally most dubious and hypocritical letters written by Lincoln. At the beginning of 1851, Lincoln was informed by three letters from relatives that his father was about to die. He replied only to the last one, remarking that he had not answered the other two on purpose because "I could write nothing that could do any good."[6] After explaining why he could not visit his father at that time he continues,

> I sincerely hope Father may yet recover his health; but at all events tell him to remember to call upon, and confide in, our great, and good, and merciful Maker; who will not turn away from him in any extremity. He notes the fall of a sparrow, and numbers the hairs of our heads; and He will not forget the dying man, who puts his trust in Him. Say to him that if we could meet now, it is doubtful whether it would not be more painful than pleasant; but that if it be his lot to go now, he will soon have a joyous [meeting] with many loved ones gone before; and where [the rest] of us, through the help of God, hope ere-long [to join] them.[7]

Anyone who has read all of Lincoln's published letters must be struck by the difference both in tone and in content between all the others and this one. Its tone changes from coldness to a religious fervor not to be found anywhere in Lincoln's writings. Even if one is reluctant to sit in moral judgment without full knowledge of the circumstances, one cannot but find extraordinary, especially in a man of Lincoln's compassion and moral sensitivity, this indifference in feeling and passivity in action in the face of one's father's approaching death. The fervent invocation of divine intervention, unique among Lincoln's utterances on religion, serves to compensate for the lack of filial love and even human feeling, similarly unique—with one exception—in Lincoln's writings. In other words, the expression of religious faith has the appearance of hypocrisy.

Yet while Lincoln was indifferent to religion as dogma and organization, he was profoundly and consistently aware of the existential human condition from which the religious impulse made rational in dogma and visible in organization, springs: the finiteness of man in knowledge and action. Man must act without knowing much of the present and anything of the future. He must act in the belief, which turns out to be an illusion, that he can mold events to his intention and purposes. In truth, as Lincoln put it on April 4, 1864: "I claim not to have controlled events, but confess plainly that events have controlled me."[8] Man is in the hands of a higher power, and it is an illusion to think that he, rather than that power, is in control.

The experience of insecurity and even powerlessness, while in apparent full control of the implements of power, is an experience common to all sane statesmen and military leaders. They are called upon to make decisions of the utmost gravity without adequate knowledge of their consequences. In order to withstand the pressures of their responsibilities, at odds with their ability to discharge them with confidence, and to be able to act at all, these leaders are in need of reassuring themselves that a higher power, however defined, will ultimately decide in their favor. That need for reassurance has throughout history manifested itself in different ways. Superstitions, such as astrology and the examination of the flights of birds and of the entrails of animals, have over long periods of history served to establish in the minds of the political actor the conviction that the act he was about to perform was in harmony with the design of the higher power. The search for, and the assurance of, divine inspiration and the invocation of divine support have performed a similar function. On the eve of the Battle of Naseby, Cromwell wrote that when he arrived on the field of battle, he prayed, God smiled at him, and he gave the order to attack.

Lincoln's approach to the problem was different. As concerns his ability to know the designs of the higher power, he was thoroughly skeptical. As concerns his ability to influence those designs, he was thoroughly fatalistic.

Sometimes the expression of his skepticism was cautious, sometimes it was blunt. On November 15, 1861, the historian George Bancroft wrote him a letter whose last paragraph reads as follows: "Your administration has fallen upon times which should be remembered as long as human events find a record. I sincerely wish to you the glory of perfect success. Civil War is the instrument of Divine Providence to root out social slavery; posterity will not be satisfied with the result, unless the consequences of the war shall effect an increase of free states. This is the universal expectation and hope of men of all parties."[9] Lincoln's reply is completely non-committal: "The main thought in the closing paragraph of your letter is one which does not escape my attention, and with which I must deal in all due caution and with the best judgment I can bring to it."[10]

More explicitly negative is the answer he gives on September 13, 1862 to the *Emancipation Memorial Presented by Chicago Christians of All Denominations:*

> The subject presented in the memorial is one upon which I have thought much for weeks past and I might even say for months. I am approached with the most opposite opinions and advice and that by religious men, who are equally certain that they represent the Divine will. I am sure that either the one or the other class is mistaken in that belief and perhaps in some respects both. I hope it

will not be irreverent for me to say that if it is probable that God would reveal his will to others, on a point so connected with my duty, it might be supposed he would reveal it directly to me; for, unless I am more deceived in myself than I often am, it is my earnest desire to know the will of Providence in this matter. *And if I can learn what it is I will do it!* These are not, however, the days of miracles, and I suppose it will be granted that I am not to expect a direct revelation. I must study the plain physical facts of the case, ascertain what is possible and learn what appears to be wise and right.[11]

This statement is obviously an elaboration of a private *Meditation on the Divine Will* written at the beginning of the same month: "In great contests each party claims to act in accordance with the will of God. Both *may* be, and one *must* be wrong. God can not be *for,* and *against* the same thing at the same time."[12]

The same thought is reflected in the Second Inaugural Address with reference to the two parties in the Civil War: "Both read the same Bible, and pray to the same God; and each invokes His aid against the other. It may seem strange that any men should dare to ask a just God's assistance in wringing their bread from the sweat of other men's faces; but let us judge not that we be not judged. The prayers of both could not be answered; that of neither has been answered fully."[13]

Even more cautious and ironic, unmasking religious claims on behalf of slavery as ideologies of self-interest, is the *Fragment On Pro-Slavery Theology* of October 1, 1858, another of those compositions Lincoln wrote for his own edification: "The sum of pro-slavery theology seems to be this: 'Slavery is not universally *right,* nor yet universally *wrong;* it is better for *some* people to be slaves; and, in such cases, it is the Will of God that they be such.'"

He added:

Certainly there is no contending against the Will of God; but still there is some difficulty in ascertaining and applying it, to particular cases. For instance we will suppose the Rev. Dr. Ross has a slave named Sambo, and the question is 'Is it the Will of God that Sambo shall remain a slave, or be set free?' The Almighty gives no audible answer to the question, and his revelation—the Bible— gives none—or, at most, none but such as admits of a squabble, as to its meaning. No one thinks of asking Sambo's opinion on it. So, at last, it comes to this, that Dr. Ross is to decide the question. And while he consider[s] it, he sits in the shade, with gloves on his hands, and subsists on the bread that Sambo is earning in the burning sun. If he decides that God wills Sambo to continue a slave, he thereby retains his own comfortable position; but if he decides that God wills Sambo to be free, he thereby has to walk out of the shade, throw off his gloves, and delve for his own bread. Will Dr. Ross be activated by that perfect impartiality, which has ever been considered most favorable to correct decisions? But slavery is good for some people!!! As a good thing, slavery is strikingly peculiar in this, that it is the only good thing which no man ever seeks the good of, for *himself*.

Nonsense! wolves devouring lambs not because it is good for their own greedy maws, but because it [is] good for the lambs!!![14]

In a similar negative vein, as concerns the invocation of religion for personal ends, is the record of an interview which Lincoln wrote down afterwards again for his personal use. A woman comes to him and asks for the release of her husband from jail on the ground that he was a religious man." Lincoln ordered the release of the prisoner and then said to the petitioner: 'You say your husband is a religious man; tell him when you meet him, that I say I am not much of a judge of religion, but that, in my opinion, the religion that sets men to rebel and fight against their government, because, as they think, that government does not sufficiently help *some* men to eat their bread on the sweat of *other* men's faces, is not the sort of religion upon which people can get to heaven!'"[15]

However, here as elsewhere, Lincoln's skepticism as to the human ability to know the divine design was qualified by his resolution to preserve the Union and by his moral opposition to slavery. When he was presented on June 2, 1863, by members of the Presbyterian General Assembly with resolutions supporting the government, he replied:

It has been my happiness to receive testimonies of a similar nature, from I believe, all denominations of Christians. They are all loyal, but perhaps not in the same degree, or in the same num-bers; but I think they all claim to be loyal. This to me is most gratifying, because from the beginning I saw that the issues of our great struggle depended on the Divine interposition and favor. If we had that, all would be well. . . . In every case, and at all hazards, the Government must be perpetuated. Relying, as I do, upon the Almighty Power, and encouraged as I am by these reso-lutions which you have just read, with the support which I receive from Christian men, I shall not hesitate to use all the means at my control to secure the termination of this rebellion, and will hope for success.[16]

Thus Lincoln assumed that whatever else God wills he cannot will slavery and the destruction of America. The same conviction was most forcefully expressed in the Second Inaugural Address: "If we shall suppose that American Slavery is one of those offences which, in the providence of God, must needs come, but which, having continued through His appointed time, He now wills to remove, and that He gives to both North and South, this terrible war, as the woe due to those by whom the offence came, shall we discern therein any departure from those divine attributes which the believers in a Living God always ascribe to Him?"[17]

This address, containing both expressions of Lincoln's skepticism and religious condemnation of slavery, also expresses Lincoln's predominant attitude toward divine providence: fatalism: "Fondly do we hope—fervently do we pray—that this mighty scourge of war may speedily pass away. Yet, if God wills that it continue, until all the wealth piled by the bond-man's two hundred and fifty years of unrequited toil shall be sunk, and until every drop of blood drawn with the lash, shall be paid by another drawn with the sword, as was said three thousand years ago, so still it must be said the judgments of the Lord, are true and righteous altogether."[18]

This fatalistic reliance upon the will of an inaccessible God appears time and again in Lincoln's utterances. For instance on October 24, 1863, he addressed the Baltimore Presbyterian Synod saying: "I have often wished that I was a more devout man than I am. Nevertheless, amid the greatest difficulties of my Administration, when I could not see any other resort, I would place my whole reliance in God, knowing that all would go well, and that He would decide for the right."[19]

This identification of his own position with the will of God, unknown and unknowable, became more pronounced as the Civil War wore on without decision, a bloody stalemate seemingly without end. He argued with himself that these tribulations were not his personal responsibility, but were the will of God. Thus he wrote to a Quaker lady on October 26, 1862:

We are indeed going through a great trial—a fiery trial. In the very responsible position in which I happen to be placed, being a humble instrument in the hands of our Heavenly Father, as I am, and as we all are, to work out his great purposes, I have desired that all my works and acts may be according to his will, and that it might be so, I have sought his aid—but if after endeavoring to do my best in the light which he affords me, I find my efforts fail, I must believe that for some purpose unknown to me, He wills it otherwise. If I had had my way, this war would never have been commenced; If I had been allowed my way this war would have been ended before this, but we find it still continues; and we must believe that He permits it for some wise purpose of his own, mysterious and unknown to us; and though with our limited under-standings we may not be able to comprehend it, yet we cannot but believe, that he who made the world still governs it.[20]

Almost two years later, on September 4, 1864, he elaborated his position in a letter to the same lady:

The purposes of the Almighty are perfect, and must prevail, though we erring mortals may fail to accurately perceive them in advance. We hoped for a happy termination of this terrible war long before this; but God knows best, and has ruled otherwise. We shall yet acknowledge His wisdom and our own error therein. Meanwhile we must work earnestly in the best light He gives us, trusting that so working still conduces to the great ends He or-dains. Surely He intends some great good to follow this mighty convulsion, which no mortal could make, and no mortal could stay.[21]

In his *Meditation on the Divine Will,* a short composition for his own use, he wrote on September 2, 1862:

In the present civil war it is quite possible that God's purpose is something different from the purpose of either party—and yet the human instrumentalities, working just as they do, are of the best adaptation to effect His purpose. I am almost ready to say this is probably true—that God wills this contest, and wills that it shall not end yet. By his mere quiet power, on the minds of the now contestants, He could have either *saved* or *destroyed* the Union without a human contest. Yet the contest began. And having be-gun He could give the final victory to either side any day. Yet the contest proceeds.[22]

In a similar vein he wrote to a journalist on April 4, 1864: "Now, at the end of three years' struggle the nation's condition is not what either party, or any man devised, or expected. God alone can claim it.

Whither it is tending seems plain. If God now wills the removal of a great wrong, and wills also that we of the North as well as you of the South, shall pay fairly for our complicity in that wrong, impartial history will find therein new cause to attest and revere the justice and goodness of God."[23] The same fatalism is even more strongly expressed shortly before his death. He wrote on March 20, 1865: "Fondly do we hope—fervently do we pray—that this mighty scourge of war may speedily pass away. Yet, if God wills that it continue until all the wealth piled by the bondman's two hundred and fifty years of unrequited toil shall be sunk, and until every drop of blood drawn with the lash shall be paid by another drawn with the sword, as was said three thousand years ago, so still it must be said: 'The judgments of the Lord are true, and righteous altogether.' "[24]

Skepticism and fatalism, then, are the dominant moods of Lincoln's religiosity. References to "God," "Almighty God," "the Lord," "the Savior," "Providence" appear routine and add nothing to the substance of Lincoln's religiosity. It is worthy of note, whatever the significance, that the Gettysburg Address as prepared by Lincoln did not contain the words "under God." Lincoln added them when he spoke, and they are in all of Lincoln's later revisions.[25]

Similarly, the frequent references to biblical persons and events in Lincoln's utterances are very likely without religious significance. They are made for the purpose of literary illustration, sometimes with ironic effect. Thus during the presidential election contest of 1864, the supporters of Frémont tried to split the Republican Party by calling a convention at Cleveland, one week before the regular Republican Convention was scheduled to meet. While the promoters expected thousands to attend, only 400 came, less than 200 from out of town. Lincoln, when informed of the fiasco, reached for his Bible, leafed through it to I Samuel XXII, 2, and read: "And every one that was in distress, and every one that was in debt, and every one that was discontented, gathered themselves unto him; and he became a captain over them: and there were with him about four hundred men."[26]

Lincoln tried to reconcile himself to the responsibility he bore for the Civil War—the terrible suffering it caused, the enormous destruction it wrought, the threat it entailed for the very existence of the nation and the risk of failure, ever present virtually until the end of his life—by his belief in a higher power whose designs are inscrutable and who guides the affairs of men toward unknown ends. Thus the Civil War with all the evil that it entailed was really the responsibility of a higher power, whose instrument he was. It willed the war and would end it one way or other when it willed that it end. The most mortal men, such as

Lincoln, could do was to work to the best of their ability toward the end which they expected to be the design of the higher power: the restoration of the Union. God governs the world according to his own designs which can neither be known nor influenced by man. Thus in one sense man is a forlorn actor on the stage of the world; for he does not know the nature of the plot and the outcome of the play written by an inaccessible author. But he is also a confident and self-sufficient actor; for he knows that there is a script, however unknown and unknowable its content, and he can do no more than act out what he believes the script to require.

III. DETACHMENT

Lincoln's detachment from the higher power corresponds to, and in a profound sense is of one piece with, his detachment from himself and from the human world around him. Unaware of any particular, favored relationship to the higher power and unable to invoke the higher power on behalf of a particular position or action, he faced himself and the world alone, beholding himself and the world with complete detachment, undistorted by the belief in divine favors which might have aroused his intellect and emotions to partisanship. He is in a profound sense alone, alone under the higher power with whom he cannot communicate and who does not communicate with him, alone with himself, alone with his fellowmen. Detached from the intellectual and emotional crutches which enable the common run of men to move around, Lincoln must rely upon his own inner intellectual and emotional resources, both engaged at times to the limits of human endurance. Nothing outside himself sustains him, except, as we have seen, his fatalism and, as we shall see, his faith in the unique worth of America.

Out of these resources Lincoln fashions four basic attitudes toward himself and the world: objectivity, humility, humor, and compassion. These attitudes are organically related to one another, stemming as they do from the common source of detachment.

(1) LINCOLN'S OBJECTIVITY

Lincoln was first of all objective toward himself. He was able to look at himself as if he were another person, and to analyze himself not only without emotion but also with remarkable intellectual impartiality. Lincoln suffered at least three great emotional crises which brought him close to suicide. The first was the death of Ann Rutledge, which put him in such a state of depression that his friends watched over him twenty-four hours a day because they were afraid he would commit suicide. The second is the annulment of his engagement to Mary Todd, after which he wrote on January 23, 1841 in a letter to his friend John T. Stuart:

> I am now the most miserable man living. If what I feel were equally distributed to the whole human family, there would not be one cheerful face on the earth. Whether I shall ever be better I can not tell; I awfully forebode I shall not. To remain as I am is impossible; I must die or be better, it appears to me. The matter you speak of on my account, you may attend to as you say, unless you shall hear of my condition forbidding it. I say this, because I fear I shall be unable to attend to any business here, and a change of scene might help me. If I could be myself, I would rather remain at home with Judge Logan. I can write no more.[27]

Considering Lincoln's psychological situation, it is remarkable that he could, albeit not very profoundly, analyze his position at all and lay out the alternatives open to him.

Take another example, much less traumatic. Somebody paints a picture of him, when he was already in the last year of his presidency, and on December 30, 1864, he writes to the painter, "Your picture presented by Mr. Lutz is, in the main, very good. From a line immediately above the eye-brows, downward it appears to me perfect. Above such line I think it is not so good,—that is, while it gives perhaps a better fore-head, it is not quite true to the original. If you were present I could tell you wherein, but I can not well do so on paper. The next best thing I suppose would be to carefully study a photograph."[28] Those of us who have had their pictures painted and had some mixed reaction to them are not likely to write such an almost anatomical analysis of their own face, as it has been presented by someone else.

Lincoln was much interested in the theater, an interest that cost him his life. He received a volume on Shakespeare, written by an actor named James A. Hackett. Lincoln thanked him on August 17, 1863, in these words:

> For one of my age, I have seen very little of the drama. The first presentation of Falstaff I ever saw was yours here, last winter or spring. Perhaps the best compliment I can pay is to say, as I truly can, I am very anxious to see it again. Some of Shakespeare's plays I have never read; while others I have gone over perhaps as frequently as any unprofessional reader. Among the latter are *Lear, Richard Third, Henry Eighth, Hamlet,* and especially *Macbeth.* I think nothing equals *Macbeth.* It is wonderful. Unlike you

18

gentlemen of the profession, I think the soliloquy in Hamlet commencing 'O, my offence is rank' surpasses that commencing 'To be, or not to be.' But pardon this small attempt at criticism. I should like to hear you pronounce the opening speech of Richard the Third. Will you not soon visit Washington again? . . ."[29]

This letter was published first by Hackett for private circulation, then by the newspapers, and created a storm of ridicule. The newspapers scoffed at this uneducated man from the wilds of Kentucky who assumes to be able to judge Shakespeare. Mr. Hackett was, of course, embarrassed and wrote Lincoln a letter of apology. Here is Lincoln's answer of November 2, 1863, "My note to you I certainly did not expect to see in print; yet I have not been much shocked by the newspaper comments upon it. Those comments constitute a fair specimen of what has occurred to me through life. I have endured a great deal of ridicule without much malice; and have received a great deal of kindness, not quite free from ridicule. I am used to it."[30]

Most of us would be incensed that this personal letter was published at all, and we would also be incensed at the reception it received from the press. For Lincoln this is an event which really does not concern him, which really does not touch him as a person. He looks at it as though it had happened to someone else or did not happen at all.[31]

This uneducated man, who, in spite of no more than one year of formal schooling all told, was a master of the English language himself, did not hesitate to express his fascination with English literature with the same detachment from himself, i.e., the absence of self-consciousness about his lack of formal competence. This was the same attitude with which he approached all the more important issues of his life. He was able to establish the same kind of distance in the political sphere. He was elected to Congress in 1846 and wrote to his close friend Joshua F. Speed: "Being elected to Congress, though I am very grateful to our friends for having done it, has not pleased me as much as I expected."[32] When he competed for the Presidential nomination, he wrote to Senator Trumbull on April 29, 1860: "As you request, I will be entirely frank. The taste *is* in my mouth a little; and this, no doubt, disqualifies me, to some extent, to form correct opinions."[33] In other words, he recognized that the involvement of his self with itself, this lack of detachment from himself, detracted from his sound judgment. Thus he paid tribute to what was indeed his principal virtue, the source of all the others.

He arrived in Washington as President and the people serenaded him. What did he say to thank the serenaders? "I suppose that I may take this as a compliment paid to me, and as such please accept my thanks for it. I have reached the city of Washington under circumstances considerably differing from those under which any other man has ever reached it. I have reached it for the purpose of taking an official position amongst the people almost all of whom were opposed to me, and are yet opposed to me, as I suppose."[34]

Imagine the President, who has just been elected in the face of a threatening rebellion on behalf of slavery, coming into the District of Columbia where slavery is legal, and finding himself serenaded by the supporters of slavery in Washington. He does not try to gloss over that situation in order to obscure its absurdity. He does not offer any concessions, nor does he ask for any from his audience. Quite to the contrary, by defining the situation in all its unique starkness, he emphasizes its absurdity. He looks at himself, at the crowd, and their mutual relations and not only recognizes but also articulates his extraordinary position with complete objectivity: I am alone, you are all against me.

Then Lincoln waged a Civil War which saddled him with the almost crushing burden of its enormous bloodletting, its long-drawn-out inconclusiveness, and its domestic and international repercussions—all in good measure a result of the incompetence of his generals. On July 1st 1862, he called for 300,000 volunteers "so as to bring this unnecessary and injurious civil war to a speedy and satisfactory conclusion."[35]

Imagine any other President fighting a war widely regarded to be "unnecessary and injurious" and calling for volunteers to fight it. Would he not appeal to the people to fight "a necessary and beneficial war" in order to obtain the maximum response? Lincoln does not allow the objective expression of his judgment as to the merits of the war to be qualified by the practical need to induce volunteers to join the ranks.

It is that very same objectivity that allowed Lincoln to understand the position of the enemy and, hence, contemplate it with detachment rather than passion. The most profound manifestation of that objectivity is to be found in Lincoln's *Address at Sanitary Fair, Baltimore, Maryland* of April 18, 1864:

> The world has never had a good definition of the word liberty, and the American people, just now, are much in want of one. We all declare for liberty; but in using the same *word* we do not all mean the same *thing*. With some the word liberty may mean for each man to do as he pleases with himself, and the product of his labor; while with others the same word may mean for some men to do as they please with other men, and the product of other men's labor. Here are two, not only different, but incompatible things

called by the same name—liberty. And it follows that each of the things is, by the respective parties, called by two different and incompatible names—liberty and tyranny.

And Lincoln concluded: "The shepherd drives the wolves from the sheep's throat, for which the sheep thanks the shepherd as a *liberator,* while the wolf denounces him for the same act as the destroyer of liberty, especially as the sheep was a black one. Plainly the sheep and the wolf are not agreed upon a definition of the word liberty; and precisely the same difference prevails to-day among us human creatures, even in the North, and all professing to love liberty . . ."[36]

This utterance is remarkable first of all by its deep understanding of the relative nature of the concept of freedom, determined as it is by interest and power, and second, by the objective analysis of the political situation to which the concept is applied.

Political freedom, then, has two different and incompatible meanings according to whether we think of the holder or the subject of political power. Freedom for the holder of political power signifies the opportunity to exercise political domination; freedom for the subject means the absence of such domination. Not only are these two conceptions of freedom mutually exclusive in logic, but they are also incapable of coexisting in fact within any particular sphere of action. One can only be realized at the expense of the other, and the more there is of the one the less there is bound to be of the other.

It follows that universal and absolute freedom is a contradiction in terms. In the political realm, the freedom of one is always paid for by the lack of freedom of somebody else. The political master can have his freedom only at the price of the freedom of those who are subject to him; the latter can be free only if the master is made to sacrifice his freedom as a master.

In any given society not everyone can be as free as everyone else. Every society must decide for itself who shall have what freedom. The kind of freedom a particular society is able to realize in a particular period of its history, then, depends upon the kind of political order under which it lives. The nature of that particular order, in turn, is determined by the fundamental values with which that society identifies itself and which it attempts to realize through the medium of politics. In short, the kind of liberty a society enjoys is determined by the kind of political justice it seeks. Liberty cannot be defined without justice, and it can only be realized by a particular political order informed by a particular sense of justice.

All attempts at realizing freedom have throughout history derived from one of two incompatible conceptions of justice: one, minoritarian; the other, equalitarian.

The minoritarian conception of justice assumes that only a minority, determined by birth, supernatural charisma, or qualifications of achievement, is capable of finding and understanding the truth about matters political and of acting successfully on it. The majority, not so endowed, is subject to the will of the minority, both for its own sake and for the sake of the whole commonwealth. From Plato and Aristotle to the modern justifications of aristocratic and totalitarian government, the denial of political freedom for the majority has derived from a conception of political justice which limits to a minority the ability and, hence, the right to enjoy political freedom.

This conception determines not only the over-all character of political society but also the specific nature of its institutions. It claims for these institutions the attribute of freedom, if not in good faith, at least in good logic. To what Lincoln experienced in the controversies over slavery we can add our experiences with totalitarian arguments.

In order to appreciate fully Lincoln's objectivity in this disquisition on liberty, one must keep in mind that Lincoln was not preaching a sermon to a disinterested audience but that he was speaking as the head of a government that had embarked upon a civil war in defense of one particular concept of freedom. In spite of his position as the leading partisan of one concept of freedom, assigned to him by history, he looks at the philosophic and moral battlefield from what one might call a stratospheric point of view. He recognized the relative justice of each side and, at this point at least, refrains from passing judgment on the relative merits of the case. Again imagine a President of the United States during the First or Second World War or during the Vietnam War presenting to the public the relative philosophic and moral merits of the two positions at war and let it go at that!

Lincoln's objectivity in the historic contest in which he was engaged is matched by the detachment of his own person from the public controversies in which he was involved. While his political ambition was pronounced and his political acumen and his ability at political maneuver were outstanding, he would subordinate his personal welfare to the political cause he was fighting for. Observing that the masses of the people were concerned only about military success and remained indifferent towards the Negro, he remarked to William Ellery Channing and Moncure D. Conway: "We shall need all the anti-slavery feeling in the country and more; you can go home and try to bring the people to your views; and you may say anything you like about me, if that will help. Don't spare me!"[37]

22

Lincoln showed a similar detachment in a matter of much greater political importance for himself in his competition with Salmon P. Chase, Secretary of the Treasury, for the presidential nomination in 1864. Chase, whose ability was exceeded only by his ambition to be President, had the support of Senator Pomeroy, who had organized a committee of Chase's political friends and published a circular promoting Chase's candidacy and opposing Lincoln's renomination. Chase wrote Lincoln—contrary to fact—that he had had no knowledge of the circular before he saw it in print, and suggested his resignation if Lincoln should be dissatisfied with this "action or position." Here is the relevant passage of Lincoln's reply of February 29, 1864:

> My knowledge of Mr. Pomeroy's letter having been made *public* came to me only the day you wrote; but I had, in spite of myself, known of it's *existence* several days before. I have not yet read it, and I think I shall not. I was not shocked, or surprised by the appearance of the letter, because I had had knowledge of Mr. Pomeroy's Committee, and of secret issues which I supposed came from it, and of secret agents who I supposed were sent out by it, for several weeks. I have known just as little of these things as my own friends have allowed me to know. They bring the documents to me, but I do not read them—they tell me what they think fit to tell me, but I do not inquire for more. I fully concur with you that neither of us can be justly held responsible for what our respective friends may do without our instigation or countenance; and I assure you, as you have assured me, that no assault has been made upon you by my instigation, or with my countenance.
>
> Whether you shall remain at the head of the Treasury Department is a question which I will not allow myself to consider from any standpoint other than my judgment of the public service; and, in that view, I do not perceive occasion for a change.[38]

However, Chase's presidential ambitions proved to be incompatible with his presence in Lincoln's cabinet, and he resigned in June 1864. Yet Lincoln never relinquished his objectivity and later in the year nominated Chase for the position of Chief Justice of the United States. To criticism he replied: "Mr. Chase is a very able man. He is a very ambitious man and I think on the subject of the presidency a little insane. He has not always behaved very well lately and people say to me, 'Now is the time to *crush him out*.' Well, I'm not in favor of crushing anybody out! If there is anything that a man can do and do it well, I say let him do it. Give him a chance."[39]

The source of this personal detachment was a strength of personality which afforded Lincoln detachment and objectivity both with regard to persons and issues. Thus he could reply on October 5, 1863 to a radical delegation from Missouri and Kansas, pleading its case against the conservatives:

> One side ignored the *necessity,* and magnified the evils of the system; while the other ignored the evils, and magnified the necessity; and each bitterly assailed the motives of the other. I could not fail to see that the controversy enlarged in the same proportion as the professed Union-men there distinctly took sides in two opposing political parties. I exhausted my wits, and very nearly my patience also, in efforts to convince both that the evils they charged on each other, were inherent in the case, and could not be cured by giving either party a victory over the other. . . . I do not feel justified to enter upon the broad field you present in regard to the political differences between radicals and conservatives. From time to time I have done and said what appeared to me proper to do and say. The public knows it all. It obliges nobody to follow me, and I trust it obliges me to follow nobody. The radicals and conservatives, each agree with me in some things, and disagree in other. I could wish both to agree with me in all things; for then they would agree with each other, and would be too strong for any foe from any quarter. They, however, choose to do otherwise, and I do not question their right. I too shall do what seems to be my duty. I hold whoever commands in Missouri, or elsewhere, responsible to me, and not to either radicals or conservatives. It is my duty to hear all; but at last, I must within my sphere, judge what to do, and what to forbear.[40]

However, Lincoln's objectivity manifested itself most strikingly at the very beginning of his national political career in the congressional debates and votes on the Mexican War. Lincoln spoke repeatedly and sharply against the official version of the origins of the war and introduced and supported a number of resolutions putting the responsibility for the war on President Polk. That position was completely at odds with the opinion prevailing in his constituency; he was vehemently attacked as a modern Benedict Arnold, and it was widely expected that his political career would not extend beyond his first term in Congress. His personal and political friends expressed their misgivings in letters. Lincoln's replies consistently argued in favor of truth against expediency. Thus he wrote on February 1, 1848, to William H. Herndon:

> That vote affirms that the war was unnecessarily and unconstitutionally commenced by the President; and I will stake my life, that if you had been in my place, you would have voted just as I did. Would you have voted what you felt you knew to be a lie? I know you would not. Would you have gone out of the House— skulked the vote? I expect not. If you had skulked one vote, you would have had to skulk many more, before the end of the session. Richardson's resolutions, introduced before I made any move, or gave any vote upon the subject, make the direct question of the justice of the war; so that no man can be silent if he would. You are compelled to speak; and your only alternative is to tell the *truth* or tell a *lie*. I can not doubt which you would do.[41]

In a similar vein he wrote to Usher F. Linder on March 22, 1848: "Their very first act in congress was to present a preamble declaring that war existed by the act of Mexico, and the whigs were obliged to vote on it—and this policy is followed up by them; so that they are compelled to *speak* and their only option is whether they will, when they do speak, tell the *truth,* or tell a foul, villainous, and bloody falsehood."[42]

It was not only the truth about the Mexican War that concerned Lincoln but also its justice. The Reverend John M. Peck, a prominent Illinois clergyman, made an oration of which Lincoln had received a copy, in celebration of the victory of Buena Vista. In that oration, Peck declared: "In view of *all* the facts, the conviction to my mind is irresistible, that the Government of the United States committed no aggression on Mexico."[43] Without any visible compulsion Lincoln wrote the author on May 24, 1848, commenting on this particular passage:

> Not in view of *all* the facts. There are facts which you have kept out of view. It is a fact, that the United States Army, in marching to the Rio Grande, marched into a peaceful Mexican settlement, and frightened the inhabitants away from their homes and their growing crops.
>
> It is a fact, that Fort Brown, opposite Matamoras, was built by that army, within a Mexican cotten-field, on which, at the time the army reached it, a young cotten crop was growing and which crop was wholly destroyed, and the field itself greatly, and permanently injured, by ditches, embankments, and the like.

It is a fact, that when the Mexicans captured Capt. Thorton and his command, they found and captured them within another Mexican field.

Now I wish to bring these facts to your notice, and to ascertain what is the result of your reflection upon them. If you *deny* that they *are* facts, I think I can furnish proof which shall convince you that you are mistaken.

If you *admit* that they are facts, then I shall be obliged for a reference to any law of language, law of states, law of nations, law of morals, law of religion,—any law human or divine, in which an authority can be found for saying those facts constitute '*no aggression.*'

Possibly you consider those acts too small for notice. Would you venture to so consider them, had they been committed by any nation on earth, against the humblest of our people? I know you would not. Then I ask, is the precept 'Whatsoever ye would that men should do to you, do ye even so to them' obsolete?—of no force?—of no application?[14]

Lincoln's objectivity is a quality that manifests itself on all occasions small and large. Four examples, in ascending order of importance, will illustrate the pervasive character of that quality.

Lincoln's Postmaster General, Montgomery Blair, asked for the President's preference as to whether his brother, General Frank Blair, ought to occupy his seat in Congress or to remain in the field. Lincoln's advice is in a letter of November 2, 1863:

My wish, then, is compounded of what I believe will be best for the country, and best for him. And it is, that he will come here, put his military commission in my hands, take his seat, go into caucus with our friends, abide the nominations, help elect the nominees, and thus aid to organize a House of Representatives which will really support the government in the war. If the result shall be the election of himself as Speaker, let him serve in that position; if not, let him re-take his commission, and return to the Army. For the country this will heal a dangerous schism; for him, it will relieve from a dangerous position. By a misunderstanding, as I think he is in danger of being permanently separated from those with whom only he can ever have a real sympathy—the sincere opponents of slavery. It will be a mistake if he shall allow the provocations offered him by insincere time-servers, to drive him out of the house of his own building. He is young yet. He has abundant talent—quite enough to occupy all his time, without devoting any to temper. He is rising in military skill and usefulness. His recent appointment to the command of a corps, by one so competent to judge as Gen. Sherman, proves this. In that line he can serve both the country and himself more profitably than he could as a member of congress on the floor. The foregoing is what I would say, if Frank Blair were my brother instead of yours.[45]

After the Battle of Stone River, the Secretary of War telegraphed General Rosecrans: "Anything you and your command want you can have." The General thereupon submitted a list of requests which were not acted upon and complained to Lincoln. One of the complaints concerned the removal of Major Larned, which the General attributed to the hatred of Colonel Andrews. One of the requests was that Rosecrans' appointment as Major General, taking effect as of March 21, 1862, be predated to December 1861, so that he might outrank General Grant. Lincoln disposed of the complaint and the request on March 17, 1863 with these arguments:

And as to Gen. Andrews, I have, in another connection, felt a little agrieved, at what seemed to me, his implicit following the advice and suggestions of Major Larned—so ready are we all to cry out, and ascribe motives, when our own toes are pinched.

Now, as to your request that your Commission should date from December 1861. Of course you expected to *gain* something by this; but you should remember that precisely so much as you should gain by it others would lose by it. If the thing you sought had been exclusively ours, we would have given it cheerfully; but being the right of other men, we having a merely arbitrary power over it, the taking it from them and giving it to you, became a more delicate matter, and more deserving of consideration. Truth to speak, I do not appreciate this matter of rank on paper, as you officers do. The world will not forget that you fought the battle of "Stone River" and it will never care a fig whether you rank Gen. Grant on paper, or he so, ranks you.[46]

During the early phase of the Civil War, Union public opinion was sharply divided between the supporters of Secretary of War Stanton and General McClellan in assessing blame for the failures and defeats of the Union armies. Lincoln took a position in this controversy on August 6, 1862 in a meeting of citizens in front of the Capitol:

I am very little inclined on any occasion to say anything unless I hope to produce some good by it. The only thing I think of just now not likely to be better said by some one else, is *a matter in which we have heard some other persons blamed for what I did myself.* There has been a very wide-spread attempt to have a quarrel between Gen. McClellan and the Secretary of War. *Now, I occupy a position that enables me to observe, at least, these two gentlemen are not nearly so deep in the quarrel as some pretending to be their friends.* Gen. McClellan's attitude is such that, in the very selfishness of his nature, he cannot but wish to be successful, and I hope he will—and the Secretary of War is in precisely the same situation. If the military commanders in the field cannot be successful, not only the Secretary of War, but myself for the time being the master of them both, cannot be but failures. I know Gen. McClellan wishes to be successful, and I know he does not wish it any more than the Secretary of War for him, and both of them together no more than I wish it. Sometimes we have a dispute about how many men Gen. McClellan has had, and those who would disparage him say that he has had a very large number, and those who would disparage the Secretary of War insist that Gen. McClellan has had a very small number. The basis for this is, *there is always a wide difference, and on this occasion, perhaps, a wider one between the grand total on McClellan's rolls and the men actually fit for duty;* and those who would disparage him talk of the grand total on paper, and those who would disparage the Secretary of War talk of those at present fit for duty. Gen. McClellan *has sometimes asked for things that the Secretary of War did not give him.* Gen. McClellan is not to blame for asking what he wanted and needed, and the Secretary of War *is not to blame for not giving when he had none to give.* And I say here, as far as I know, *the Secretary of War has withheld no one thing at any time in my power to give him.* I have no accusation against him. *I believe he is a brave and able man,* and I stand here, as justice requires me to do, *to take upon myself what has been charged on the Secretary of War, as withholding from him.*[47]

In order to appreciate fully the objectivity of this statement one must remember how sorely Lincoln was tried both by the actions and manner of these two subordinates, to the point that soon afterwards he felt he had to relieve McClellan of his command.

When changes in the military command were not followed by changes in the adverse fortunes of war, Carl Schurz, the leader of the

German Americans and at the time Brigadier General of Volunteers, wrote Lincoln a letter, criticizing his conduct of the war. Here are the relevant passages of Lincoln's reply of November 24, 1862:

> I understand you *now* to be willing to accept the help of men, who are not republicans, provided they have heart in it. Agreed. I want no others. But who is to be the judge of hearts, or of heart in it? If I must discard my own judgment, and take yours, I must also take that of others; and by the time I should reject all I should be advised to reject, I should have none left, republicans, or others— not even yourself. For, be assured, my dear sir, there are men who have heart in it that think you are performing your part as poorly as you think I am performing mine. I certainly have been dissatisfied with the slowness of Buell and McClellan; but before I relieved them I had greater fears I should not find successors to them, who would do better; and I am sorry to add, that I have seen little since to relieve those fears. I do not clearly see the prospect of any more rapid movements. I fear we shall at last find out that the difficulty is in our case, rather than in particular generals. I wish to disparage no one—certainly not those who sympathize with me; but I must say I need success more than I need sympathy, and that I have not seen the so much greater evidence of getting success from my sympathizers, than from those who are denounced as the contrary. It does seem to me that in the field the two classes have been very much alike, in what they have done, and what they have failed to do. In sealing their faith with their blood, Baker, an(d) Lyon, and Bohlen, and Richardson, republicans, did all that men could do; but did they any more than Kearney, and Stevens, and Reno, and Mansfield, none of whom were republicans, and some, at least of whom, have been bitterly, and repeatedly, denounced to me as secession sympathizers? I will not perform the ungrateful task of comparing cases of failure.[48]

(2) LINCOLN'S HUMILITY

The same disposition of detachment that manifests itself as objectivity in relations between the self and the things and persons of the outside world becomes humility when applied to the self, that is, when the self looks at itself, its appearance, its qualities, its actions in comparison with others. Most men are proud of themselves when they behold the results of that self-inspection and comparison. Their ego inflates their own merits at the expense of others. They are proud of themselves and unjust towards others. It is the rare humble man who sees himself as he ought to be seen in view of his objective merits. He neither yields to the inflated claims of his ego, nor does he make concessions to the adulation and denigrations of others. He is as objective towards himself as he is towards the outside world. His humility is the absence of the pride with which most men look at themselves in comparison with others, elevating themselves at the expense of others.

In Lincoln, humility appears in six different manifestations: as modesty, self-disparagement, admission of ignorance, admission of error, recognition of defects and fatalism.

Lincoln says of himself in his address to the New York Legislature of February 18, 1861: "It is true that while I hold myself without mock modesty, the humblest of all individuals that have ever been elevated to the Presidency, I have a more difficult task to perform than any one of them."[49] While many of these public expressions of modesty contain no doubt at least an element of insincerity as one would expect of a politician, there are many others where circumstances point to the absence of dissimulation. The autobiography which Lincoln wrote in 1858 for the Dictionary of Congress covers four printed lines. When the Republicans began to think of Lincoln as a possible Presidential candidate, Jesse W. Fell, who was Adlai Stevenson's great-grandfather, asked Lincoln for an autobiographical sketch. The sketch itself is a monument to Lincoln's detachment manifesting itself both in complete objectivity and modesty, aside from being a classic of English exposition and a moving description of Lincoln's early circumstances. Let me only quote what Lincoln says about his education: "Of course when I came of age I did not know much. Still somehow, I could read, write, and cipher to the Rule of Three; but that was all. I have not been to school since. The little advance I now have upon this store of education, I have picked up from time to time under the pressure of necessity."[50] The accompanying letter of December 20, 1859 makes explicit the modesty of the sketch: "Herewith is a little sketch, as you requested. There is not much of it, for the reason, I suppose, that there is not much of me.

"If any thing be made out of it, I wish it to be modest, and not to go beyond the material. If it were thought necessary to incorporate any thing from any of my speeches, I suppose there would be no objection. Of course it must not appear to have been written by myself."[51]

During the election campaign of 1860, a judge asked permission to dedicate a book of his to Lincoln. Lincoln replied on October 13, 1860: "Gratefully accepting the proffered honor, I give the leave, begging only that the inscription may be in modest terms, not representing me as a man of great learning, or a very extraordinary one in any respect."[52]

When the returns of the Second Presidential Election of 1864 showed Lincoln's decisive victory over McClellan, Lincoln dictated on November 9, 1864 the following dispatch to Dr. Anson G. Henry: "With returns and States of which are confident, the re-election of the President is considered certain, while it is not certain that McClellan has carried any State, though the chances are that he has carried New Jersey and Kentucky."[53] His secretary, Noah Brooks, reports: "When I had written the despatch at the President's dictation, I passed it to him for his signature; but he declined to 'blow his own horn,' as he expressed it, and said: 'You sign the message, and I will send it.' "[54] When the Secretary of War suggests that the Adjutant General be in regular attendance upon him Lincoln replies on January 22, 1862: "On reflection I think it will not do as a rule for the Adjutant General to attend me wherever I go; not that I have any objection to his presence, but that it would be an uncompensating incumbrance both to him and me. When it shall occur to me to go anywhere, I wish to be free to go at once, and not to have to notify the Adjutant General, and wait till he can get ready. It is better too, for the public service, that he shall give his time to the business of his office, and not to personal attendance on me."[55]

If humility is looking with detachment on oneself, keeping one's ego in check, self-disparagement is giving oneself less than one's due: it is humility with a vengeance. It is the attempt not to appear better than one is, which would be pride, but to appear only as good as one thinks one deserves, which is to appear inferior to what people expect one to be.

Lincoln's utterances abound in expressions of such self-depreciation, and while one must make allowance for the politician's deliberate coyness, these expressions are too frequent and too pointed to be dismissed as political ploys. Lincoln's self-disparagement extends from his physical appearance to his ability as a statesman and his position as President.

It was, of course, obvious to his contemporaries that Lincoln was neither handsome nor elegant, a defect which did not prevent him from being elected President in 1860. Yet time and again at the many stops he made on his trip to Washington as President Elect, he makes a point of calling the attention of the audience to the unattractiveness of his appearance. Thus on February 14, 1861 he remarked from the balcony of the Monongahela House in Pittsburgh: ". . . and I have made my appearance now only to afford you an opportunity of seeing as clearly as may be, my beautiful countenance!"[56] At Painesville, Ohio, he said on February 16, 1861: "I have stepped out upon this platform that I may see you and that you may see me, and in the arrangement I have the best of the bargain."[57] Lincoln appears to have been particularly fond of this formulation, for he repeats it frequently.[58]

On the same historic trip, Lincoln questions repeatedly his ability to discharge his duties as President. Thus he remarks in Poughkeepsie on February 19, 1861: "I do not think that they have chosen the best man to conduct our affairs, now—I am sure they did not".[59] Time and again he harps on that theme. Thus he says on February 22, 1861 in Harrisburg, Pennsylvania: "As I have often had occasion to say, I repeat to you—I am quite sure I do not deceive myself when I tell you I bring to the work an honest heart; I dare not tell you that I bring a head sufficient for it."[60] On February 26, 1861 in his reply to the Committee of Congress Reporting the Electoral Count he states his "distrust of my own ability to perform the required duty under the most favorable circumstances, now rendered doubly difficult by existing national perils."[61]

Even before he was elected President, he voiced doubt at times about his intellectual abilities. In one of the Douglas debates on October 13, 1858, he referred to a remark of Douglas in these terms: "He did not make a mistake, in one of his early speeches, when he called me an amiable man, though perhaps he did when he called me an intelligent man."[62] Concerning a local political task he writes to Norman B. Judd on December 14, 1859: ". . . I shall attend to it as well as I know how, which, God knows, will not be very well."[63]

Lincoln expressed repeatedly similar doubts about his ability to speak. Invited to give a lecture, the man who debated Douglas replied on April 7, 1860:

> I am not a professional lecturer—I have never got up but one lecture; and that, I think, rather a poor one."[64] As President, he said on July 4, 1861 at a review of New York Regiments: "Gentlemen, I appear before you in obedience to your call; not, however, to make a speech. I have made a great many poor speeches in my life, and I feel considerably relieved now to know that the dignity of the position in which I have been placed does not permit me to expose myself any longer. I therefore take shelter, most gladly, in standing back and allowing you to hear speeches from gentlemen who are so very much more able to make them than myself. I thank you for the kindness of your call, but I must keep good my

word, and not be led into a speech, as I told you I did not appear for that purpose.[65]

In response to a serenade by an Ohio delegation to the Republican Convention, he said on June 9, 1864: "I have just been saying, and will repeat it, that the hardest of all speeches I have to answer is a serenade. I never know what to say on these occasions."[66] Lincoln expressed not only his doubts as to his ability to speak, but also his fear to make mistakes when speaking. At the opening of the Patent Office Fair on February 22, 1864, he remarked according to *The New York Tribune:* "There was great objection to his saying anything, for necessarily, in consequence of his position, everything went into print. If he made any mistake it might do both himself and the nation harm. It was very difficult to say sensible things."[67]

When in the spring of 1859 personal and political friends suggested that he consider the presidential nomination, Lincoln denied his qualifications for the office. The private character of his denials excludes the possibility that they were not genuine and made only for political effect. Thus he wrote on April 16, 1859 to Thomas J. Pickett, a newspaper editor from Illinois: "As to the other matter you kindly mention, I must, in candor, say I do not think myself fit for the Presidency. I certainly am flattered, and gratified, that some partial friends think of me in that connection; but I really think it best for our cause that no concerted effort, such as you suggest, should be made."[68] On July 28, 1859 he wrote to Samuel Galloway, an attorney with whom he had a business correspondence: "I must say that I do not think myself fit for the Presidency."[69] Writing almost a year later on April 6, 1860 to Richard M. Corwine, another lawyer, he was somewhat less categorical but still diffident: "Remembering that when not a very great man begins to be mentioned for a very great position, his head is very likely to be a little turned, . . ."[70] When he is formally notified of the nomination of May 19, 1860 by the Committee of the Republican National Convention he was still diffident: "Deeply, and even painfully sensible of the great responsibility which is inseparable from that [this high] honor—a responsibility which I could almost wish had fallen upon some one of the far more eminent men and experienced statesmen whose distinguished names were before the Convention. . . ."[71] As President he liked to underplay his personal power, pointing to the temporary character of his holding the office. Thus on his way to Washington as President Elect, he said in Indianapolis on February 11, 1861: "I, as already intimated, am but an accidental instrument, temporary, and to serve but for a limited time . . ."[72] And he elaborated on this theme the next day in Lawrenceburg, Indiana: "I have been selected to fill an important office for a brief period, and am now, in your eyes, invested with an influence which will soon pass away; but should my administration prove to be a very wicked one, or what is more probable, a very foolish one, if you, the PEOPLE, are but true to yourselves and to the Constitution, there is but little harm I can do, *thank God!*"[73] He went further on February 14, 1861 in Steubenville, Ohio: "Though the majority may be wrong, and I will not undertake to say that they were not wrong in electing me, yet we must adhere to the principle that the majority shall rule. By your Constitution you have another chance in four years. No great harm can be done by us in that time—in that time there can be nobody hurt. If anything goes wrong, however, and you find you have made a mistake, elect a better man next time. There are plenty of them."[74] He returned to the theme on July 4, 1862 in his remarks to a delegation of veterans of 1812 when he referred to himself as "(for the time being), the head of the government."[75]

In his relations with the military during the Civil War, Lincoln was firm in his assertion of presidential authority and diffident with regard to substantive military decisions. When in June 1863, during one of the most severe crises of the war, the animosity between Generals Hooker, the Commander of the Army of the Potomac, and Halleck, the General-in-Chief, came into the open, Lincoln wired Hooker on June 16, 1863: "To remove all misunderstanding, I now place you in the strict military relation to Gen. Halleck, of a commander of one of the armies, to the General-in-Chief of all the armies. I have not intended differently; but as it seems to be differently understood, I shall direct him to give you orders, and you to obey them."[76] Yet on the same day he wrote a polite and understanding letter to Hooker which ends with this statement: "As it looks to me, Lee's now returning toward Harper's Ferry gives you back the chance that I thought McClellan lost last fall. Quite possibly I was wrong both then and now; but, in the great responsibility resting upon me, I cannot be entirely silent. Now, all I ask is that you will be in such mood that we can get into our action the best cordial judgment of yourself and General Halleck, with my poor mite added, if indeed he and you shall think it entitled to any consideration at all."[77] On October 16, 1863 he wrote to Halleck, making one of his frequent suggestions for military operations: "If Gen. Meade can now attack him (Lee) on a field no worse than equal for us, and will do so with all the skill and courage, which he, his officers and men possess, the honor will be his if he succeeds, and the blame may be mine if he fails."[78]

The pattern for the diffidence in military matters was set by him in the early stage of the Civil War. After McClellan had been appointed Commander-in-Chief, in addition to his command of the Army of the Potomac, Lincoln conferred with him frequently at his headquarters. One night, Lincoln, Seward, and Hay came to McClellan's house to confer with him. They waited for an hour until the General arrived. A servant told him who was waiting and McClellan went immediately upstairs without taking notice of his visitors. Half an hour later, a servant was sent upstairs to remind the General of his visitors. The servant returned to tell the President that the General had gone to bed. On the way home, Hay expressed his indignation at this arrogance, eliciting Lincoln's response that this was no time for points of etiquette and personal dignity. "I will hold McClellan's horse," he remarked later, "if he will only bring us success." However, from then onwards, Lincoln called McClellan to the White House when he wanted to see him.[79]

The same diffidence revealed itself when the issue was not a matter of affairs of state but of personal concern close to Lincoln's heart. Thus he wrote to Grant on January 19, 1865:

> Please read and answer this letter as though I was not President, but only a friend. My son, now in his twenty second year, having graduated at Harvard, wishes to see something of the war before it ends. I do not wish to put him in the ranks, nor yet to give him a commission, to which those who have already served long, are better entitled, and better qualified to hold. Could he, without embarrassment to you, or detriment to the service, go into your Military family with some nominal rank, I, and not the public, furnishing his necessary means? If no, say so without the least hesitation, because I am as anxious, and as deeply interested, that you shall not be encumbered as you can be yourself.[80]

To appreciate fully the revelation of Lincoln's character through this letter, one must remember how Lincoln was set upon with demands for patronage, military and otherwise, and to what extent he yielded to them, frequently regardless of merit.

While Lincoln's judgment in military matters was frequently sound and even brilliant and far superior to that of many of his generals and while he asserted during the last phase of the Civil War a powerful influence upon military strategy, he never tired to emphasize vis-à-vis his generals that they were the experts and he a mere ignorant layman. Thus he wrote on May 9, 1862 with regard to the reorganization of the

Army: "Of course, I did not, on my own judgment, pretend to understand the subject."[81] On September 19, 1863 he wrote to Halleck with regard to an inquiry of General Meade: "I am not prepared to order, or even advise an advance in this case, wherein I know so little of particulars, and wherein he, in the field, thinks the risk is so great, and the promise of advantage so small."[82] That disclaimer, however, did not prevent him from launching in the same letter into a brilliant analysis of the military situation, his strategic preferences clearly stated. On April 30, 1864, he wrote to Grant on whose thinking and actions he had a great and sometimes determining influence: "Not expecting to see you again before the Spring campaign opens, I wish to express, in this way, my entire satisfaction with what you have done up to this time, so far as I understand it. The particulars of your plans I neither know, or seek to know. You are vigilant and self-reliant; and, pleased with this, I wish not to obtrude any constraints or restraints upon you. While I am very anxious that any great disaster, or the capture of our men in great numbers, shall be avoided, I know these points are less likely to escape your attention than they would be mine."[83]

The disclaimers derived from ignorance are not limited to military matters. In a major address in Pittsburgh on February 15, 1861, Lincoln said of the tariff: "I must confess that I do not understand this subject in all its multiform bearings, but I promise you that I will give it my closest attention, and endeavor to comprehend it more fully."[84] Referring to the tariff bill, he repeated: "I confess I do not understand the precise provisions of this bill."[85]

Nor did Lincoln hesitate to admit to doubt and indecision. An article in *The North American Review* had criticized Lincoln's policy "practically to concede to any rebel who might choose to profess loyalty, rights under the Constitution whose corresponding obligations he repudiated."[86] Lincoln replied on January 16, 1864: "I have never had a theory that secession could absolve States or people from their obligations. Precisely the contrary is asserted in the inaugural address; and it was because of my belief in the continuation of these *obligations,* that I was puzzled, for a time, as to denying the legal *rights* of those citizens who remained individually innocent of treason or rebellion."[87]

Lincoln's diffidence extends from his general ability to the possibility and actuality of error in specific instances. At the very beginning of his political career, when running for the Illinois General Assembly, he told the citizens of Sangamo County on March 9, 1832: "However, upon the subjects of which I have treated, I have spoken as I thought. I may be wrong in regard to any or all of them; but holding it a sound maxim, that it is better to be only sometimes right, than at all times wrong, so soon as I discover my opinions to be erroneous, I shall be ready to renounce them."[88] Addressing the Wisconsin State Agricultural Society on September 30, 1859 he says: "And in such suggestions by me, quite likely very little will be new to you, and a large part of the rest possibly already known to be erroneous."[89] When the attempt to provision Fort Sumter had failed, Lincoln wrote on May 1, 1861, to Captain Fox, Assistant Secretary of the Navy and Commander of one of the ships of the expedition, after enumerating the causes of the failure: ". . . by an accident, for which you were in no wise responsible, and possibly I, to some extent was, you were deprived of a war vessel with her men, which you deemed of great importance to the enterprize."[90] After the victory at Vicksburg, Lincoln, on July 13, 1863, wrote to Grant, recapitulating their divergent battle plans and ending with these words: "I now wish to make the personal acknowledgment that you were right, and I was wrong."[91] On December 24, 1863 Lincoln wrote to General Banks: "I deeply regret to have said or done anything which could give you pain, or uneasiness. . . . My error has been that it did not occur to me that Gov. Shepley or any one else would set up a claim to act independently of you; and hence I said nothing expressly upon the point. Language has not been guarded at a point where no danger was thought of. . . . This, in it's liability to be misconstrued, it now seems was an error in us."[92] On August 9, 1864, he writes to General Butler: "In your paper of February you fairly notified me that you contemplated taking a popular vote; and, if fault there be, it was my fault that I did not object then, which I probably should have done, had I studied the subject as closely as I have since done."[93] The same willingness to admit error extends even to minor matters of courtesy. Thus Lincoln wrote to General Sigel on February 5, 1863: "Gen. Schurz thinks I was a little cross in my late note to you. If I was, I ask pardon. If I do get up a little temper I have no sufficient time to keep it up."[94] And he writes to William Lloyd Garrison on February 7, 1865: "I have your kind letter of the 21st of January, and can only beg that you will pardon the seeming neglect occasioned by my constant engagements. When I received the spirited and admirable painting 'Waiting for the Hour' I directed my Secretary not to acknowledge its arrival at once, preferring to make my personal acknowledgment of the thoughtful kindness of the donors; and waiting for some leisure hour, I have committed the discourtesy of not replying at all."[95]

These diffident manifestations of Lincoln's humility are the expression of a basic fatalistic disposition. Things will turn out as they must, he seems to say, and they are not likely to turn out in my favor. So he ends his communication to the people of Sangamo County already quoted, in which he asks them to vote for him, with these words anticipating defeat: "But if the good people in their wisdom shall see fit to keep me in the background, I have been too familiar with disappointments to be very much chagrined."[96] He wrote on May 7, 1849 to George W. Rives who bought a federal appointment: "You overrate my capacity to serve you. Not one man recommended by me has yet been appointed to any thing, little or big, except a few who had no opposition."[97] After his defeat by Douglas, he wrote on November 19, 1858 to Anson G. Henry: "I am glad I made the late race. It gave me a hearing on the great and durable question of the age, which I could have had in no other way; and though I now sink out of view, and shall be forgotten, I believe I have made some marks which will tell for the cause of civil liberty long after I am gone."[98] When all these claims to insignificance had been invalidated by history, Lincoln could still in 1864 look at himself as the object of fate rather than the molder of history: "I claim not to have controlled events but confess plainly that events have controlled me."[99]

(3) LINCOLN'S HUMOR

Lincoln's humor, in two of its manifestations, was nothing more than a particular expression of his detachment and humility. As we have seen before, detachment is a prerequisite for objectivity and for the ability to see things as they are rather than as they appear to be because they are made to take on certain appearances by dint of convention or self-interest. The juxtaposition between appearance and reality, to which we are exposed unprepared, can create a humorous effect. Accustomed to look at the appearance of a thing as though it were its reality, we are shocked and maybe amused, when we are suddenly made aware of the distinction. Thus, to a telegram suggesting General Allen be appointed Quarter Master General, Lincoln replies on September 15, 1863: "What nation do you desire Gen. Allen to be made Quarter-Master-General of? This nation already has a Quarter-Master-General."[100] When Lincoln, returning from Gettysburg with a mild form of smallpox, found the White House shunned by the usual horde of office seakers, he remarked that he now had something he could give to everybody.[101] Lincoln received a telegram reading: "The following lines will give you to understand what is justice & what is truth to all men. Equal Rights & Justice to all white men in the United States forever. White men is in class number one & black men is in class number two & must be governed by white men forever." Nicolay replied in Lincoln's name on August 6, 1864: "The President has received yours of yesterday, and is kindly paying attention to it. As it is my business to assist him whenever I can, I will thank you to inform me, for his use, whether you are either a white man or black one, because in either case, you can not be regarded as an entirely impartial judge. It may be that you belong to a third or fourth class of *yellow* or *red* men, in which case the impartiality of your judgment would be more apparant."[102]

When Lincoln learned that a brigadier general had been captured in bed, he said according to the *New York Times* of March 11, 1863, "that he did not mind the loss of the Brigadier as much as he did the loss of the horses. 'For,' said he, 'I can make a much better Brigadier in five minutes, but the horses cost a hundred and twenty-five dollars apiece.' "[103]

Lincoln used a similar technique when he dealt on June 20, 1848, in his speech to the House of Representatives on internal improvements, with the issue of inequality: "I make no special allusion to the present president when I say there are few stronger cases in this in this [*sic*] world, of 'burthen to the many, and benefit to the few'—of 'inequality'—than the presidency itself is by some thought to be. An honest laborer digs coal at about seventy cents a day, while the president digs abstractions at about seventy dollars a day. The *coal* is clearly worth more than the *abstractions,* and yet what a monstrous inequality in the prices!"[104] To Governor Gamble Lincoln sent the following reply on July 28, 1862: "You ask four Regiments for Gen. Schofield, and he asks the same of the Sec. of War. Please raise them for me, as I have them not, nor can have, till some governor gives them to me."[105] And to General McClellan he telegraphed: "I have just read your despatch about sore tongued and fatiegued (sic) horses. Will you pardon me for asking what the horses of your army have done since the battle of Antietam that fatigue anything?"[106]

The same contrast between pretense and appearance, on the one hand, and reality, on the other, makes for the comic effect of Lincoln's humility. That effect was potentially inherent in many examples of self-disparagement given above.[107] It only requires an explicit justaposition between appearance and reality in order to make the comic element explicit. A prosecuting attorney wanted to prevent an indictment Lincoln had written from being crushed; for "Quashing an Indct. written by a prominent candidate for the Presidency of the U.S. by a *little court* like Col. [David] Davis' will not sound well in history." Lincoln replied: "If, after all, the indictment shall be quashed, it will only prove that my *forte* is as a Statesman, rather than as a Prosecutor."[108]

Finally, Lincoln uses humor for rhetorical purposes, revealing through the punning, paradoxical, or ironic use of language, a meaning which ordinary usage does not yield. Thus he ends a speech in the House of Representatives on January 5, 1848, by saying: "He had no desire, he could assure gentlemen, ever to be out of order—though he never could keep long *in* order."[109] On his way to Washington at Leaman Place, Pennsylvania, on February 22, 1861, after making his disparaging standard remark about his appearance,[110] he brings his wife, much smaller than he, to the platform with the words that he had decided to give them "the long and the short of it!"[111] A member of the Illinois legislature proposed "That the nomination of Samuel McHatton, for County Surveyor of Schuyler county . . . be vacated for the reason that said office was not vacant at the time said nomination was made." Lincoln replied: "That if, as appeared to be the opinion of legal gentlemen, there was no danger of the new surveyor's ousting the old one as long as he persisted not to die—he would suggest the propriety of letting matters remain as they were, so that if the old surveyor should hereafter conclude to die, there would be a new one ready made without troubling the legislature."[112]

(4) LINCOLN'S COMPASSION

Lincoln's detachment from the world around him and from himself was also one of the sources of his most striking and pervasive attitudes towards his fellow men: his compassion. He loved nobody and nothing in particular, with the exception of some immediate members of his family and, as we shall see, of America as defined in the Declaration of Independence. But because he did not allow himself to be involved with love—or for that matter hate—in the affairs of other men, he could afford to behold all of them with a detachment that opened up the other source of his compassion: his respect for, and sympathy with, all human beings as such. Thus his compassion in action, especially with regard to death sentences, had an unsentimental and even unemotional quality, while it was infused with concern for each human being whose life was in his hands. Lincoln discharged this awesome responsibility with the same combination of complete detachment and love for all mankind with which one might imagine God meting out justice on the day of last judgment.

His general attitude is expressed in the words he uttered when he saw a line of wounded soldiers file by in Washington: "Look yonder at those poor fellows. I cannot bear it. This suffering, this loss of life is dreadful."[113] The number of court-martial sentences, especially those imposing the death sentence for desertion or cowardice, was enormous. In one year, there were 30,000 of them. They had all to be disposed of by the President. Lincoln examined all of them with a diligence to be expected from a trial judge. John Hay tells of six hours of a humid July day spent on such examination.[114]

The pattern that emerged clearly favored the avoidance of the death penalty if the circumstances even remotely justify it. That is obvious, both from general policy and from the disposition of individual cases. It was also obvious to Lincoln who in a letter to General Butler of August 9, 1864, refered to the Attorney General as "constantly restraining . . . my tendency to clemency for rebels and rebel sympathizers."[115] On February 26, 1864, in General Orders Number 76 the President directed "that the sentences of all deserters, who have been condemned by Court Martial to death, and that have not been otherwise acted upon by him, be mitigated to imprisonment during the war."[116] Innumerable Confederate soldiers were released from prison on Lincoln's orders: "Let this man take the oath and be discharged."[117]

To give only a few examples of individual action: concerning a private sentenced to be shot for desertion, Lincoln orders on July 18, 1863: "Let him fight instead of being shot."[118] One of the last official actions he performed before he died was to sign the pardon of a deserter with the words: "Well, I think the boy can do us more good above ground than under ground."[119]

Three episodes will show to what lengths Lincoln went to make sure that nobody's life was taken without just cause. On April 11, 1863, he wired General Mitchell: "Is there a soldier by the name of 'John R. Minnick' of Wynkoop's Cavalry, under sentence of death, by a Court-Martial, or Military Commission, in Nashville? and, if so, what was his offence? and when is he to be executed?"[120] On December 29, 1864, he sent the following telegram to General Butler: "There is a man in Co. I. 11th. Conn. Vols. 1 Brigade 3. Division 24th. Army Corps. at Chapins Farm, Va, under the assumed name of Wm. Stanley, but whose real name is Frank R. Judd; and who is under arrest, and probably about to be tried for desertion. He is the son of our present Minister to Prussia, who is a close personal friend of Senator Trumbull and myself. We are not willing for the boy to be shot, but we think it as well that his trial go regularly on, suspending execution until further order from me & reporting to me."[121] He followed this telegram up with another one to General Ord on January 19, 1865: "You have a man in arrest for desertion passing by the name of Stanley—William Stanley I think—but whose real name is different. He is the son of so close a friend of mine that I must not let him be executed. Please let me know what is his present and prospective condition."[122]

Compassion pure and simple takes the place of justice in the case of Andrews who had been sentenced to be shot. Lincoln wrote on January 7, 1864: "The case of Andrews is really a very bad one, as appears by the record already before me. Yet before receiving this I had ordered his punishment commuted to imprisonment for during the war at hard labor, and had so telegraphed. I did this, not on any merit in the case, but because I am trying to evade the butchering business lately."[123]

Yet Lincoln's compassion could also be tempered by justice as this letter to General Rosecrans shows: "A Major Wolf, as it seems, was under sentence, in your Department, to be executed in retaliation for the murder of a Major Wilson; and I, without any particular knowledge of the facts, was induced by appeals for mercy, to order the suspension of his execution until further order. Understanding that you so desire, this letter places the case again within your control, with the remark only that I wish you to do nothing merely for revenge, but that what you may do, shall be solely done with reference to the security of the future."[124] In the usual vein of pure compassion Lincoln wrote on March 17, 1863, to the Attorney General: "I understand a Danville, Illinoisian, by the name of Lyman Guinnip, is under an indictment at Louisville, something about slaves. I knew him slightly. He was not of bad character at home, and I scarcely think he is guilty of any real crime. Please try if you can not slip him through."[125] When a colonel is dismissed because he ordered slaves to be returned to their owners, Lincoln writes on January 20, 1863, to the Secretary of War: "I have a strong inclination to give Col. McHenry another chance. What says the Sec. of War?"[126] On March 1, 1864, he writes to the Secretary of War: "A poor widow, by the name of Baird, has a son in the Army, that for some offence has been sentenced to serve a long time without pay, or at most, with very little pay. I do not like this punishment of withholding pay—it falls so very hard upon poor families. After he has been serving in this way for several months, at the tearful appeal of the poor Mother, I made a direction that he be allowed to enlist for a new term, on the same conditions as others. She now comes, and says she can not get it acted upon. Please do it."[127]

The same compassion extends to minor matters. Lincoln had an upset stomach attributed to bad drinking water. Special water was ordered but did not arrive. The Quartermaster in charge apologized and wrote to Lincoln that he would call the officer responsible "to account for his bad management." Lincoln replied on March 24, 1865: "I am not at all impatient, and hope Major James will not reproach himself or deal harshly with the officer having the matter in charge.

Doubtless he, too, has met some unexpected difficulty."[128] On December 16, 1862, he wrote to General Curtis: "N. W. Watkins, of Jackson, Mo. (who is half brother to Henry Clay) writes me that a Col. of ours has driven him from his home at Jackson. Will you please look into the case, and restore the old man to his home, if the public interest will admit?"[129]

Lincoln was not only concerned with the penalties meted out but also with the effect of the penalties upon the transgressors. Captain Cutts had been sentenced to be dismissed from the service. Here is what Lincoln wrote to him on October 26, 1863:

> Although what I am now to say is to be, in form, a reprimand, it is not intended to add a pang to what you have already suffered upon the subject to which it relates. You have too much of life yet before you, and have shown too much of promise as an officer, for your future to be lightly surrendered. You were convicted of two offences. One of them, not of great enormity, and yet greatly to be avoided, I feel sure you are in no danger of repeating. The other you are not so well assured against. The advice of a father to his son 'Beware of entrance to a quarrel, but being in, bear it that the opposed may beware of thee,' is good, and yet not the best. Quarrel not at all. No man resolved to make the most of himself, can spare time for personal contention. Still less can he afford to take all the consequences, including the vitiating of his temper, and the loss of self-control. Yield larger things to which you can show no more than equal right; and yield lesser ones, though clearly your own. Better give your path to a dog, than be bitter by him in contesting for the right. Even killing the dog would not cure the bite.
>
> In the mood indicated deal henceforth with your fellow men, and especially with your brother officers; and even the unpleasant events you are passing from will not have been profitless to you.[130]

Lincoln's compassion, as this letter shows, did not manifest itself only in action, especially with regard to the punishment to be meted out, but embraced the human being in distress trying to alleviate his suffering. The most famous example is Lincoln's letter of November 21, 1864, to Mrs. Bixby,[131] who was presumed to have lost five sons in the Civil War. In fact only two died in battle. One is supposed to have died in prison as a deserter, another deserted and survived, and one was honorably discharged from the Army. More importantly, it is in my judgment by no means the most eloquent and Lincolnesque letter of this kind, a fact which tends to support the claim that it was actually composed by John Hay.

What distinguishes the letters that bear the stamp of Lincoln's mind and character is the practical wisdom that gives the expression of compassion a therapeutic function. Thus he writes on December 23, 1862, to Fanny McCullough:

It is with deep grief that I learn of the death of your kind and brave Father; and, especially, that it is affecting your young heart beyond what is common in such cases. In this sad world of ours, sorrow comes to all; and, to the young, it comes with bitterest agony, because it takes them unawares. The older have learned to ever expect it. I am anxious to afford some alleviation of your present distress. Perfect relief is not possible, except with time. You can not now realize that you will ever feel better. Is not this so? And yet it is a mistake. You are sure to be happy again. To know this, which is certainly true, will make you some less miserable now. I have had experience enough to know what I say; and you need only to believe it, to feel better at once. The memory of your dear Father, instead of an agony, will yet be a sad sweet feeling in your heart, of a purer, and holier sort than you have known before.[132]

Or he writes on June 28, 1862, to Quintin Campbell, the son of a cousin of Mrs. Lincoln, who had just entered West Point:

Your good mother tells me you are feeling very badly in your new situation. Allow me to assure you it is a perfect certainty that you will, very soon, feel better—quite happy—if you only stick to the resolution you have taken to procure a military education. I am older than you, have felt badly myself, and *know*, what I tell you is true. Adhere to your purpose and you will soon feel as well as you ever did. On the contrary, if you falter, and give up, you will lose the power of keeping any resolution, and will regret it all your life. Take the advice of a friend, who, though he never saw you, deeply sympathizes with you, and stick to your purpose.[133]

On January 1, 1863, Lincoln wrote to the Secretary of War:

Yesterday a piteous appeal was made to me by an old lady of genteel appearance, saying she had, with what she thought sufficient assurance that she would not be disturbed by the government, fitted up the two South Divisions of the old Duff Green building in order to take boarders, and has boarders already in it, & others, including M.C.s. engaged, and that now she is ordered to be out of it by Saturday the 3rd. Inst.; and that, independently of the ruin it brings on her, by her lost out-lay, she neither has, nor can find another shelter for her own head. I know nothing about it myself, but promised to bring it to your notice.[134]

Nowhere has the fusion of compassion and justice, characteristic of Lincoln, more impressively manifested itself than in the case of the Sioux Indians who rose in 1862 against the government of Minnesota, killing more than three hundred fifty settlers. Three hundred Indians were sentenced to death, and General Pope transmitted their names to Lincoln for approval of the death sentence. Lincoln replied on November 10, 1862: "Your despatch giving the names of three hundred Indians condemned to death, is received. Please forward, as soon as possible the full and complete record of these convictions. And if the record does not fully indicate the more guilty and influential, of the culprits, please have a careful statement made on these points and forwarded to me."[135] Lincoln was pressed by Pope, the governor, and the congressional representatives of Minnesota to order the immediate execution of all condemned Indians, and they painted a gruesome picture of the anarchy and massacres that would occur if it were not done. Lincoln did nothing. On December 1, 1862, he wrote to the Judge Advocate General: "Three hundred Indians have been sentenced to death in Minnesota by a Military Commission, and execution only awaits my action. I wish your legal opinion whether if I should conclude to execute only a part of them, I must myself designate which, or could I leave the designation to some officer on the ground?"[136] On December 11, 1862, Lincoln reported to the Senate the action he had taken:

Anxious to not act with so much clemency as to encourage another outbreak on the one hand, nor with so much severity as to be real cruelty on the other, I caused a careful examination of the records of trials to be made, in view of first ordering the execution of such as had been proved guilty of violating females. Contrary to my expectations, only two of this class were found. I then directed a further examination, and a classification of all who were proven to have participated in *massacres,* as distinguished from participation in *battles.* This class numbered forty, and included the two convicted of female violation. One of the number is strongly recommended by the Commission which tried them, for commutation to ten years' imprisonment. I have ordered the other thirty-nine to be executed on Friday, the 19th. instant."[137]

(5) LINCOLN'S JUSTICE

We have thus far spoken of the fusion between compassion and justice in Lincoln's actions. Yet Lincoln's actions are also formed by justice pure and simple, without the attenuation of compassion—legal justice in the sense of respect for the law and moral justice in the sense of fair and equitable dealing. The motto of Lincoln's dedication to legal justice might well be contained in the message of January 16, 1863, to the Secretary of War, concerning a lieutenant dismissed from the service because of being absent without leave: "Injustice has probably been done in this case. Sec. of War please examine it."[138] In application of this principle, Lincoln had written four days earlier to the Secretary of War: "Dr. Thomas Sim, has been dismissed from the service for being in this City contrary to a general order. His afflicted wife assures me he had a pass from Gen. Sickles, commander of his Division, for 48 hours, and that within the 48 hours he was refused the 15 days absence he asked, and reported to Gen. Sickles, who extended his time so as to take the Dr. with him, and that he reached the army in less than twelve additional hours to the original 48, allowed him. Please see the lady."[139] When the issue of legal blame for a military disaster—the loss of a division at Winchester—was raised, Lincoln wrote on October 27, 1863: "Serious blame is not necessarily due to every serious disaster, and I can not say that in this case, any of their officers is deserving of serious blame. No Court-Martial is deemed necessary or proper in the case."[140]

That sense of justice applies with equal force to the enemies in the war. Thus Lincoln wrote on January 20, 1865, to General Reynolds: "It would appear by the accompanying papers that Mrs. Mary E. Morton is the owner, independently of her husband, of a certain building, premises and furniture, which she, with her children, has been occupying and using peaceably during the war, until recently, when the Provost-Marshal, has, in the name of the U.S. government, seized the whole of said property, and ejected her from it. It also appears by her statement to me, that her husband went off in the rebellion at the beginning, wherein he still remains. . . .

"The true rule for the Military is to seize such property as is needed for Military uses and reasons, and let the rest alone. Cotton and other staple articles of commerce are seizable for military reasons. Dwelling houses & furniture are seldom so. If Mrs. Morton is playing traitor, to the extent of practical injury, seize her, but leave her house to the courts. Please revise and adjust this case upon these principles."[141]

On January 2, 1863, he wrote to General Curtis concerning Dr. McPheter:

> The charges are all general—that he has a rebel wife and rebel relations, that he sympathizes with rebels and that he exercises rebel influence. Now, after talking with him, I tell you frankly, I believe he does sympathize with the rebels; but the question remains whether such a man, of unquestioned good moral character, who has taken such an oath as he has, and can not even be charged of violating it, and who can be charged with no other specific act or omision, can, with safety to the government be exiled, upon the suspicion of his secret sympathies. But I agree that this must be left to you who are on the spot; and if, after all, you think the public good requires his removal, my suspension of the order is withdrawn, only with this qualification that the time during the suspension, is not to be counted against him. I have promised him this.[142]

Lincoln insists that violations of the law, committed in furtherance of the war, must be justified by absolute necessity. Thus in a memorandum on military arrests he writes on May 17, 1861: "Unless the *necessity* for these arbitrary arrests is *manifest,* and *urgent,* I prefer they should cease."[143] Concerning the confused and near anarchic situation in Missouri, Lincoln wrote to Charles O. Drake, head of a radical committee from Missouri and Kansas: "To restrain contraband intelligence and trade, a system of searches, seizures, permits, and passes, had been introduced. . . . That there was a necessity for something of the sort was clear; but that it could only be justified by stern necessity, and that it was liable to great abuse in administration, was equally clear."[144] Lincoln admits the dubious legality of certain measures necessitated by the war in his message to Congress of July 4, 1861:

> Recurring to the action of the government, it may be stated that, at first, a call was made for seventy-five thousand militia; and rapidly following this, a proclamation was issued for closing the ports of the insurrectionary districts by proceedings in the nature of Blockade. So far all was believed to be strictly legal. At this point the insurrectionists announced their purpose to enter upon the practice of privateering.

Other calls were made for volunteers, to serve three years, unless sooner discharged; and also for large additions to the regular Army and Navy. These measures, whether strictly legal or not, were ventured upon, under what appeared to be a popular demand, and a public necessity; trusting, then as now, that Congress would readily ratify them. It is believed that nothing has been done beyond the constitutional competency of Congress.[145]

Yet Lincoln defended strenuously, and it seems to me convincingly, the one measure which had aroused the most criticism on legal grounds: the suspension of the writ of habeas corpus:

Soon after the first call for militia, it was considered a duty to authorize the Commanding General, in proper cases, according to his discretion, to suspend the privilege of the writ of habeas corpus; or, in other words, to arrest, and detain, without resort to the ordinary processes and forms of law, such individuals as he might deem dangerous to the public safety. This authority has purposely been exercised but very sparingly. Nevertheless, the legality and propriety of what has been done under it, are questioned; and the attention of the country has been called to the proposition that one who is sworn to 'take care that the laws be faithfully executed,' should not himself violate them. Of course some consideration was given to the questions of power, and propriety, before this matter was acted upon. The whole of the laws which were required to be faithfully executed, were being resisted, and failing of execution, in nearly one-third of the States. Must they be allowed to finally fail of execution, even had it been perfectly clear, that by the use of the means necessary to their execution, some single law, made in such extreme tenderness of the citizen's liberty, that practically, it relieves more of the guilty, than of the innocent, should, to a very limited extent, be violated? To state the question more directly, are all the laws, *but one,* to go unexecuted, and the government itself go to pieces, lest that one be violated? Even in such a case, would not the official oath be broken, if the government should be overthrown, when it was believed that disregarding the single law, would tend to preserve it? But it was not believed that this question was presented. It was not believed that any law was violated. The provision of the Constitution that 'The privilege of the writ of habeas corpus, shall not be suspended unless when, in cases of rebellion or invasion, the public safety may require it,' is equivalent to a provision—is a provision—that such privilege may be suspended when, in cases of rebellion, or invasion, the public safety *does* require it. It was decided that we have a case of rebellion, and that the public safety does require the qualified suspension of the privilege of the writ which was authorized to be made. Now it is insisted that Congress, and not the Executive, is vested with this power. But the Constitution itself, is silent as to which, or who, is to exercise the power; and as the provision was plainly made for a dangerous emergency, it cannot be believed the framers of the instrument intended, that in every case, the danger should run its course, until Congress could be called together; the very assembling of which might be prevented, as was intended in this case, by the rebellion.[146]

When it came to legal rules to be enacted, Lincoln combined legal principle with compassion and practicality. Thus he wrote to the Secretary of War on February 5, 1864: "On principle I dislike an oath which requires a man to swear he *has* not done wrong. It rejects the Christian principle of forgiveness on terms of repentance. I think it is enough if the man does no wrong *hereafter.*"[147] On November 2, 1863, he wrote to the governor of Maryland: "I revoke the first of the three propositions in Gen. Schenck's general order No. 53; not that it is wrong in principle, but because the military being, of necessity, exclusive judges as to who shall be arrested, the provision is too liable to abuse."[148] On October 1, 1863, he writes to General Schofield: "Under your recent order, which I have approved, you will only arrest individuals, and suppress assemblies, or newspapers, when they may be working *palpable* injury to the Military in your charge; and, in no other case will you interfere with the expression of opinion in any form, or allow it to be interfered with violently by others. In this, you have a discretion to exercise with great caution, calmness, and forbearance."[149] But he added:

> With the matters of removing the inhabitants of certain counties *en masse;* and of removing certain individuals from time to time, who are supposed to be mischievous, I am not now interfering, but am leaving to your own discretion.
>
> Nor am I interfering with what may still seem to you to be necessary restrictions upon trade and intercourse.
>
> I think proper, however, to enjoin upon you the following:
>
> Allow no part of the Military under your command, to be engaged in either returning fugitive slaves, or in forcing, or enticing slaves from their homes; and, so far as practicable, enforce the same forbearance upon the people.[150]

The epitome of Lincoln's combination of legal principle, compassion and practicality is found in the instructions of March 18, 1864, to the Secretary of War concerning prisoners of war, dismissal of officers, rebel sympathizers, women wanting to pass the lines, and two special cases:

I am so pressed in regard to prisoners of war in our custody, whose homes are within our lines, and who wish to not be exchanged, but to take the oath and be discharged, that I hope you will pardon me for again calling up the subject. My impression is that we will not ever force the exchange of any of this class; that taking the oath, and being discharged, none of them will again go to the rebellion, but the rebellion again coming to them, a considerable percentage of them, probably not a majority, would rejoin it; that by a cautious discrimination the number so discharged would not be large enough to do any considerable mischief in any event; would relieve distress in, at least some meritorious cases; and would give me some relief from an intolerable pressure. I shall be glad therefore to have your cheerful assent to the discharge of those whose names I may send, which I will only do with circumspection. In using the strong hand, as now compelled to do, the government has a difficult duty to perform. At the very best, it will by turns do both too little and too much. It can properly have no motive of revenge, no purpose to punish merely for punishment's sake. While we must, by all available means, prevent the overthrow of the government, we should avoid planting and cultivating too many thorns in the bosom of society. These general remarks apply to several classes of cases, on each of which I wish to say a word.

First, the dismissal of officers when neither incompetency, nor intentional wrong, nor real injury to the service, is imputed. In such cases it is both cruel and impolitic, to crush the man, and make him and his friends permanent enemies to the administration if not to the government itself. I think of two instances. One wherein a Surgeon, for the benefit of patients in his charge, needed some lumber, and could only get it by making a false certificate wherein the lumber was denominated 'butter & eggs' and he was dismissed for the false certificate. The other a Surgeon by the name of Owen who served from the beginning of the war till recently, with two servants, and without objection, when upon discovery that the servants were his own *sons*, he was dismissed.

Another class consists of those who are known or strongly suspected, to be in sympathy with the rebellion. An instance of this is
the family of Southern, who killed a recruiting officer last autumn,
in Maryland. He fled, and his family are driven from their home,
without a shelter or crumb, except when got by burthening our
friends more than our enemies. Southern had no justification to kill
the officer; and yet he would not have been killed if he had proceeded in the temper and manner agreed upon by yourself and
Gov. Bradford. But this is past. What is to be done with the
family? Why can they not occupy their old home, and excite much
less opposition to the government than the manifestation of their
distress is now doing? If the house is really needed for the public
service; or if it has been regularly confiscated and the title
transferred, the case is different.

Again, the cases of persons, mostly women, wishing to pass our
lines, one way or the other. We have, in some cases, been appar-
antly, if not really, inconsistent upon this subject—that is, we have
forced some to go who wished to stay, and forced others to stay
who wished to go. Suppose we allow all females, with ungrown
children of either sex, to go South, if they desire, upon absolute
prohibition against returning during the war; and all to come North
upon the same condition of not returning during the war, and the
additional condition of taking the oath.

I wish to mention two special cases—both of which you well
remember. The first is that of Yocum. He was unquestionably
guilty. No one asking for his pardon pretends the contrary. What
he did, however, was perfectly lawful, only a short while before,
and the change making it unlawful had not, even then been fully
accepted in the public mind. It is doubtful whether Yocum did not
suppose it was really lawful to return a slave to a loyal owner,
though it is certain he did the thing secretly, in the belief that his
superiors would not allow it if known to them. But the great point
with me is that the severe punishment of five years at hard labor in
the Penitentiary is not at all necessary to prevent the repetition of
the crime by himself or by others. If the offence was one of frequent recurrence, the case would be different; but this case of
Yocum is the single instance which has come to my knowledge. I
think that for all public purposes, and for all proper purposes, he
has suffered enough.

The case of Smithson is troublesome. His wife and children are
quartered mostly on our friends, and exciting a great deal of sym-

pathy, which will soon tell against us. What think you of sending him and his family South, holding the sentence over him to be reinforced if he returns during the war.[151]

Lincoln was aware of that quality of detachment—this awareness being itself a function of that detachment—which allowed him to meet a hostile, fallible and cruel world with compassion rather than passion. On the eve of the presidential election of 1864, Lincoln observed to John Hay: "It is singular that I, who am not a vindictive man, should always, except once, have been before the people in canvasses marked by great bitterness. When I came to Congress it was a quiet time, but always, except that, the contests in which I have been prominent have been marked with great rancor."[152] When one of his companions exalted over a victory in Maryland, Lincoln replied: "You have more of that feeling of personal resentment than I. Perhaps I have too little of it, but I never thought it paid. A man has no time to spend half his life in quarrels. If any man ceases to attack me I never remember the past against him."[153]

In the whole printed record there is only one expression of concern for himself. He writes on May 12, 1864, to Senator Pomeroy, who is competing with Senator Lane for patronage: "I did not doubt yesterday that you desired to see me about the appointment of Assessor in Kansas. I wish you and Lane would make a sincere effort to get out of the mood you are in. I[t] does neither of you any good—it gives you the means of tormenting my life out of me, and nothing else.[154]

(6) LINCOLN'S TOUGHNESS

One would completely misunderstand Lincoln's character were one to attribute his compassion to weakness, sentimentality, or just good nature. His compassion sprang, as we have tried to show, from his detachment which allowed him to look at and act upon, his fellow man without love or hatred, but with indiscriminate sympathy, that is, with justice. Thus the counterfoil to that detachment is toughness where the same detachment and justice required it. We have seen that he commuted untold death sentences, but he also approved those where justice appeared to require approval. Thus he reports in his annual message to Congress of December 3, 1861, that "one captain, taken with a cargo of Africans on board his vessel, has been convicted of the highest grade of offence under our laws, the punishment of which is death."[155] But even here toughness was tempered with compassion as the following proclamation attests:

Whereas, it appears that at a Term of the Circuit Court of the United States of America for the Southern District of New York held in the month of November A.D. 1861, Nathaniel Gordon was indicted and convicted for being engaged in the Slave Trade, and was by the said Court sentenced to be put to death by hanging by the neck, on Friday the 7th day of February, A.D. 1862.

And whereas, a large number of respectable citizens have earnestly besought me to commute the said sentence of the said Nathaniel Gordon to a term of imprisonment for life, which application I have felt it to be my duty to refuse;

And whereas, it has seemed to me probable that the unsuccessful application made for the commutation of his sentence may have prevented the said Nathaniel Gordon from making the necessary preparation for the awful change which awaits him:

Now, therefore, be it known, that I, Abraham Lincoln, President of the United States of America, have granted and do hereby grant unto him, the said Nathaniel Gordon, a respite of the above recited sentence, until Friday the twenty-first day of February, A.D. 1862, between the hours of twelve o'clock at noon and three o'clock in the afternoon of the said day, when the said sentence shall be executed.[156]

When five enlisted men, who had enlisted for the purpose of deserting after receiving a bounty were sentenced to death and applied to Lincoln for mercy, Lincoln telegraphed General Meade: "Walter, Rainese, Faline, Lae, & Kuhne appeal to me for mercy, without giving any ground for it whatever. I understand these are very flagrant cases, and that you deem their punishment as being indispensable to the service. If I am not mistaken in this, please let them know at once that their appeal is denied."[157] In the case of Dr. Wright Lincoln approved the death sentence:

Upon the presentation of the record in this case and the examination thereof, aided by the report thereon of the Judge-Advocate-General, and on full hearing of counsel for the accused, being satisfied that no proper question remained open except as to the insanity of the accused, I caused a very full examination to be made on that question, upon a great amount of evidence, including all offered by counsel of accused, by an expert of high reputation in that professional department, who thereon reports to me, as his opinion, that the accused Dr. David M. Wright, was not insane prior to or on the 11th day of July, 1863, the date of the homicide of Lieutenant Sanborn; that he has not been insane since, and is not insane now (October 7, 1863). I therefore approve the finding and sentence of the military commission, and direct that the major-general in command of the department including the place of trial, and wherein the convict is now in custody, appoint time and place and carry said sentence into execution.[158]

When application was made for Mrs. Wright to have an interview with the President, Lincoln wrote to General Foster on October 17, 1863: "It would be useless for Mrs. Dr. Wright to come here. The subject is a very painful one, but the case is settled."[159]

Similarly, when Surgeon-General Hammond was dismissed by court martial, his wife went to the White House to ask for an interview with the President. Lincoln sent her card back with the following inscription: "Under the circumstances, I should prefer not seeing Mrs. Hammond."[160] He also refused to see Hammond himself by not replying to his letter applying for an interview for himself.[161] In a memorandum of September 10, 1863, he rejected out of hand the protestation of innocence of a man who had been fined for selling liquor to soldiers: "I can not listen to a man's own story, unsupported by any evidence, who has been convicted of violating the law; because that would put an end to all law."[162]

Lincoln could also be tough in politics. In reply to a letter of resignation by Gibson, the United States Solicitor in the Court of Claims, Lincoln wrote on July 25, 1864, the following letter which he had John Hays sign:

According to the request contained in your note, I have placed Mr. Gibson's letter of resignation in the hands of the President. He has read the letter, and says he accepts the resignation, as he will be glad to do with any other which may be tendered, as this is, for the purpose of taking an attitude of hostility against him. He says he was not aware that he was so much indebted to Mr. Gibson for having accepted the office at first, not remembering that he ever pressed him to do so, or that he gave it otherwise than as was usual, upon request made on behalf of Mr. Gibson. He thanks Mr. Gibson for his acknowledgment that he has been treated with personal kindness and consideration; and he says he knows of but two small draw-backs upon Mr. Gibson's right to still receive such treatment, one of which is that he never could learn of his giving much attention to the duties of his office, and the other is this studied attempt of Mr. Gibson's to stab him.[163]

(7) LINCOLN'S TOUGHNESS AND JUSTICE

Toughness and justice combined in Lincoln's handling of the case of Vallandigham. Vallandigham was a Democratic member of Congress from Ohio, who passionately opposed the war and its conduct by the Lincoln administration. He was arrested on orders of General Burnside and sentenced by a Military Commission to confinement for the duration of the war. A federal judge denied a motion for a writ of habeas corpus. This action created a storm of indignation and Lincoln commuted the sentence to banishment within the Confederate lines. Lincoln, obviously doubtful of the necessity for the original sentence, telegraphed General Burnside: "All the cabinet regretted the necessity of arresting, for instance, Vallandigham, some perhaps, doubting, that there was a real necessity for it—but, being done, all were for seeing you through with it."[164]

What is significant for our purpose are the arguments Lincoln put forward to justify the action. Thus he writes on June 12, 1863, to a committee from Albany, New York, which had passed a resolution sharply critical of Lincoln's interpretation of the Constitution in the Vallandigham case:

> They assert [It is asserted] in substance that Mr. Vallandigham was . . . seized and tried 'for no other reason than words addressed to a public meeting, in criticism of the course of the administration. . . . Now, if there be no mistake about this . . . then I concede that the arrest was wrong. But the arrest, as I understand, was made for a very different reason. Mr. Vallandigham avows his hostility to the war on the part of the Union; and his arrest was made because he was laboring, with some effect, to prevent the raising of troops, to encourage desertions from the army, and to leave the rebellion without an adequate military force to suppress it. He was not arrested because he was damaging the political prospects of the administration . . . but because he was damaging the army. . . . He was warring upon the military; and this gave the military constitutional jurisdiction to lay hands upon him. . . .
>
> Long experience has shown that armies can not be maintained unless desertion shall be punished by the severe penalty of death. The case requires, and the law and the constitution, sanction this punishment. Must I shoot a simple-minded soldier boy who deserts, while I must not touch a hair of a wiley agitator who induces him to desert? . . . I think that in such a case, to silence the agitator, and save the boy, is not only constitutional, but, withal, a great mercy.[165]

The Ohio Democratic State Convention passed a similar resolution to which Lincoln replied on June 29, 1863, repeating in substance his arguments in reply to the Albany resolution:

> I expressed the opinion that the constitution is different, *in its application* in cases of Rebellion or Invasion, involving the Public Safety, from what it is in times of profound peace and public security; and this opinion I adhere to, simply because, by the constitution itself, things may be done in the one case which may not be done in the other. . . .
>
> You claim that men may, if they choose, embarrass those whose duty it is, to combat a giant rebellion, and then be dealt with in turn, only as if there was no rebellion. The constitution itself rejects this view. The military arrests and detentions, which have been made, including those of Mr. V. which are not different in principle from the others, have been for *prevention,* and not for *punishment*—as injunctions to stay injury, as proceedings to keep the peace—and hence, like proceedings in such cases, and for like reasons, they have not been accompanied with indictments, or trials by juries, nor, in a single case by any punishment whatever, beyond what is purely incidental to the prevention. The original sentence of imprisonment in Mr. V.'s case, was to prevent injury to the Military service only, and the modification of it was made as a less disagreeable mode to him, of securing the same prevention.[166]

Lincoln's toughness comes particularly to the fore in his relations with his family. It is sometimes mitigated by kindness, sometimes borders on indifference, and almost always results from a detached and penetrating analysis of the situation which appears to leave Lincoln no choice but to be tough. Thus he writes to his father on December 24, 1848: "I very cheerfully send you the twenty dollars, which sum you say is necessary to save your land from sale. It is singular that you should have forgotten a judgment against you; and it is more singular that the plaintiff should have let you forget it so long, particularly as I suppose you have always had property enough to satisfy a judgment of that amount. Before you pay it, it would be well to be sure you have not paid it; or, at least, that you can not prove you have paid it."[167] On the same date he writes to his step-brother John D. Johnston:

Your request for eighty dollars, I do not think it best, to comply with now. . . . You are not *lazy,* and still you *are* an idler. . . . You do not very much dislike to work; and still you do not work much, merely because it does not seem to you that you could get much for it. This habit of uselessly wasting time, is the whole difficulty; and it is vastly important to you, and still more so to your children that you should break this habit. It is more important to them, because they have longer to live, and can keep out of an idle habit before they are in it; easier than they can get out after they are in.

You are now in need of some ready money; and what I propose is, that you shall go to work, 'tooth and nails' for some body who will give you money [for] it. Let father and your boys take charge of things at home—prepare for a crop, and make the crop; and you go to work for the best money wages, or in discharge of any debt you owe, that you can get. And to secure you a fair reward for your labor, I now promise you, that for every dollar you will, between this and the first of next May, get for your own labor, either in money, or in your own indebtedness, I will then give you one other dollar. Now if you will do this, you will soon be out of debt, and what is better, you will have a habit that will keep you from getting in debt again. But if I should now clear you out, next year you will be just as deep in as ever. You say you would almost give your place in Heaven for $70 or $80. Then you value your place in Heaven very cheaply. . . . You have always been kind to me, and I do not now mean to be unkind to you. On the contrary, if you will but follow my advice, you will find it worth more than eight times eighty dollars to you.[168]

In a similar vein, Lincoln wrote on November 4, 1851, to the same step-brother:

When I came into Charleston day-before yesterday I learned that you are anxious to sell the land where you live, and move to Missouri. . . . What can you do in Missouri, better than here? Is the land any richer? Can you there, any more than here, raise corn, & wheat & oats, without work? Will any body there, any more than here, do your work for you? If you intend to go to work, there is no better place than right where you are; if you do not intend to go to work, you can not get along any where.

Now do not misunderstand this letter. I do not write it in any unkindness. I write it in order, if possible, to get you to *face* the truth—which truth is, you are destitute because you had *idled*

57

away all your time. Your thousand pretences for not getting along better, are all non-sense—they deceive no body but yourself. *Go to work* is the only cure for your case.[169]

On November 9, 1851, Lincoln wrote concerning Johnston's son: "As to Abram, I do not want him *on my own account;* but I understand he wants to live with me so that he can go to school, and get a fair start in the world, which I very much wish him to have. When I reach home, if I can make it convenient to take him, I will take him, provided there is no mistake between us as to the object and terms of my taking him."[170]

Indifference gets the better of toughness in the letter of January 12, 1851, again addressed to his stepbrother:

On the day before yesterday I received a letter from Harriett, written at Greenup. She says she has just returned from your house; and that Father [is very] low, and will hardly recover. She also s[ays] you have written me two letters; and that [although] you do not expect me to come now, yo[u wonder] that I do not write. I received both your letters, and although I have not answered them, it is no [t because] I have forgotten them, or been uninterested about them—but because it appeared to me I could write nothing which could do any good. You already know I desire that neither Father or Mother shall be in want of any comfort either in health or sickness while they live; and I feel sure you have not failed to use my name, if necessary, to procure a doctor, or any thing else for Father in his present sickness. My business is such that I could hardly leave home now, if it were not, as it is, that my own wife is sick-abed. (It is a case of baby-sickness, and I suppose is not dangerous.)[171]

The letter ends with that unique religious invocation noted above.[172]

IV. PRACTICALITY

Lincoln's political philosophy is not the result of theoretical reflection and study nor even of experience, but of innate qualities of character and mind. From the qualities of his character we turn now to the qualities of his mind. The qualities of his mind are as extraordinary as the quality of his character. His sheer brainpower must have exceeded that of all other Presidents, Jefferson included. The manifestations are the more astounding as Lincoln's mind was virtually untrained, his sporadic formal elementary schooling having amounted altogether to about one year. That extraordinary intelligence revealed itself in a philosophic understanding of public issues, in a judicious concern with politically relevant detail, in a mastery of political manipulation in military judgment, and in an interest in technological innovation. We shall examine each in turn.

(1) LINCOLN'S UNDERSTANDING OF PUBLIC ISSUES

Lincoln's philosophic understanding of public issues revealed itself not only in his pronouncements on slavery and the preservation of the union but also in his discussion of limited technical issues. Not only did he relate concrete issues to broader philosophical principles but he pointed up connections between moral principles and self-interest. Early in his political career, on December 26, 1839, he made a public speech on whether to use the Sub-Treasury or the National Bank as the federal instrument of financial administration. He explained:

> I now come to the proposition, that it [the Sub-Treasury] would be less secure than a National Bank, as a depository of the public money. The experience of the past, I think, proves the truth of this. And here, inasmuch as I rely chiefly upon experience to establish it, let me ask, how is it that we know any thing—that any

event will occur, that any combination of circumstances will produce a certain result—except by the analogies of past experience? What has once happened, will invariably happen again, when the same circumstances which combined to produce it, shall again combine in the same way. We all feel that we know that a blast of wind would extinguish the flame of the candle that stands by me. How do we know it? We have never seen this flame thus extinguished. We know it, because we have seen through all our lives, that a blast of wind extinguishes the flame of a candle whenever it is thrown fully upon it. Again, we all . . . *know* that we have to die. How? We have never died yet. We know it, because we know, or at least think we know, that of all the beings, just like ourselves, who have been coming into the world for six thousand years, not one is now living who was here two hundred years ago. . . . we know nothing of what will happen in future, but by the analogy of experience. . . . We then, do not say . . . that Bank officers are more honest than Government officers, selected by the same rule. What we do say, is, that the *interest* of the Sub-Treasurer is *against his duty*—while the *interest* of the Bank is *on the side of its duty*. Take instances—a Sub-Treasurer has in his hands one hundred thousand dollars of public money; his *duty* says—'You ought to pay this money over'—but his *interest* says, 'You ought to run away with this sum, and be a nabob the balance of your life.' And who that knows anything of human nature, doubts that, in many instances, interest will prevail over duty, and that the Sub-Treasurer will prefer opulent knavery in a foreign land, to honest poverty at home? But how different is it with a Bank. If it proves faithful to the Government, it continues its business; if unfaithful, it forfeits its charter, breaks up its business, and thereby loses more than all it can make by seizing upon the Government funds in its possession. Its *interest,* therefore, is on the side of its duty—is to be faithful to the Government, and consequently, even the dishonest amongst its managers, have no temptation to be faithless to it.[173]

He also linked human nature with honesty and virtue. In notes for a law lecture on July 24, 1850, Lincoln wrote:

The matter of fees is important, far beyond the mere question of bread and butter involved. Properly attended to, fuller justice is done to both lawyer and client. An exorbitant fee should never be claimed. As a general rule never take your whole fee in advance, nor any more than a small retainer. When fully paid beforehand, you are more than a common mortal if you can feel the same interest in the case, as if something was still in prospect for you, as well as for your client. There is a vague popular belief that lawyers are necessarily dishonest. I say vague, because when we consider to what extent confidence and honors are reposed in and conferred upon lawyers by the people, it appears improbable that their impression of dishonesty is very distinct and vivid. Yet the impression is common, almost universal. Let no young man choosing the law for a calling for a moment yield to the popular belief—resolve to be honest at all events; and if in your own judgment you cannot be an honest lawyer, resolve to be honest without being a lawyer. Choose some other occupation, rather than one in the choosing of which you do, in advance, consent to be a knave.[174]

Lincoln understood that rivalry and factionalism were a permanent part of the human scene and had to be dealt with realistically. On May 27, 1863, he wrote to General Schofield:

Having relieved Gen. Curtis and assigned you to the command of the Department of the Missouri—I think it may be of some advantage for me to state to you why I did it. I did not relieve Gen. Curtis because of any full conviction that he had done wrong by commission or omission. I did it because of a conviction in my mind that the Union men of Missouri, constituting, when united, a vast majority of the whole people, have entered into a pestilent factional quarrel among themselves, Gen. Curtis, perhaps not of choice, being the head of one faction, and Gov. Gamble that of the other. After months of labor to reconcile the difficulty, it seemed to grow worse and worse until I felt it my duty to break it up some how; and as I could not remove Gov. Gamble, I had to removed Gen. Curtis. Now that you are in the position, I wish you to undo nothing merely because Gen. Curtis or Gov. Gamble did it; but to exercise your own judgment, and do *right* for the public interest. Let your military measures be strong enough to repel the invader and keep the peace, and not so strong as to unnecessarily harrass and persecute the people. It is a difficult *role,* and so much greater will be the honor if you perform it well. If both factions, or neither, shall abuse you, you will probably be about right. Beware of being assailed by one, and praised by the other.[175]

(2) ATTENTION TO DETAIL

Lincoln combined his concern for general principles with meticulous attention for practical detail. His plans for political campaigns are strikingly modern in their emphasis on organization and empirical detail. Here is Lincoln's plan for the political campaign of 1840:

1st. Appoint one person in each county as county captain, and take his pledge to perform promptly all the duties assigned him.

Duties of the County Captain

1st. To procure from the poll-books a separate list for each Precinct of all the names of all those persons who voted the Whig ticket in August.
2nd. To appoint one person in each Precinct as Precinct Captain, and, by a personal interview with him, procure his pledge, to perform promptly all the duties assigned him.
3rd. To deliver to each Precinct Captain the list of names as above, belonging to his Precinct; and also a written list of his duties.

Duties of the Precinct Captain

1st. To Divide the list of names delivered him by the County Captain, into Sections of ten who reside most convenient to each other.
2nd. To appoint one person of each Section as Section Captain, and by a personal interview with him, procure his pledge to perform promptly all the duties assigned him.
3rd. To deliver to each Section Captain the list of names belonging to his Section and also a written list of his duties.

Duties of the Section Captain.

1st. To see each man of his Section face to face, and procure his pledge that he will for no consideration (impossibilities excepted) stay from the polls on the first monday in November; and that he will record his vote as early on the day as possible.
2nd. To add to his Section the name of every person in his vicinity who did not vote with us in August, but who will vote with us in the fall, and take the same pledge of him, as from the others.
3rd. To task himself to procure at least such additional names to his Section."[176]

That plan is supplemented by the campaign circular of January 31, 1840:

> After due deliberation, the following is the plan of organization, and the duties required of each county committee.
>
> 1st. To divide their county into small districts, and to appoint in each a sub-committee, whose duty it shall be to make a perfect list of all the voters in their respective districts, and to ascertain with certainty for whom they will vote. . . .
>
> 2nd. It will be the duty of said sub-committee to keep a CONSTANT WATCH on the DOUBTFUL VOTERS. . . .
>
> 3rd. It will also be their duty to report to you, at least once a month, the progress they are making, and on election days see that every Whig is brought to the polls.
>
> 4th. The sub-committees should be appointed immediately; and by the last of April, at least, they should make their first report.
>
> 5th. On the first of each month hereafter, we shall expect to hear from you. After the first report of your sub-committees, unless there should be found a great many doubtful voters, you can tell pretty accurately the manner in which your county will vote. . . .
>
> 6th. When we hear from all the counties, we shall be able to tell with *similar* accuracy, the political complexion of the State. This information will be forwarded to you as soon as received.
>
> 7th. Enclosed is a prospectus for a newspaper to be published until after the Presidential election. It will be SUPERINTENDED BY OURSELVES, and every Whig in the State MUST take it. It will be published so low that every one can afford it. . . .
>
> 8th. Immediately after my election in your county, you must inform us of its results; and as early as possible after any general election, we will give you the like information.
>
> 9th. A Senator in Congress is to be elected by our next Legislature. Let no local interests divide you, but select candidates that can succeed.
>
> 10th. Plan of operations will of course be CONCEALED FROM EVERYONE except OUR GOOD FRIENDS, who of right ought to know them.[177]

It would be wrong to associate Lincoln with political philosophers who talked only of high principles and were indifferent to painstaking efforts to implement them.

During one campaign Lincoln received a letter from Joseph Gilles-
pie, candidate for the State Senate, predicting that Douglas would
carry the votes of at least half the Americans ["Know-Nothings"] in the
district for the Democratic candidate. Lincoln replied on July 25, 1858:

> Your doleful letter of the 18th. was received on my return from
> Chicago last night. I do hope you are worse scared than hurt,
> though you ought to know best. We must not lose that district. We
> must make a job of it, and save it. Lay hold of the proper agencies
> and secure all the Americans you can, at once. I do hope, on
> closer inspection, you will find they are not half gone. Make a little
> test. Run down one of the poll-books of the Edwardsville precinct,
> and take the first hundred known American names. Then quietly
> ascertain how many of them are actually going for Douglas. I think
> you will find less than fifty. But even if you find find [sic] fifty,
> make sure of the other fifty—that is, make sure of all you can at all
> events. We will set other agencies to work, which shall compen-
> sate for the loss of a good many Americans.[178]

Nor was Lincoln beyond offering hard evidence for the practical
results of a moral and political enterprise. To a Senator who opposed
the compensated emancipation of slaves, he replied on March 14, 1862:

> As to the expensiveness of the plan of gradual emancipation
> with compensation, proposed in the late Message, please allow me
> one or two brief suggestions.
> Less than one half-day's cost of this war would pay for all the
> slaves in Delaware at four hundred dollars per head:
> Thus, all the slaves in Delaware,
> By the Census of 1860, are   1798
> 400
> _____
> Cost of the slaves . . . . $ 719,200
> One day's cost of the war . . . .   2,000,000[179]

His instructions to military and political subordinates left nothing to
chance but were highly detailed.

On February 15, 1864, Lincoln wrote to General Sickles:

> I wish you to make a tour for me (principally for observation and
> information) by way of Cairo and New Orleans, and returning by
> the Gulf and Ocean. . . . Please ascertain . . . what is being done, if
> anything, for reconstruction—how the Amnesty proclamation

works, if at all—what practical hitches, if any, there are about it—whether deserters come in from the enemy, what number has come in at each point since the Amnesty, and whether the ratio of their arrival is any greater *since* than before the Amnesty—what deserters report generally, and particularly, whether, and to what extent, the Amnesty is known within the rebel lines. Also learn what you can as to the colored people—how they get along as soldiers, as laborers in our service, on leased plantations, and as hired laborers with their old masters, if there be such cases. Also learn what you can about the colored people within the rebel lines. Also get any other information you may consider interesting, and, from time to time, send me what you may deem important to be known here at once, and be ready to make a general report on your return.[180]

(3) POLITICAL MANIPULATION

Lincoln's concern for empirical data and analysis of detail was informed by a profound understanding of the nature of politics and rendered practical by extraordinary political astuteness. On June 20, 1848, in a speech in the House of Representatives, he laid down the principle on which political judgments must oftentimes be based. "The true rule, in determining to embrace, or reject any thing, is not whether it have *any* evil in it; but whether it have more of evil, than of good. There are few things *wholly* evil, or *wholly* good. Almost everything, especially of governmental policy, is an inseparable compound of the two; so that our best judgment of the preponderance between them is continually demanded. On this principle the president, his friends, and the world generally, act on most subjects. Why not apply it, then, upon this question? Why, as to improvements, magnify the *evil,* and stoutly refuse to see any *good* in them?"[181]

Charles A. Dana, an outstanding journalist who worked for the administration during the Civil War, wrote later: "Lincoln was a supreme politician. He understood politics because he understood human nature. . . . There was no flabby philanthrophy about Abraham Lincoln. He was all solid, hard, keen intelligence combined with goodness."[182]

As member of the Illinois legislature, Lincoln wrote on April 4, 1839, to William S. Waite in defense of a new revenue law, meritorious in itself but on which he offered shrewd political analysis: "I believe it can be sustained, because it does not increase the tax upon the *'many poor'* but upon the *'wealthy few'* by taxing the land that is worth $50 or $100 per acre, in proportion to its value, insted of, as heretofore, no more than that which was worth but $5 per acre. . . . If, however, the wealthy should, regardless of the justness of the complaint, as men often are, when interest is involved in the question, complain of the change, it is still to be remembered, that *they* are not sufficiently numerous to carry the elections."[183]

In preparation of the Republican National Convention he wrote on July 6, 1859, to Schuyler Colfax:

My main object in such conversation would be to hedge against divisions in the Republican ranks generally, and particularly for the contest of 1860. The point of danger is the temptation in different localities to *'platform'* for something which will be popular just there, but which, nevertheless, will be a firebrand elsewhere, and especially in a National convention. Massachusetts republicans should have looked beyond their noses; . . . tilting against foreigners would ruin us in the whole North-West. New-Hampshire and Ohio should forbear tilting against the Fugitive Slave law in such as [to] utterly overwhelm us in Illinois with the charge of enmity to the constitution itself. Kansas, in her confidence that she can be saved to freedom on 'squatter sovereignty'—ought not to forget that to prevent the spread and nationalization of slavery is a national concern, and must be attended to by the nation. In a word, in every locality we should look beyond our noses; and at least say *nothing* on points where it is probable we shall disagree.[184]

Lincoln was capable of eliminating damaging passages from letters and making it appear that no change had been made. He and Horace Greeley planned to publish their correspondence about the possibility of peace negotiations at Niagara Falls in the form of a pamphlet. Lincoln wrote Greeley on August 9, 1864: "Herewith is a full copy of the correspondence, and which I have had privately printed, but not made public. The parts of your letters which I wish suppressed, are only those which, as I think, give too gloomy an aspect to our cause, and those which present the carrying of elections as a motive of action. I have, as you see, drawn a red pencil over the parts I wish suppressed."[185] Yet the pamphlet ended with the following statement: "The foregoing is absolutely the whole record of the case ever seen by the President."[186] Greeley refused to agree to this arrangement, and the pamphlet was not published. It can not be denied that Lincoln's motives were patriotic. As he wrote to Henry J. Raymond, who urged on Lincoln the publication of the full correspondence, on August 15, 1864: "I have proposed to Mr. Greeley that the Niagara correspondence be published, suppressing only the parts of his letters over which the red-pencil is drawn. . . . He declines giving his consent to the publication of his letters unless these parts be published with the rest. I have concluded that it is better for *me* to submit, for the time, to the consequences of the false position in which I consider he has placed me, than to subject the *country* to the consequences of publishing these discouraging and injurious parts."[187] Political morality and right and wrong had to be subordinated to what was good for the country and Lincoln was prepared to withhold certain facts, even denying that they had been withheld, if it served the national interest. He never wavered in his belief that truth-telling was linked with higher purposes which politically included the preservation of the union.

Probably the most brilliant demonstration of Lincoln's political astuteness was his settlement of the Cabinet crisis that threatened to tear his administration apart at the end of 1862. The war was going badly, and the Union troops had suffered a disastrous and bloody defeat at Fredericksburg. Lincoln and Seward, the member of the Cabinet closest to him, were blamed. The demands for Seward to resign were widespread, and there was even serious talk of asking for Lincoln's resignation. The caucus of the Republican senators selected a committee of nine to present their grievances to Lincoln and ask for a reorganization of the Cabinet, meaning primarily Seward's resignation. That agitation was inspired and encouraged by Chase, the Secretary of the Treasury, who aspired to Seward's dominant influence in the Cabinet and even to replacing Lincoln as President. Seward tendered his resignation. Lincoln, after receiving the demands of the committee on December 18, 1862, called a meeting of the Cabinet, not attended by Seward, in which he defended his policies and received agreement from all members that they had rarely disagreed on fundamental policies. With the support of the Cabinet thus secured, Lincoln received the committee of senators again on December 19, in the presence of the whole Cabinet, with the exception of Seward. Lincoln told the senators of the harmony reigning in the Cabinet and thereby disarmed Chase who was reduced to equivocation. When Lincoln asked at the end of the session how many were still in favor of Seward's resignation, only four responded in the affirmative. Thus Seward was saved and Chase discredited.

The next day, Chase told Lincoln that he had been so grieved by the events of the previous night that he had prepared his resignation. "Where is it," asked Lincoln. "I brought it with me," Chase replied, holding a letter in his hand. "Let me have it," said Lincoln and snatched it from the hand of the hesitant Chase. "This," Lincoln said, "cuts the Gordian knot." Lincoln rejected Stanton's resignation who tendered it after Chase did, and he sent identical notes to Seward and Chase, rejecting theirs. Lincoln sums the situation up by saying: "I can rite now. I've got a pumpkin in each end of my bag."[188]

(4) MILITARY JUDGMENT

Lincoln's extraordinary intellectual powers are most strikingly revealed in his judgment on military matters. Military strategy and tactics are generally considered to be highly technical and esoteric issues on which only experts can form a competent judgment. While Lincoln read up on military matters at the beginning of the Civil War, it is obvious that the opinions he voiced both on the general nature of the war and on specific strategic and tactical issues stemmed more from his innate ability to understand and judge correctly the weight and interplay of political and military forces than from his efforts at professional study. Thus he stated with classic simplicity in a letter to General Buell of January 13, 1862, his "general idea of this war to be that we have the *greater* numbers, and the enemy has the *greater* facility of concentrating forces upon points of collision; that we must fail, unless we can find some way of making *our* advantage an over-match for *his;* and that this can only be done by menacing him with superior forces at *different* points, at the *same* time."[189]

In a "Memorandum on Joseph Hooker's Plan of Campaign Against Richmond" of c. April 6–10, 1863, he dealt critically with two alternative battle plans.

My opinion is, that just now, with the enemy directly ahead of us, there is *no* eligible route for us into Richmond; and consequently a question of preference between the Rappahannock route, and the James River route is a contest about nothing. Hence our prime object is the enemies' army in front of us, and is not with, or about, Richmond—at all, unless it be incidental to the main object.

What then? The two armies are face to face with a narrow river between them. Our communications are shorter and safer than are those of the enemy. For this reason, we can, with equal powers fret him more than he can us. I do not think that by raids towards Washington he can derange the Army of the Potomac at all. He has no distant operations which can call any of the Army of the Potomac away; we have such operations which may call him away, at least in part. While he remains in tact, I do not think we

should take the disadvantage of attacking him in his entrench-
ments; but we should continually harrass and menace him, so that
he shall have no leisure, nor safety in sending away detachments.
If he weakens himself, then pitch into him.[190]

Lincoln expressed the same philosophy in a telegram to General
Hooker of June 10, 1863: "If left to me, I would not go South of the
Rappahannock, upon Lee's moving North of it. If you had Richmond
invested to-day, you would not be able to take it in twenty days;
meanwhile, your communications, and with them, your army would be
ruined. I think *Lee's* Army, and not *Richmond,* is your true objective
point. If he comes towards the Upper Potomac, follow on his flank, and
on the inside track, shortening your lines, whilst he lengthens his. Fight
him when opportunity offers. If he stays where he is, fret him, and fret
him."[191]

In his military planning, Lincoln demonstrated the same gift he displayed in his approach to politics of combining the "big picture" with a
meticulous attention to detail. An example is a "Memorandum for a
Plan of Campaign" of October 1, 1861. He ordered:

On, or about the 5th of October, (the exact day to be determined
hereafter) I wish a movement made to seize and hold a point on the
Railroad connecting Virginia and Tennessee, near the Mountain
pass called Cumberland Gap.

That point is now guarded against us by Zolicoffer, with 6000 or
8000, rebels at Barboursville, Kentucky, say twentyfive miles
from the Gap towards Lexington.

We have a force of 5000 or 6000, under General Thomas, at
Camp Dick Robinson, about twentyfive miles from Lexington, and
seventyfive from Zollicoffer's camp on the road between the two,
which is not a Railroad, anywhere between Lexington and the
point to be seized—and along the whole length of which the Union
sentiment among the people largely predominates.

We have military possession of the Railroads from Cincinnati to
Lexington, and from Louisville to Lexington, and some Home
Guards under General Crittenden are on the latter line.

We have possession of the Railroad from Louisville to Nashville, Tenn, so far as Muldrough's Hill, about forty miles, and the
rebels have possession of that road all South of there. At the Hill
we have a force of 8000 under Gen. Sherman; and about an equal
force of rebels is a very short distance South, under under [sic]
Gen. Buckner.

We have a large force at Paducah, and a smaller at Fort-Holt, both on the Kentucky side, with some at Bird's Point, Cairo, Mound City, Evansville, & New Albany, all on the other side; and all which, with the Gun-Boats on the River, are, perhaps, sufficient to guard the Ohio from Louisville to it's mouth.

About supplies of troops, my general idea is that all from Wisconsin, Minnesota, Iowa, Illinois, Missouri, and Kansas, not now elsewhere, be left to *Fremont*.

All from Indiana and Michigan, not now elsewhere, be sent to Anderson at Louisville.

All from Ohio, needed in Western Virginia be sent there; and any remainder, be sent to Mitchell at Cincinnati, for Anderson.

All East of the Mountains be appropriated to McClellan, and to the coast.

As to movements, my idea is that the one for the coast, and that on Cumberland Gap be simultaneous; and that, in the mean time, preparation, vigilant watching, and the defensive only be acted upon—(this however, not to apply to Fremonts operations in Northern and middle Missouri)—that before these movements, Thomas and Sherman shall respectively watch, but not attack Zollicoffer, and Buckner.

That when the coast and Gap movements shall be ready, Sherman is merely to stand fast; while all at Cincincinnati [sic], and all at Louisville with all on the lines, concentrate rapidly at Lexington, and thence to Thomas' camp joining him, and the whole thence upon the Gap.

It is for the Military men to decide whether they can find a pass through the mountains at or near the Gap, which can not be defended by the enemy, with a greatly inferior force, and what is to be done in regard to this.

The Coast and Gap movements made, Generals McClellan and Fremont, in their respective Departments, will avail themselves of any advantages the diversions may present."[192]

On June 28, 1862, Lincoln wrote to Seward: "My view of the present condition of the War is about as follows:

The evacuation of Corinth, and our delay by the flood in the Chicahominy, has enabled the enemy to concentrate too much force in Richmond for McClellan to successfully attack. In fact there soon will be no substantial rebel force any where else. But if we send all the force from here to McClellan, the enemy will, before we can know of it, send a force from Richmond and take Washington. Or, if a large part of the Western Army be brought here to McClellan, they will let us have Richmond, and retake Tennessee, Kentucky, Missouri &c. What should be done is to hold what we have in the West, open the Mississippi, and, take Chatanooga & East Tennessee, without more—a reasonable force should, in every event, be kept about Washington for it's protection. Then let the country give us a hundred thousand new troops in the shortest possible time, which added to McClellan, directly or indirectly, will take Richmond, without endangering any other place which we now hold—and will substantially end the war. I expect to maintain this contest until successful, or till I die, or am conquered, or my term expires, or Congress or the country forsakes me; and I would publicly appeal to the country for this new force, were it not that I fear a general panic and stampede would follow—so hard is it to have a thing understood as it really is. I think the new force should be all, or nearly all infantry, principally because such can be raised most cheaply and quickly.[193]

Lincoln maintained his overall view of the war against the pressure of special geographic interests. Thus he wrote on September 29, 1861, to Governor Morton of Indiana: "As to Kentucky, you do not estimate that state as more important than I do; but I am compelled to watch all points. While I write this I am, if not in *range,* at least in *hearing* of cannon-shot, from an army of enemies more than a hundred thousand strong. I do not expect them to capture this city; but I *know* they would, if I were to send the men and arms from here, to defend Louisville, of which there is not a single hostile armed soldier within forty miles, nor any force known to be moving upon it from any distance."[194]

Lincoln was equally concerned with organization and recruitment. In the "Memorandum on Furloughs" he wrote in November, 1862: "The Army is constantly depleted by company officers who give their men leave of absence in the very face of the enemy, and on the eve of an engagement, which is almost as bad as desertion. At this very moment there are between seventy and one hundred thousand men absent on furlough from the Army of the Potomac. The army, like the nation, has become demoralized by the idea that the war is to be ended, the nation united, and peace restored, by *strategy,* and not by hard desperate fighting. Why, then, should not the soldiers have furloughs?"[195]

On July 3, 1862, Lincoln writes to the Union governors:

I should not want the half of three hundred thousand new

troops, if I could have them *now*. If I had fifty thousand additional troops here *now,* I believe I could substantially close the war in two weeks. But *time* is *every-thing;* and if I get fifty thousand new men in a month, I shall have lost twenty thousand old ones during the same month, having gained only thirty thousand, with the difference between old and new troops still against me. The quicker you send, the fewer you will have to send. *Time* is everything. Please act in view of this. The enemy having given up Corinth, it is not wonderful that he is thereby enabled to check us for a time at Richmond.[196]

One of the great handicaps Lincoln faced in the conduct of the war was the quality of his generals. While Lincoln as a matter of principle deferred to the technical competence of the military leaders and emphasized that he was giving advice but not orders, he did not hesitate to pit his judgment against that of the generals. On July 8, 1863, he wrote to General Lorenzo Thomas: "The forces you speak of will be of no immagineable service, if they can not go forward with a little more expedition. Lee is now passing the Potomac faster than the forces you mention are passing Carlyle. Forces now beyon[d] Carlyle, to be joined by regiments still at Harrisburg, and the united force again to join Pierce somewhere, and the whole to move down the Cumberland Valley, will, in my unprofessional opinion, be quite as likely to capture the Man-in-the-Moon, as any part of Lee's Army."[197]

Lincoln's deepest concern was with General George B. McClellan. His main faults, in Lincoln's eyes, were excessive caution, overestimation of the enemy, and complaints about lack of support. Three letters addressed to McClellan give an insight into Lincoln's military thought and his relations with his generals. On February 3, 1862, he wrote:

You and I have distinct, and different plans for a movement of the Army of the Potomac—yours to be down the Chesapeake, up the Rappahannock to Urbana, and across land to the terminus of the Railroad on the York River—, mine to move directly to a point on the Railroad South West of Manassas.

"If you will give me satisfactory answers to the following questions, I shall gladly yield my plan to yours.

1st. Does not your plan involve a greatly larger expenditure of *time,* and *money* than mine?

2nd. Wherein is a victory *more certain* by your plan than mine?

3rd. Wherein is a victory *more valuable* by your plan than mine?

4th. In fact, would it not be *less* valuable, in this, that it would break no great line of the enemie's communications, while mine would?

5th. In case of disaster, would not a safe retreat be more difficult by your plan than by mine?

Yours truly

A. Lincoln[198]

In an accompanying memorandum, dated February 3, 1862, Lincoln added:

. . . once more let me tell you, it is indispensable to *you* that you strike a blow. I am powerless to help this. You will do me the justice to remember I always insisted, that going down the Bay in search of a field, instead of fighting at or near Mannassas, was only shifting, and not surmounting, a difficulty—that we would find the same enemy, and the same, or equal, intrenchments, at either place. The country will not fail to note—is now noting—that the present hesitation to move upon an intrenched enemy, is but the story of Manassas repeated.

I beg to assure you that I have never written you, or spoken to you, in greater kindness of feeling than now, nor with a fuller purpose to sustain you, so far as in my most anxious judgment, I consistently can. *But you must act.*[199]

On October 13, 1862, Lincoln wrote again to McClellan:

You remember my speaking to you of what I called your over-cautiousness. Are you not over-cautious when you assume that you can not do what the enemy is constantly doing? Should you not claim to be at least his equal in prowess, and act upon the claim?

As I understand, you telegraph Gen. Halleck that you can not subsist your army at Winchester unless the Railroad from Harper's Ferry to that point be put in working order. But the enemy does now subsist his army at Winchester at a distance nearly twice as great from railroad transportation as you would have to do without the railroad last named. He now wagons from Culpepper C.H. which is just about twice as far as you would have to do from Harper's Ferry. He is certainly not more than half as well provided with wagons as you are. I certainly should be pleased for you to have the advantage of the Railroad from Harper's Ferry to

73

Winchester, but it wastes all the remainder of autumn to give it to you; and, in fact ignores the question of *time,* which can not, and must not be ignored.

Again, one of the standard maxims of war, as you know, is 'to operate upon the enemy's communications as much as possible without exposing your own.' You seem to act as if this applies *against* you, but can not apply in your *favor.* Change positions with the enemy, and think you not he would break your communication with Richmond within the next twentyfour hours? You dread his going into Pennsylvania. But if he does so in full force, he gives up his communications to you absolutely, and you have nothing to do but to follow, and ruin him; if he does so with less than full force, fall upon, and beat what is left behind all the easier.

Exclusive of the water line, you are now nearer Richmond than the enemy is by the route that you *can,* and he *must* take. Why can you not reach there before him, unless you admit that he is more than your equal on a march. His route is the arc of a circle while yours is the chord. The roads are as good on yours as on his. . . .

Recurring to the idea of going to Richmond on the inside track, the facility of supplying from the side away from the enemy is remarkable—as it were, by the different spokes of a wheel extending from the hub towards the rim—and this whether you move directly by the chord, or on the inside arc, hugging the Blue Ridge more closely. The chord-line, as you see, carries you by Aldie, Hay-Market, and Fredericksburg; and you see how turn-pikes, railroads, and finally, the Potomac by Acquia Creek, meet you at all points from Washington. The same, only the lines lengthened a little, if you press closer to the Blue Ridge part of the Way. The gaps through the Blue Ridge I understand to be about the following distances from Harper's Ferry, towit: Vestal's five miles; Gregorie's, thirteen, Snicker's eighteen, Ashby's, twenty-eight, Mannassas, thirty-eight, Chester fortyfive, and Thornton's fifty-three. I should think it preferable to take the route nearest the enemy, disabling him to make an important move without your knowledge, and compelling him to keep his forces together, for dread of you. The gaps would enable you to attack if you should wish. For a great part of the way, you would be practically between the enemy and both Washington and Richmond, enabling us to spare you the greatest number of troops from here. When at length, running for Richmond ahead of him enables him to move this way; if he does so, turn and attack him in rear. But I think he should be engaged long before such point is reached. It is all easy if our troops march as well as the enemy; and it is unmanly to say they can not do it.

This letter is in no sense an order.[200]

(5) TECHNOLOGICAL INNOVATIONS

What stands out in Lincoln's approach to political and military problems is not only practicality through attention to empirical detail, but also modernity in a spontaneous awareness of the importance of technological innovations. He expressed this awareness in two "Lectures on Discoveries and Inventions" of April 6, 1858, and February 11, 1859, the second being a revised version of the first. The initial passage of the first will give the flavor of the whole.

> All creation is a mine, and every man, a miner.
>
> The whole earth, and all *within* it, *upon* it, and *round about* it, including *himself,* in his physical, moral, and intellectual nature, and his susceptabilities, are the infinitely various 'leads' from which, man, from the first, was to dig out his destiny.
>
> In the beginning, the mine was unopened, and the miner stood *naked,* and *knowledgeless,* upon it.
>
> Fishes, birds, beasts, and creeping things, are not miners, but *feeders* and *lodgers,* merely. Beavers build houses; but they build them in nowise differently, or better now, than they did, five thousand years ago. Ants, and honey-bees, provide food for winter; but just in the *same way* they did, when Solomon refered the sluggard to them as patterns of prudence.
>
> Man is not the only animal who labors; but he is the only one who *improves* his workmanship. This improvement, he effects by *Discoveries,* and *Inventions.* His first important discovery was the fact that he was naked; and his first invention was the fig-leaf-apron. This simple article—the apron—made of leaves, seems to have been the origin of clothing.[201]

Lincoln went on to pass in review the major discoveries and inventions made by man since Biblical times, referring frequently to passages from the Bible. The second lecture is both more political and more philosophical than the first. Lincoln praises "Young America" for having "a great passion—a perfect rage—for the 'new' ", and contrasts it favorably with the "Old Fogy."

> The great difference between Young America and Old Fogy, is the result of *Discoveries, Inventions,* and *Improvements.* These, in turn, are the result of *observation, reflection* and

experiment. . . . ever since water has been boiled in covered vessels, men have seen the lids of the vessels rise and fall a little, with a sort of fluttering motion, by force of the steam; but so long as this was not specially observed, and reflected and experimented upon, it came to nothing. At length however, after many thousand years, some man observes this long-known effect of hot water lifting a pot-lid, and begins a train of reflection upon it. He says . . . 'the force that lifts the pot-lid, will lift any thing else, which is no heavier than the pot-lid.' 'And, as man has much hard lifting to do, can not this hot-water power be made to help him?' He has become a little excited on the subject, and he fancies he hears a voice answering 'Try me' He does try it; and the *observation, reflection,* and *trial* gives to the world the control of that tremendous, and now well known agent, called steam-power. This is not the actual history in detail, but the general principle.[203]

Lincoln goes on to discuss at length the importance of speech, writing and printing for "facilitating all other inventions and discoveries."[204]

On his trip by railroad to Washington after his election to the presidency, Lincoln in a speech at Lafayette, Indiana, on February 11, 1861, spoke about technological progress: "We have seen great changes within the recollection of some of us who are the older. When I first came to the west, some 44 or 45 years ago, at sundown you had completed a journey of some 30 miles which you had commenced at sunrise, and thought you had done well. Now only six hours have elapsed since I left my home in Illinois where I was surrounded by a large concourse of my fellow citizens, almost all of whom I could recognize, and I find myself far from home surrounded by the thousands I now see before me, who are strangers to me."[205]

Lincoln's interest in technology also had practical results. In 1835–6, Lincoln surveyed and planned the new city of Petersburg a few miles from New Salem. The enterprise was so successful that New Salem became a ghost town within a few years.[206] Lincoln applied for, and received in 1849, a patent for what appears to be a rather complicated contrivance presenting "an improved method of lifting vessels over shoals."[207]

Lincoln's interest in, and aptitude for, modern technology came to the fore during the Civil War. What is impressive is Lincoln's personal involvement in technical innovations. It is not enough that they are introduced; he must see how they work. He was very much interested in the new breech-loading rifle, watched its firing near the White

House, and tried it out himself. He wrote to Stanton on August 9, 1862: "I have examined and seen tried the 'Rafael Repeater' and consider it a decided improvement upon what was called the 'Coffee Mill Gun' in these particulars that it dispenses with the great cost and liability to loss of the Steel cartridges and that it is better arranged to prevent the escape of gas. . . . While I do not order it into the service I think it well worthy of the attention of the Ordnance Bureau and should be rather pleased if it should be decided to put it into the service."[208]

On June 13, 1863, Lincoln wrote to Gideon Welles: "Sec. of Navy, please allow the bearer, Mr. Lyman, to take his new cannon into the Navy-Yard where I wish to see it fired next week."[209] The day before, he had telegraphed General Hooker: "Major-General Hooker: If you can show me a trial of the incendiary shells on Saturday night, I will try to join you at 5 p.m. that day. Answer."[210]

That curiosity to find out for himself how a new device was working was but a particular manifestation of Lincoln's interest in making use of new inventions in order to win the war. He argued in his message to Congress of December 8, 1863: "The change that has taken place in naval vessels and naval warfare, since the introduction of steam as a motive-power for ships-of-war, demands either a corresponding change in some of our existing navy yards, or the establishment of new ones, for the construction and necessary repair of modern naval vessels. No inconsiderable embarrassment, delay, and public injury have been experienced from the want of such governmental establishments.[211]

On January 9, 1864, he wrote to Admiral Dahlgren: "Capt. Lavender wishes to show you a contrivance of his for discovering, and aiding to remove, under-water obstructions to the passage of vessels, and has sufficiently impressed me to induce me to send him to you."[212] On May 9, 1863, he wrote to: "Mr. Watson, Assistant Secretary of War, please see the bearer, who is the man of whom I spoke in reference to a diving invention."[213] In a "Memorandum Concerning Harbor Defenses", Lincoln writes on April 4, 1863: "I have a single idea of my own about harbor defences. It is a Steam-ram, built so as to sacrifice nearly all capacity for carrying, to those of speed and strength, so as to be able to split any vessel having hollow enough in her to carry supplies for a voyage of any distance. Such ram, of course could not her self carry supplies for a voyage of considerable distance; and her business would be to guard a particular harbour, as a Bull-dog guards his master's door."[214] Lincoln ordered the testing of a wrought iron cannon constructed by a Mr. Aimes[215] and promoted assiduously the testing of a new gunpowder invented by Isaac R. Diller, a druggist.

V. POLITICAL PHILOSOPHY

Lincoln conceived of government, in the tradition of nineteenth century liberalism, as a utilitarian institution, subsidiary to the activities of the individual. As he put it in his "Fragment on Government" of July 1, 1854,

> The legitimate object of government, is to do for a community of people, whatever they need to have done, but can not do, *at all,* or can not, *so well do,* for themselves—in their separate, and individual capacities.
>
> In all that the people can individually do as well for themselves, government ought not to interfere.
>
> The desirable things which the individuals of a people can not do, or can not well do, for themselves, fall into two classes: those which have relation to *wrongs,* and those which have not. Each of these branch off into an infinite variety of subdivisions.
>
> The first—that in relation to wrongs--embraces all crimes, misdemeanors, and non-performance of contracts. The other embraces all which, in its nature, and without wrong, requires combined action, as public roads and highways, public schools, charities, pauperism, orphanage, estates of the deceased, and the machinery of government itself.
>
> From this it appears that if all men were just, there still would be *some,* though not *so much,* need of government.[216]

(1) DEMOCRACY

Democracy is distinguished from other forms of government by the principle of political equality: there are no permanent rulers and nobody is permanently excluded from ruling. Lincoln gave this concept a striking formulation in his "Definition of Democracy": "As I would not be a *slave,* so I would not be a *master.* This expresses my idea of democracy. Whatever differs from this, to the extent of the difference, is no democracy."[217] Democratic government is government by the will of the people. As Lincoln put it in "Response to a Serenade" of October 19, 1864, "Their will, constitutionally expressed, is the ultimate law for all. If they should deliberately resolve to have immediate peace even at the loss of their country, and their liberty, I know not the power or the right to resist them. It is their own business, and they must do as they please with their own."[218]

In practical application, the will of the people expresses itself through the will of the majority. In order to avoid despotism, the rule of the majority is subject to constitutional restraints; in order to avoid anarchy, the minority must acquiesce in the rule of the majority. Thus Lincoln declared in the final text of the First Inaugural Address of March 4, 1861:

> If, by the mere force of numbers, a majority should deprive a minority of any clearly written constitutional right, it might, in a moral point of view, justify revolution—certainly would, if such right were a vital one. . . . If the minority will not acquiesce, the majority must, or the government must cease. There is no other alternative; for continuing the government, is acquiescence on one side or the other. If a minority, in such case, will secede rather than acquiesce, they make a precedent which, in turn, will divide and ruin them; for a minority of their own will secede from them, whenever a majority refuses to be controlled by such minority.[219]

The ultimate expression of the people's will is free elections.

> This war is an appeal, by you, from the ballot to the sword; and a great object with me has been to teach the futility of such appeal— to teach that what is decided by the ballot, can not be reversed by the sword—to teach that there can be no successful appeal from a fair election, but to the next election.[220]

In such a democratic order, the powers of the President are narrowly circumscribed.

> The Chief Magistrate derives all his authority from the people, and they have conferred none upon him to fix terms for the separation of the States. The people themselves can do this also if they choose; but the executive, as such, has nothing to do with it. His

duty is to administer the present government, as it came to his hands, and to transmit it, unimpaired by him, to his successor. . . .

By the frame of the government under which we live, this same people have wisely given their public servants but little power for mischief; and have, with equal wisdom, provided for the return of that little to their own hands at very short intervals.

While the people retain their virtue, and vigilence, (sic.) no administration, by any extreme of wickedness or folly, can very seriously injure the government, in the short space of four years.[221]

The foundation of American politics is constitutionalism enshrined in the Constitution: "Don't interfere with anything in the Constitution. That must be maintained, for it is the only safeguard of our liberties."[222] Yet the effectiveness of the Constitution to protect the rights of the people depends upon the strength of the government. Here democracy faces a dilemma: "It has long been a grave question whether any government, not *too* strong for the liberties of its people, can be strong *enough* to maintain its own existence, in great emergencies."[223]

The liberties of the people which the Constitution seeks to protect are at the service of a social system that aims at maximizing substantive—in contrast to merely legal—equality in the sense of equality of opportunity. As Lincoln put it in his Message to Congress of July 4, 1861, with reference to the Civil War:

This is essentially a People's contest. On the side of the Union, it is a struggle for maintaining in the world, that form, and substance of government, whose leading object is, to elevate the condition of men—to lift artificial weights from all shoulders—to clear the paths of laudable pursuit for all—to afford all, an unfettered start, and a fair chance, in the race of life. Yielding to partial, and temporary departures, from necessity, this is the leading object of the government for whose existence we contend.[224]

Lincoln dwells particularly upon the application of this principle to labor. He concludes from his own experience in "Fragment on Free Labor" that:

We know, Southern men declare that their slaves are better off than hired laborers amongst us. How little they *know,* whereof they *speak!* There is no permanent class of hired laborers amongst us. Twentyfive (sic.) years ago, I was a hired laborer. The hired laborer of yesterday, labors on his own account to-day; and will hire others to labor for him to-morrow. Advancement— improvement in condition—is the order of things in a society of equals. As Labor is the common *burthen* of our race, so the effort of *some* to shift their share of the burthen on to the shoulders of *others,* is the great, durable, curse of the race. Originally a curse for transgression upon the whole race, when, as by slavery, it is concentrated on a part only, it becomes the double-refined curse of God upon his creatures.

Free labor has the inspiration of hope; pure slavery has no hope. The power of hope upon human exertion, and happiness, is wonderful. The slave-master himself has a conception of it; and hence the system of *tasks* among slaves. The slave whom you can not drive with the lash to break seventy-five pounds of hemp in a day, if you will task him to break a hundred, and promise him pay for all he does over, he will break you a hundred and fifty. You have substituted *hope,* for the *rod.* And yet perhaps it does not occur to you that to the extent of your gain in the case, you have given up the slave system, and adopted the free system of labor.[225]

Lincoln made the same point in his speech at Indianapolis of September 19, 1859:

The speaker himself had been a hired man twenty-eight years ago. He didn't think he was worse off than a slave. He might not be doing as much good as he could, but he was now working for himself. He thought the whole thing was a mistake. There was a certain relation between capital and labor, and it was proper that it existed. Men who were industrious and sober, and honest in the pursuit of their own interests, should after a while accumulate capital, and after that should be allowed to enjoy it in peace, and if they chose, when they had accumulated capital, to use it to save themselves from actual labor and hire other people to labor for them, it was right. They did not wrong the man they employed, for they found men who have not their own land to work upon or shops to work in, and who were benefitted by working for them as hired laborers, receiving their capital for it.

If a hired laborer worked as a true man, he saved means to buy land of his own, a shop of his own, and to increase his property. For a new beginner, this was the true, genuine principle of free labor. A few men that own capital, hire others, and thus establish the relation of capital and labor rightfully. The hired laborer, with his ability to become an employer, must have every precedence over him who labors under the inducement of force.[226]

The same theme is elaborated in Lincoln's "Address Before the Wisconsin State Agricultural Society" at Milwaukee, Wisconsin, on September 30, 1859:

Again, as has already been said, the opponents of the *'mud-sill'* theory insist that there is not, of necessity, any such thing as the free hired laborer being fixed to that condition for life. There is demonstration for saying this. Many independent men, in this assembly, doubtless a few years ago were hired laborers. And their case is almost if not quite the general rule.[227]

(2) THE UNIQUENESS OF AMERICA

Lincoln was of course profoundly aware of the peculiar character of the American polity, which is not founded upon dynastic succession, ethnic affinity, religious community, or even clearly defined geographical limits, but upon a moral principle laid down in the Declaration of Independence. That awareness is perhaps most eloquently expressed in another of those communications Lincoln wrote to himself, in the form of a "Fragment on the Constitution and the Union." That fragment was obviously stimulated by a letter of Alexander H. Stevens, a supporter of slavery, who wrote Lincoln on December 30, 1860:

In addressing you thus, I would have you understand me as being not a personal enemy, but as one who would have you do what you can to save our common country. A word fitly spoken by you now would be like 'apples of gold in pictures of silver.'[218]

After receiving this letter, Lincoln wrote sometime in the beginning of January:

All this is not the result of accident. It has a philosophical cause. Without the *Constitution* and the *Union,* we could not have attained the result; but even these, are not the primary cause of our great prosperity. There is something back of these, entwining itself more closely about the human heart. That something, is the principle of 'Liberty to all'—the principle that clears the *path* for all—

gives *hope* to all—and, by consequence, *enterprize,* and *industry* to all.

The *expression* of that principle, in our Declaration of Independence, was most happy, and fortunate. *Without* this, as well as *with* it, we could have declared our independence of Great Britain; but *without* it, we could not, I think, have secured our free government, and consequent prosperity. No oppressed, people will *fight,* and *endure,* as our fathers did, without the promise of something better, than a mere change of masters.

The assertion of that *principle,* at *that time,* was *the* word, 'fitly spoken' which has proved an "apple of gold" to us. The *Union,* and the *Constitution,* are the *picture of silver,* subsequently framed around it. The picture was made, not to *conceal,* or *destroy* the apple, but to *adorn,* and *preserve* it. The *picture* was made *for* the apple—*not* the apple for the picture.

So let us act, that neither *picture,* or *apple* shall ever be blurred, or bruised or broken.[229]

Lincoln connected this moral root of America with its subsequent happy history and, more particularly, its ability to absorb millions of immigrants, as he set forth in his speech of July 10, 1858:

We are now a mighty nation, we are thirty—or about thirty millions of people, and we own and inhabit about one-fifteenth part of the dry land of the whole earth. We run our memory back over the pages of history for about eighty-two years and we discover that we were then a very small people in point of numbers, vastly inferior to what we are now, with a vastly less extent of country,—with vastly less of everything we deem desirable among men,—we look upon the change as exceedingly advantageous to us and to our posterity, and we fix upon something that happened away back, as in some way or other being connected with this rise of prosperity. We find a race of men living in that day whom we claim as our fathers and grandfathers; they were iron men, they fought for the principle that they were contending for; and we understood that by what they then did it has followed that the degree of prosperity that we now enjoy has come to us. We hold this annual celebration to remind ourselves of all the good done in this process of time of how it was done and who did it, and how we are historically connected with it; and we go from these meetings in better humor with ourselves—we feel more attached the other to the other, and more firmly bound to the country we inhabit. In every way we are better men in the age, and race, and country in which we live for these celebrations. But after we have done all this we have not yet reached the whole. There is something else connected with it. We have besides these men—descended by blood from our ancestors—among us perhaps half our people who are not descendants at all of these men, they are men who have come from Europe—German, Irish, French and Scandinavian— men that have come from Europe themselves, or whose ancestors have come hither and settled here, finding themselves our equals in all things. If they look back through this history to trace their connection with those days by blood, they find they have none, they cannot carry themselves back into that glorious epoch and make themselves feel that they are part of us, but when they look through that old Declaration of Independence they find that those old men say that 'We hold these truths to be self-evident, that all men are created equal,' and then they feel that that moral senti- ment taught in that day evidences their relation to those men, that it is the father of all moral principle in them, and that they have a right to claim it as though they were blood of the blood, and flesh of the flesh of the men who wrote that Declaration, (loud and long continued applause) and so they are. That is the electric cord in that Declaration that links the hearts of patriotic and liberty-loving men together, that will link those patriotic hearts as long as the love of freedom exists in the minds of men throughout the world.[230]

In his annual message to Congress of December 8, 1863, Lincoln stressed the economic importance of immigration:

I again submit to your consideration the expediency of establish- ing a system for the encouragement of immigration. Although this source of national wealth and strength is again flowing with greater freedom than for several years before the insurrection occurred, there is still a great deficiency of laborers in every field of industry, especially in agriculture and in our mines, as well of iron and coal as of the precious metals. While the demand for labor is thus increased here, tens of thousands of persons, destitute of re- munerative occupation, are thronging our foreign consulates, and offering to emigrate to the United States if essential, but very cheap, assistance can be afforded them. It is easy to see that, under the sharp discipline of civil war, the nation is beginning a new life. This noble effort demands the aid, and ought to receive the attention and support of the government.[231]

In the same message, however, Lincoln warned against the abuse of the ease with which American citizenship can be acquired.

There is reason to believe that many persons born in foreign countries, who have declared their intention to become citizens, or who have been fully naturalized, have evaded the military duty required of them by denying the fact, and thereby throwing upon the government the burden of proof. . . .

There is also reason to believe that foreigners frequently become citizens of the United States for the sole purpose of evading duties imposed by the laws of their native countries, to which, on becoming naturalized here, they at once repair, and though never returning to the United States, they still claim the interposition of this government as citizens. Many altercations and great prejudices have heretofore arisen out of this abuse. It is therefore, submitted to your serious consideration. It might be advisable to fix a limit, beyond which no Citizen of the United States residing abroad may claim the interposition of his government.

The right of suffrage has often been assumed and exercised by aliens, under pretences of naturalization, which they have disavowed when drafted into the military service. I submit the expediency of such an amendment of the law as will make the fact of voting an estoppel against any plea of exemption from military service, or other civil obligation, on the ground of alienage.[232]

At the same time, Lincoln was opposed to any kind of discrimination against naturalized citizens. When asked about his reaction to a discriminatory constitutional amendment adopted by Massachusetts, Lincoln wrote to Dr. Theodore Canisius, a German-American publisher, on May 17, 1859:

Understanding the spirit of our institutions to aim at the *elevation* of men, I am opposed to whatever tends to *degrade* them. I have some little notoriety for commiserating the oppressed condition of the negro; and I should be strangely inconsistent if I could favor any project for curtailing the existing rights of *white men,* even though born in different lands, and speaking different languages from myself.[233]

Lincoln elaborated on this theme in a speech in New Haven on March 6, 1860:

I am glad to see that a system of labor prevails in New England under which laborers CAN strike when they want to (Cheers), where they are not obliged to work under all circumstances, and are not tied down and obliged to labor whether you pay them or not! (Cheers) I *like* the system which lets a man quit when he wants to, and wish it might prevail everywhere. (Tremendous applause) One of the reasons why I am opposed to Slavery is just here. What is the true condition of the laborer? I take it that it is best for all to leave each man free to acquire property as fast as he can. Some will get wealthy. I don't believe in a law to prevent a man from getting rich; it would do more harm than good. So while we do not propose any war upon capital, we do wish to allow the humblest man an equal chance to get rich with everybody else. (Applause) When one starts poor, as most do in the race of life, free society is such that he knows he can better his condition; he knows that there is no fixed condition of labor, for his whole life. I am not ashamed to confess that twenty five years ago I was a hired laborer, mauling rails, at work on a flat-boat—just what might happen to any poor man's son! (Applause.) I want every man to have the chance—and I believe a black man is entitled to it—in which he *can* better his condition—when he may look forward and hope to be a hired laborer this year and the next, work for himself afterward, and finally to hire men to work for him! That is the true system. Up here in New England, you have a soil that scarcely sprouts black-eyed beans, and yet where will you find wealthy men so wealthy, and poverty so rarely in extremity? There is not another such place on earth! (Cheers.) I desire that if you get too thick here, and find it hard to better your condition on this soil, you may have a chance to strike and go somewhere else, where you may not be degraded, nor have your family corrupted by forced rivalry with negro slaves. I want you to have a clean bed, and no snakes in it! (Cheers) Then you can better your condition, and so it may go on and on in one ceaseless round so long as man exists on the face of the earth![234]

As a philosophy of equal opportunity emerged from his own personal experience, so Lincoln saw it confirmed in the experiences of others. Thus in his "Eulogy on Henry Clay" of July 26, 1852, he declared:

Mr. Clay's lack of a more perfect early education, however it may be regretted generally, teaches at least one profitable lesson; it teaches that in this country, one can scarcely be so poor, but that, if he *will,* he *can* acquire sufficient education to get through the world respectably.[235]

In his "Message to Congress in Special Session" of July 4, 1861, Lincoln looked to the Union army and to its adversaries in the south for further evidence of equality:

So large an army as the government has now on foot, was never before known, without a soldier in it, but who had taken his place there, of his own free choice. But more than this: there are many single Regiments whose members, one and another, possess full practical knowledge of all the arts, sciences, professions, and whatever else, whether useful or elegant, is known in the world; and there is scarcely one, from which there could not be selected, a President, a Cabinet, a Congress, and perhaps a Court, abundantly competent to administer the government itself. Nor do I say this is not true, also, in the army of our late friends, now adversaries, in this contest. . . .[236]

In his "Speech to the 166th Ohio Regiment" of August 22, 1864, Lincoln returned to his own present experience as the ground on which the nation must be preserved:

It is not merely for to-day, but for all time to come that we should perpetuate for our children's children this great and free government, which we have enjoyed all our lives. I beg you to remember this, not merely for my sake, but for yours. I happen temporarily to occupy this big White House. I am a living witness that any one of your children may look to come here as my father's child has. It is in order that each of you may have through this free government which we have enjoyed, an open field and a fair chance for your industry, enterprise and intelligence; that you may all have equal privileges in the race of life, with all its desirable human aspirations. It is for this the struggle should be maintained, that we may not lose our birthright—not only for one, but for two or three years. The nation is worth fighting for, to secure such an inestimable jewel.[237]

This system of government set America apart from, and above, other nations. "It is said we have the best Government the world ever knew . . ."[238] Long before the Civil War raised the issue of whether the Union was worth saving, Lincoln elaborated on this theme:

> We find ourselves under the government of a system of political institutions, conducing more essentially to the ends of civil and religious liberty, than any of which the history of former times tells us. We, when mounting the stage of existence, found ourselves the legal inheritors of these fundamental blessings. We toiled not in the acquirement or establishment of them—they are a legacy bequeathed us, by a *once* hardy, brave, and patriotic, but *now* lamented and departed race of ancestors. Their's was the task (and nobly they performed it) to possess themselves, and through themselves, us, of this goodly land; and to uprear upon its hills and its valleys, a political edifice of liberty and equal rights; 'tis ours only, to transmit these, the former, unprofaned by the foot of an invader; the latter, undecayed by the lapse of time, and untorn by [usurpation—to the latest generation that fate shall permit the world to know. This task of gratitude to our fathers, justice to] ourselves, duty to posterity, and love for our species in general, all imperatively require us faithfully to perform.[239]

In reading Lincoln's expression of what is unique and enduring about American society and its government, one cannot but reflect on the differences which stand out between its enduring quality and the triviality of more contemporary statements manufactured by speechwriters and image-makers. For this reason, we return to the full breadth and depth of Lincoln's thought uttered in a quite different period of American history.

(3) THE UNION AS THE ULTIMATE VALUE

Lincoln's principal concern before and during the Civil War was to prevent the disintegration of the United States into sovereign units, that is, to preserve the union of the individual states under a central government. That concern is most movingly expressed in the "letter to Horace Greeley of August 22, 1862":

> I would save the Union. I would save it the shortest way under the Constitution. The sooner the national authority can be re-

stored; the nearer the Union will be "the Union as it was." If there be those who would not save the Union, unless they could at the same time *save* slavery, I do not agree with them. If there be those who would not save the Union unless they could at the same time *destroy* slavery, I do not agree with them. My paramount object in this struggle *is* to save the Union, and is *not* either to save or to destroy slavery. If I could save the Union without freeing *any* slave I would do it; and if I could save it by freeing some and leaving others alone I would also do that. What I do about slavery, and the colored race, I do because I believe it helps to save the Union; and what I forbear, I forbear because I do *not* believe it would help to save the Union.[240]

Even before the outbreak of the Civil War, Lincoln faced the choice between the dissolution of the Union and Civil War with apparent equanimity and obvious determination.

I have desired as sincerely as any man—I sometimes think more than any other man—that our present difficulties might be settled without the shedding of blood. I will not say that all hope is yet gone. But if the alternative is presented, whether the Union is to be broken in fragments and the liberties of the people lost, or blood be shed, you will probably make the choice, with which I shall not be dissatisfied.[241]

Even earlier Lincoln declared on July 23, 1856, in a speech at Galena, Illinois:

But the Union, in any event, won't be dissolved. We don't want to dissolve it, and if you attempt it, *we won't let you*. With the purse and sword, the army and navy and treasury in our hands and at our command, you *couldn't do it*. This Government would be very weak, indeed, if a majority, with a disciplined army and navy, and a well-filled treasury, could not preserve itself, when attacked by an unarmed, undisciplined, unorganized minority.

All this talk about the dissolution of the Union is humbug— nothing but folly. *We* WON'T dissolve the Union, and *you* SHAN'T.[242]

When Lincoln contemplated his probable defeat in the elections of 1864, he wrote to himself on August 23, 1864, a "Memorandum Concerning His Probable Failure of Re-election":

This morning, as for some days past, it seems exceedingly probable that this Administration will not be re-elected. Then it will be my duty to so co-operate with the President elect, as to save the Union between the election and the inauguration; as he will have secured his election on such ground that he can not possibly save it afterwards.[243]

When in July, 1864, General Meade congratulated his army on "driving the enemy from our soil" Lincoln said: "This is a dreadful reminiscence of McClellan; it is the same spirit that moved him to claim a great victory because 'Pennsylvania and Maryland were safe.' Will our generals never get that idea out of their heads? The whole country is our soil."[244]

When people clamored for peace, Lincoln did not lose sight of the purpose of the war. In the "Speech at Great Central Sanitary Fair, Philadelphia, Pennsylvania," of June 16, 1864, he said:

It is a pertinent question often asked in the mind privately, and from one to the other, when is the war to end? . . . . We accepted this war for an object, a worthy object, and the war will end when that object is attained. Under God, I hope it never will until that time. . . . This war has taken three years; it was begun or accepted upon the line of restoring the national authority over the whole national domain, and for the American people, as far as my knowledge enables me to speak, I say we are going through on this line if it takes three years more.[245]

On September 12, 1864, Lincoln wrote to Isaac M. Schermerhorn:

Much is being said about peace; and no man desires peace more ardently than I. Still I am yet unprepared to give up the Union for a peace which, so achieved, could not be of much duration. The preservation of our Union was *not* the sole avowed object for which the war was commenced. It was commenced for precisely the reverse object—*to destroy our Union.* . . . It is true, however, that the administration accepted the war thus commenced, for the sole avowed object of preserving our Union; and it is not true that it has since been, or will be, prossecuted by this administration, for any other object.[246]

When, from the summer of 1864 onwards, the question of peace negotiations arose, Lincoln remained adamant. On July 9, 1864, he wrote to Horace Greeley: "If you can find, any person anywhere professing to have any proposition of Jefferson Davis in writing, for peace, embracing the restoration of the Union and abandonment of slavery, what ever else it embraces, say to him he may come to me with you . . ."[247] On August 24, 1864, Lincoln wrote to Henry J. Raymond:

> You will proceed forthwith and obtain, if possible, a conference for peace with Hon. Jefferson Davis, or any person by him authorized for that purpose. . . .
>
> At said conference you will propose, on behalf this government, that upon the restoration of the Union and the national authority, the war shall cease at once, all remaining questions to be left for adjustment by peaceful modes. If this be accepted hostilities to cease at once.
> If it be not accepted, you will then request to be informed what terms, if any embracing the restoration of the Union, would be accepted.[248]

Lincoln's position with regard to the restoration of the Union never changed during the actual peace negotiations. When the delegation of the Confederacy suggested a postponement of the discussion of this issue while other issues were settled and hostilities stopped, Lincoln's reaction was negative. According to Seward,

> This suggestion, though deliberately considered, was nevertheless regarded by the President as one of armistice or truce, and he announced that we can agree to no cessation or suspension of hostilities, except on the basis of the disbandment of the insurgent forces, and the restoration of the national authority throughout all the States in the Union. . . . It was further declared by the President that the complete restoration of the national authority was an indispensable condition of any assent on our part to whatever form of peace might be proposed.[249]

To John A. Campbell, one of the representatives of the Confederacy, Lincoln wrote on April 5, 1865:

> As to peace, I have said before, and now repeat, that three things are indispensable.
> 1. The restoration of the national authority throughout all the States.
> 2. No receding by the Executive of the United States on the slav-

ery question, from the position assumed thereon, in the late Annual Message to Congress, and in preceding documents.
3. No cessation of hostilities short of an end of the war and the disbanding of all force hostile to the government.[250]

Why was the preservation of the Union and, after the outbreak of the Civil War, its restoration central to Lincoln's political thought and the overriding purpose of his statesmanship? The answer is to be found in the very nature of the American polity. According to Lincoln, whose view echoed the conviction of the Founders, the American polity is a novel experiment in statecraft, and the outcome of that experiment is important not only for America but for all mankind. Long before the issue of slavery and the Civil War put the success of the experiment in jeopardy, Lincoln warned against the dangers threatening the experiment. In his time, Lincoln saw no danger from abroad. In his "Address Before the Young Men's Lyceum of Springfield, Illinois," of January 27, 1838, having as its subject "The Perpetuation of our Political Institutions," Lincoln declared:

Shall we expect some transatlantic military giant, to step the Ocean, and crush us at a blow? Never! All the armies of Europe, Asia and Africa combined, with all the treasure of the earth (our own excepted) in their military chest; with a Buonaparte for a commander, could not by force, take a drink from the Ohio, or make a track on the Blue Ridge, in a trial of a thousand years.

At what point then is the approach of danger to be expected? I answer, if it ever reach us, it must spring up amongst us. It cannot come from abroad. If destruction be our lot, we must ourselves be its author and finisher. As a nation of freemen, we must live through all time, or die by suicide.[251]

Instead of foreign enemies, Lincoln warned against twin dangers from within: mobocracy through lynch law and personal ambition.

When men take it in their heads to day, to hang gamblers, or burn murderers, they should recollect, that, in the confusion usually attending such transactions, they will be as likely to hang or burn some one, who is neither a gambler nor a murderer [as] one who is; and that, acting upon the [exam]ple they set, the mob of tomorrow, may, an[d] probably will, hang or burn some of them, [by th]e very same mistake. And not only so; the innocent, those who have ever set their faces against violations of law in every shape, alike with the guilty, fall victims to the ravages of mob law; and thus it goes on, step by step, till all the walls erected for the defence of the persons and property of individuals, are trodden down, and disregarded. But all this even, is not the full extent of the evil. By such examples, by instances of the perpetrators of such acts going unpunished, the lawless in spirit, are encouraged to become lawless in practice; and having been used to no restraint, but dread of punishment, they thus become, absolutely unrestrained. Having ever regarded Government as their deadliest bane, they make a jubilee of the suspension of its operations; and pray for nothing so much, as its total annihilation. While, on the other hand, good men, men who love tranquility, who desire to abide by the laws, and enjoy their benefits, who would gladly spill their blood in the defence of their country; seeing their property destroyed; their families insulted, and their lives endangered; their persons injured; and seeing nothing in prospect that forebodes a change for the better; become tired of, and disgusted with, a Government that offers them no protection; and are not much averse to a change in which they imagine they have nothing to lose. Thus, then, by the operation of this mobocratic spirit, which all must admit, is now abroad in the land, the strongest bulwark of any Government, and particularly of those constituted like ours, may effectually be broken down and destroyed—I mean the *attachment* of the People. Whenever this effect shall be produced among us; whenever the vicious portion of population shall be permitted to gather in bands of hundreds and thousands, and burn churches, ravage and rob provision stores, throw printing presses into rivers, shoot editors, and hang and burn obnoxious persons at pleasure, and with impunity; depend on it, this Government cannot last. . . .

I know the American People are *much* attached to their Government;—I know they would suffer *much* for its sake;—I know they would endure evils long and patiently, before they would ever think of exchanging it for another. Yet, notwithstanding all this, if the laws be continually despised and disregarded, if their rights to be secure in their persons and property, are held by no better tenure than the caprice of a mob, the alienation of their affections from the Government is the natural consequence; and to that, sooner or later, it must come.[252]

For Lincoln, then, the breakdown of political and civil order was one point at which danger might be expected. He asked himself how danger could be overcome and order preserved:

The answer is simple. Let every American, every lover of liberty, every well wisher to his posterity, swear by the blood of the Revolution never to violate in the least particular, the laws of the country; and never to tolerate their violation by others. As the patriots of seventy-six did to the support of the Declaration of Independence, so to the support of the Constitution and Laws, let every American pledge his life, his property, and his sacred honor;—let every man remember that to violate the law, is to trample on the blood of his father, and to tear the character [charter?] of his own, and his children's liberty. Let reverence for the laws, be breathed by every American mother, to the lisping babe, that prattles on her lap—let it be taught in schools, in seminaries, and in colleges;—let it be preached from the pulpit, proclaimed in legislative halls, and enforced in courts of justice. And, in short, let it become the *political religion* of the nation; and let the old and the young, the rich and the poor, the grave and the gay, of all sexes and tongues, and colors and conditions, sacrifice unceasingly upon its altars.[253]

Then Lincoln asked what was the relationship between lawfulness and what was right. He answered:

There is no grievance that is a fit object of redress by mob law. In any case that arises, as for instance, the promulgation of abolitionism, one of two positions is necessarily true; that is, the thing is right within itself, and therefore deserves the protection of all law and all good citizens; or, it is wrong, and therefore proper to be prohibited by legal enactments; and in neither case, is the interposition of mob law, either necessary, justifiable, or excusable.[254]

Personal ambition was the other threat to the Republic's survival and the further the nation moved from its founding, the more pressing were the dangers from this source. In Lincoln's words: "That our government should have been maintained in its original form from its establishment until now, is not much to be wondered at. It had many props to support it through that period, which now are decayed, and crumbled away. Through that period, it was felt by all, to be an undecided experiment; now, it is understood to be a successful one. Then, all that sought celebrity and fame, and distinction, expected to find them in the success of that experiment. Their *all* was staked upon it:—their destiny was *inseparably* linked with it. Their ambition aspired to display before an admiring world, a practical demonstration of the truth of a proposition, which had hitherto been considered, at best no better, than problematical; namely, *the capability of a people to govern themselves.* If they succeeded, they were to be immortalized. . . . If they failed, they were to be called knaves and fools, and fanatics for a fleeting hour; then to sink and be forgotten. They succeeded. The experiment is successful; and thousands have won their deathless names in making it so. But the game is caught; and I believe it is true, that with the catching, end the pleasures of the chase. This field of glory is harvested, and the crop is already appropriated. But new reapers will arise, and *they,* too, will seek a field. It is to deny, what the history of the world tells us is true, to suppose that men of ambition and talents will not continue to spring up amongst us. And, when they do, they will as naturally seek the gratification of their ruling passion, as others have so done before them. The question then, is, can that gratification be found in supporting and maintaining an edifice that has been erected by others? Most certainly it cannot. Many great and good men sufficiently qualified for any task they should undertake, may ever be found, whose ambition would aspire to nothing beyond a seat in Congress, a gubernatorial or a presidential chair; *but such belong not to the family of the lion, or the tribe of the eagle,*[.] What! think you these places would satisfy an Alexander, a Caesar, or a Napoleon? Never! Towering genuis disdains a beaten path. It seeks regions hitherto unexplored. It sees *no distinction* in adding story to story, upon the monuments of fame, erected to the memory of others. It *denies* that it is glory enough to serve under any chief. It *scorns* to tread in the footsteps of *any* predecessor, however illustrious. It thirsts and burns for distinction; and, if possible, it will have it, whether at the expense of emancipating slaves, or enslaving freemen. Is it unreasonable then to expect, that some man possessed of the loftiest genius, coupled with ambition sufficient to push it to its utmost stretch, will at some time, spring up among us? And when such a one does, it will require the people to be united with each other, attached to the government and laws, and generally intelligent, to successfully frustrate his designs.

Distinction will be his paramount object; and although he would as willingly, perhaps more so, acquire it by doing good as harm; yet, that opportunity being past, and nothing left to be done in the way of building up, he would set boldly to the task of pulling down.²⁵⁵"

It was through the living memory of the American Revolution that personal ambition, rivalry and jealousy had been channeled away from selfish ends and to the service of the republic. For: "the jealousy, envy, and avarice, incident to our nature, and so common to a state of peace, prosperity, and conscious strength, were, for the time, in a great measure smothered and rendered inactive; while the deep rooted principles of *hate,* and the powerful motive of *revenge,* instead of being turned against each other, were directed exclusively against the British nation. And thus, from the force of circumstances, the basest principles of our nature, were either made to lie dormant, or to become the active agents in the advancement of the noblest of cause[s?]—that of establishing and maintaining civil and religious liberty."²⁵⁶

What Lincoln feared was that the fires of liberty and devotion to the common good had been weakened with the passage of time. How was liberty and union to be kept alive, he asked? His reply which he framed with an eye to the future was:

But this state of feeling *must fade, is fading, has faded,* with the circumstances that produced it. I do not mean to say, that the scenes of the revolution *are now* or *ever will be* entirely forgotten; but that like every thing else, they must fade upon the memory of the world, and grow more and more dim. . . . In history, we hope, they will be read of, and recounted, so long as the bible shall be read;—but even granting that they will, their influence *cannot be* what it heretofore has been. Even they *cannot be* so universally known, nor so vividly felt, as they were by the generation just gone to rest. At the close of that struggle, nearly every adult male had been a participator in some of its scenes. The consequence was, that of those scenes, in the form of a husband, a father, a son or a brother, a *living history was* to be found in every family—a history bearing the undubitable testimonies of its own authenticity, in the limbs mangled, in the scars of wounds received, in the midst of the very scenes related—a history, too, that could be read and understood alike by all, the wise and the ignorant, the learned and the unlearned. But *those* histories are gone. They *can* be read no more forever. They *were* a fortress of strength; but, what invading foemen could *never do,* the silent artillery of time *has done;* the levelling of its walls. They are gone. They *were* a forest of giant oaks; but the all-resistless hurricane has swept over them, and left only, here and there, a lonely trunk, despoiled of its verdure, shorn of its foliage; unshading and unshaded, to murmur in a few more gentle breezes, and to combat with its mutilated limbs, a few more ruder storms, then to sink, and be no more.

They *were* the pillars of the temple of liberty; and now, that they have crumbled away, that temple must fall, unless we, their descendants, supply their places with other pillars, hewn from the solid quarry of sober reason. Passion has helped us; but can do so no more. It will in future be our enemy. Reason, cold, calculating, unimpassioned reason, must furnish all the materials for our future support and defence. Let those [materials] be moulded into *general intelligence,* [*sound*] morality and, in particular, *a reverence for the constitution and laws;* and, that we improved to the last; that we remained free to the last; that we revered his name to the last; [that], during his long sleep, we permitted no hostile foot to pass over or desecrate [his] resting place; shall be that which to le[arn the last] trump shall awaken our WASH[INGTON.

Upon these] let the proud fabric of freedom r[est, as the] rock of its basis; and as truly as has been said of the only greater institution, *'the gates of hell shall not prevail against it.'*[257]

Lincoln did not hesitate to invoke the Constitution and popular sovereignty even against himself. He gave one example warning against the unrestrained power of the President to make war. His friend William H. Herndon had defended the proposition:

that if it shall become *necessary, to repel invasion,* the President may, without violation of the Constitution, cross the line, and *invade* the teritory [sic] of another country; and that whether such *necessity* exists in any given case, the President is to be the *sole* judge.

Against this interpretation of executive power, Lincoln replied:

Allow the President to invade a neighboring nation, whenever *he* shall deem it necessary to repel an invasion, and you allow him to do so, *whenever he may choose to say* he deems it necessary for such purpose—and you allow him to make war at pleasure. Study to see if you can fix *any limit* to his power in this respect, after you have given him so much as you propose. If, today, he should choose to say he thinks it necessary to invade Canada, to prevent the British from invading us, how could you stop him? You may say to him, 'I see no probability of the British invading us' but he will say to you 'be silent; I see it, if you dont.' [sic]

The provision of the Constitution giving the war-making power to Congress, was dictated, as I understand it, by the following reasons. Kings had always been involving and impoverishing their people in wars, pretending generally, if not always, that the good of the people was the object. This, our Constitution understood to be the most oppressive of all Kingly oppressions; and they resolved to so frame the Constitution that *no one man* should hold the power of bringing this oppression upon us. But your view destroys the whole matter, and places our President where kings have always stood.[258]

Yet while the threats to the Union for Lincoln lay within rather than outside the nation, he foresaw the role of America as defender of liberty with meaning for all mankind. In his "Eulogy on Henry Clay," Lincoln stressed the latter's dedication to the Union and to America as a model for the world: "He loved his country partly because it was his own country, but mostly because it was a free country. . . . He desired the prosperity of his countrymen partly because they were his countrymen, but chiefly to show to the world that freemen could be prosperous."[259]

It was, however, only when the threat and the actuality of civil war put the Union in jeopardy that Lincoln placed greatest emphasis on the twin arguments of the uniqueness of the American experiment and its significance for the world. In his "Address to the New Jersey Senate at Trenton, New Jersey" on February 21, 1861, he linked America's destiny with that of the world:

I recollect thinking then, boy even though I was, that there must have been something more than common that those men struggled for. I am exceedingly anxious that that thing which they struggled for; that something even more than National Independence; that something that held out a great promise to all the people of the world to all time to come; I am exceedingly anxious that this Union, the Constitution, and the liberties of the people shall be perpetuated in accordance with the original idea for which that struggle was made, and I shall be most happy indeed if I shall be an humble instrument in the hands of the Almighty, and of this, his almost chosen people, for perpetuating the object of that great struggle.[260]

The issue in the struggle between north and south was more than a national question. When the Civil War had just broken out, Lincoln said to Hay:

> For my part, I consider [that] the central idea pervading this struggle is the necessity that is upon us, of proving that popular government is not an absurdity. We must settle this question now, whether in a free government the minority have the right to break up the government whenever they choose. If we fail it will go far to prove the incapability of the people to govern themselves.[261]

Lincoln formulated the issue in his "Message to Congress in Special Session" of July 4, 1861, in philosophic terms of universal applicability:

> And this issue embraces more than the fate of these United States. It presents to the whole family of man, the question, whether a constitutional republic, or a democracy—a government of the people, by the same people—can, or cannot, maintain its territorial integrity, against its own domestic foes. It presents the question, whether discontented individuals, too few in numbers to control administration, according to organic law, in any case, can always, upon the pretences made in this case, or on any other pretences, or arbitrarily, without any pretence, break up their Government, and thus practically put an end to free government upon the earth. It forces us to ask: 'Is there, in all republics, this inherent, and fatal weakness?' 'Must a government, of necessity, be too *strong* for the liberties of its own people, or too *weak* to maintain its own existence?'[262]

Having posed the issue, Lincoln went on to articulate a principle which continues to have relevance for free governments everywhere. He explained that any republican experiment faced three tests, two of which had been met:

> Our popular government has often been called an experiment. Two points in it, our people have already settled—the successful *establishing*, and the successful administering of it. One still remains—its successful *maintenance* against a formidable [internal] attempt to overthrow it. It is now for them to demonstrate to the world, that those who can fairly carry an election, can also suppress a rebellion—that ballots are the rightful, and peaceful,

successors of bullets; and that when ballots have fairly, and constitutionally, decided, there can be no successful appeal, back to bullets; that there can be no successful appeal, except to ballots themselves, at succeeding elections. Such will be a great lesson of peace; teaching men that what they cannot take by an election, neither can they take it by a war—teaching all, the folly of being the beginners of a war.[263]

The Civil War, Lincoln declared in his "Response to Evangelical Lutherans" of May 13, 1862: "involves, in my judgment, not only the civil and religious liberties of our own dear land, but in a large degree the civil and religious liberties of mankind in many countries and through many ages."[264] Most eloquently expressed, Lincoln restated the idea of the trial of free government in the "Address Delivered at the Dedication of the Cemetery at Gettysburg" on November 19, 1863:

> Four score and seven years ago our fathers brought forth on this continent, a new nation, conceived in Liberty, and dedicated to the proposition that all men are created equal.
> Now we are engaged in a great civil war, testing whether that nation, or any nation so conceived and so dedicated, can long endure. . . . It is rather for us to be here dedicated to the great task remaining before us . . . that this nation, under God, shall have a new birth of freedom—and that government of the people, by the people, for the people, shall not perish from the earth.[265]

After the presidential election of 1864, Lincoln thought that America had passed the test. On November 10, 1864, in "Response to a Serenade," he observed: "It has long been a grave question whether any government, not *too* strong for the liberties of its people, can be strong *enough* to maintain its own existence, in great emergencies."[266] The Civil War in itself had confronted the nation with a severe test and holding an election in the midst of the strife had added to the strain. Yet elections in a democracy are a necessity even when the people are divided and at political war with one another. If the election had been postponed, that act would have proven that free government could be destroyed in rebellion. Lincoln added that human nature would not change. In future trials, the nation would face similar tests. Only brave and patriotic men can prevail. Lincoln proclaimed that: "It [the election] has demonstrated that a people's government can sustain a national election, in the midst of a great civil war. Until now it has not been known to the world that this was a possibility."[267] The election,

Lincoln explained, had shown that the American polity was sound and strong. But there were other lessons to be learned if the nation's common interest was to be rediscovered and rekindled. As the electoral victor, Lincoln expressed no self-righteousness but announced: "While I am deeply sensible to the high compliment of a re-election; and duly grateful, as I trust to Almighty God for having directed my countrymen to a right conclusion, as I think, for their own good, it adds nothing to my satisfaction that any other man may be disappointed or pained by the result."[268] Nearly a century later, another western leader, Winston S. Churchill, was to speak in similar tones of "maganimity in victory."

But perhaps Lincoln understood even more the importance of the place of compassion in the search for the common interest, the need to reunite all the people in a common effort to save "our common country." It was Lincoln who concluded: "May I ask those who have not differed with me, to join with me, in this same spirit towards those who have?"[269] Before he suffered a martyr's death, Lincoln tried to prepare the nation to understand that in any future trial, America would have strong men as well as weak, bad men as well as good. Following its trials, however, the nation ought to view its deeds not as wrongs to be revenged, but in a spirit of "malice toward none . . . charity for all."[270] For men everywhere struggling to preserve freedom, Lincoln's most enduring legacy may well be his joining of the principles of firmness in crisis and forgiveness in victory. May they survive.

PART TWO

ABRAHAM LINCOLN'S
THEOLOGICAL OUTLOOK

by

DAVID HEIN

PART 1
LINCOLN'S FAITH

INTRODUCTION

A singular feature of the ways in which men have interpreted the wars in which they have been engaged—at least up until the 1920s—is that participants and onlookers alike have often dreamed that human works would result in holy gains, that expenditures of blood and treasure could purchase cleansing and sanctification, that military victory would bring divine rewards: a reformed, regenerated, redeemed people in a united land. When T. E. Lawrence wrote in the decade following World War I of the Arab Revolt against the Turks, he told a wistful tale that intertwined strands of innocence and experience, of naive expectations and calculated fraud, of grand visions and double-dealing. "We lived many lives in those whirling campaigns, never sparing ourselves: yet when we achieved and the new world dawned," erstwhile ways reasserted themselves: Arab bickered with Arab as French and English diplomats carved up the territory for European powers. The revolt's victorious conclusion was refashioned when "the old men came out again" and redefined the triumph "in the likeness of the former world they knew. Youth could win, but had not learned to keep: and was pitiably weak against age. We stammered that we had worked for a new heaven and a new earth, and they thanked us kindly and made their peace."[i] Certainly something, however initially abstract, was produced through the uprising in the desert, a principle of freedom perhaps, that could not finally be gainsaid. But before even a part of that freedom could be effected, there was the experience of rivalry, duplicity, and Sykes-Picot. And there never was a new heaven and a new earth.

Recent commentators have described Lincoln as one who believed that the Civil War was not only an instance in which divine retributive justice was being worked out but also an experience through which the nation would be reborn, made new after a baptism of blood. Taking only the second point for now, would we not have to say that, if this were true, his faith blinded him to reality? In what way were citizens morally or spiritually better after the war? The aftermath of the Civil War rather more closely resembled the conclusion of the First World War than it did the dawning of the Endtime. H. Richard Niebuhr has written that the judgment that the Civil War brought liberty to the slaves "is questionable, for the war-won liberty of the Negro was not liberty indeed and the equality written into laws was neither complete nor practicable in an unconverted kingdom of this world." Tasks remaining after the war were as mighty as the ones that preceded it: "giving white men freedom from their fetters of pride and race fear," according "black men freedom from the hopelessness and ignorance wherewith they reinforced their masters' bondage." And there were other problems as well, especially that of "liberating the new slaves of the northern victors, the growing army in factories and cities of those who, coming from Europe or our own land, became the serfs of a new order of masters."[ii] Lincoln would have understood (in kind if not in detail) the events described by Lawrence and would not have been surprised by them. He had hopes, but his confidence did not reside in human works producing holy gains; he had faith, but not such as to be able to tally with any dispatch God's action in the war·in terms of pluses and minuses, describable goods and particular judgments.

In order to comprehend Lincoln, we need to know more about him than that he was faithful; but we shall discover nothing about him if we do not first recognize that he was a believer who trusted in the graciousness of Being. We can learn much concerning Lincoln's theological outlook just by seeing that "faith" can be defined in a certain way and that that understanding can be applied to him. In this discussion, I take "faith" to designate two distinct but related movements of the heart, mind, and will: *fiducia* and *fidelitas*. The word will be used to refer not to intellectual assent to propositions but to trust and loyalty, confidence in the One whose power is good and whose goodness is powerful, and responsible commitment to this One's cause of universal community.[iii]

Throughout his writings and speeches, Lincoln expressed his reliance on God, "overruling Providence," the Almighty Father. In his political life it is possible to see him from early days to his last day reaching out to reconcile contending factions, to heal wounds, and to build up community. He demonstrated concern not only for America but for all human beings and for their children. In all of this he took no credit for himself but repeatedly acknowledged that to God belonged the glory and the greatness, the victory and the power. Herbert Butterfield has asked "why in politics the virtues I associate with the Christian religion should be suspended: humility, charity, self-judgment, and acceptance of the problem Providence sets before one" and why there cannot be present in our leaders "a disposition not to direct affairs as a sovereign will in the world, but to make one's action a form of co-operation with Providence."[iv] In Abraham Lincoln we can see that those virtues and that disposition are not necessarily absent in statesmen, that they can be present to a significant degree.

In what follows I shall try to say some of this in more detail. Throughout, it is my intention to develop an understanding of the sixteenth President as a "witness to God," to whom the Civil War was a "fiery trial" in which many Americans suffered and died, sacrificing themselves for the sake of others. The phrase "witness to God" is another way of describing the person of faith, who is both trusting and loyal. Lincoln in his efforts both before and during the war manifested loyalty to the cause of the universal commonwealth; his devotion to God is apparent in his theocentric interpretation of experience. This reliance on the power of God has been termed "fatalism" by a number of Lincoln scholars. That is not an accurate description of his faith. We should be able to see that Lincoln responded in his being and doing not to a Determiner of his destiny that has the impersonal character of fate but rather to a Ruler of the realm of heaven and earth who is personal and caring. The God in whom Lincoln trusted acts toward his creation more like a father to his children than like a manufacturer to his products. The world this God governs is not one in which all that occurs happens blindly, without significance, but one in which there is divine activity for good and the promise of liberation, a world where persons are responsible actors and where suffering has meaning.[v]

I begin by setting forth and assessing some important features of the prevailing understanding of Abraham Lincoln's theological outlook. (So much has been written about Lincoln by so many that it would be impossible otherwise than by removing obstacles to start with a clean slate.) I suggest some difficulties with reigning interpretations before commencing my own constructive effort. The focus in presenting Lincoln's thoughts is on his own utterances and chiefly as these are found in his letters and speeches. The picture of Lincoln that emerges is that of a complex man, who, while not exactly a prophet, was a believer, and who, as such, can reveal in profound yet subtle ways what it means to confess, "I believe in God the Father Almighty. . . ."

CHAPTER I
WITNESS TO GOD

Of the numerous chroniclers of Lincoln's religious beliefs, William J. Wolf may be the best known and most important. His highly-regarded studies are up-to-date and scholarly. In the discussion that follows, I will use his writings to indicate some significant features of the prevailing interpretation of Lincoln's understanding of divine providence. Wolf's views will be supplemented by those of others to demonstrate what the standard approaches to Lincoln have been.

The first item of significance we should note is that those who have studied Lincoln and written about his beliefs have generally found that the Lincoln of the Second Inaugural was different in important and discernible ways from the younger Lincoln. Wolf joins in the consensus that points to change in Lincoln's theological outlook and claims that in the last year or final months of his life Lincoln perceived, perhaps for the first time, God's plan in the conflict. Not before did he clearly see what God's intentions for the nation actually were. This new awareness of God's purposes enabled Lincoln in his Second Inaugural Address on March 4, 1865, to employ, in Wolf's words, "the severe language of Scripture" and to hold "the nation under judgment." "For somewhat more than the last year of his life Lincoln understood the tragedy and suffering of the Civil War as God's judgment upon this evil [of slavery] and as punishment to bring about its removal." Slavery was a sin in which the whole nation had participated; because it was a national evil "judgment fell upon both sides." Wolf believes Lincoln thought "that a just God might allow the war to continue 'until all the wealth piled by the bondman's 250 years of unrequited toil shall be sunk.'" Lincoln saw, though, according to Wolf, that punishment was only part of a story that also included the "reformation" and "renewal" of the people of America "newly dedicated to the increase of freedom."[1] Change, judgment, and reformation are the lineaments of an interpretation I shall want to examine more closely. Wolf's view that

Lincoln understood the war as divine punishment for the national sin of slavery is a dominant scholarly position and a second feature in the standard treatment of Lincoln I want to examine.

This understanding of the war as a divine judgment upon both sides for the sin of tolerating slavery is one that virtually all scholars who have written about Lincoln's religious outlook have ascribed to him. Stephen B. Oates writes in his recent (1977) biography *With Malice Toward None:* "in his search for the meaning of this vast struggle, he'd come to view it finally as a divine punishment for the sin of slavery, as a terrible retribution visited by God on a guilty people. . . ."[2] Other historians and students of the period agree with Oates' view. One could cite almost identical statements by J. G. Randall, Richard Current, Timothy L. Smith, Conrad Cherry, Ronald Marstin, John Updike, Richard Hofstadter, Ernest G. Bormann, John Wesley Hill, George B. Forgie, Geoffrey C. Ward, Richard S. Emrich, and Ida Tarbell, among many others.[3]

D. Elton Trueblood writes in a recent work that Lincoln saw the war as a penalty demanded by justice in payment for the sin and guilt of slavery. He refers to Lincoln as "the theologian of American anguish" and says that as the days passed the President became more and more convinced of the truth of this answer to the question of the war's meaning; it was an answer he was finally able to state "with amazing firmness." Lincoln, Trueblood says, "grew convinced that our universe, far from demonstrating a merely mechanical order, is a theater for the working out of the moral law."[4] In his understanding of Lincoln's having arrived at this conviction after a long period during which Lincoln could see little more than, as it were, "puzzling reflections in a mirror,"[5] Trueblood is at one with Wolf.

Something interesting happens when we turn to the reputed element of national spiritual transformation in Lincoln's interpretation of the Civil War. In their depiction of the President as a biblical prophet pronouncing the righteous judgment of God upon an immoral, insensitive nation, some commentators have seen Lincoln acting like a prophet in linking the nation's pardon and rebirth to its repentance. Thus Trueblood can write: "Terrible as it was, the ordeal might, Lincoln believed, turn into a blessing if it could induce true humility."[6] David D. Anderson, a historian, voices a similar view when he writes of Lincoln's theological understanding of the war that it "became both a punishment and a purging, perhaps prefatory to another resurgence of greatness under God if man were able and willing to accept and build upon the righteous punishment of God.'"[7] This view of Lincoln as one who held that contrition, change of direction, and restitution were preconditions for God's deliverance of the nation, for his blessing, is a highly problematic reading of the available evidence.

The scraps of evidence on which this judgment relies are found in documents like the March 30, 1863, proclamation for a National Fast Day to be observed on the following 30th of April. These documents, which were probably composed at least in part by Secretary of State William H. Seward, request the people's prayers in altogether conventional and expected ways. It is possible to juxtapose them with the President's statements from the same or later periods in letters and elsewhere and see that his personal views on the subject of God's actions in history and the purposes and consequences thereof were profoundly different from the theological ideas presented in these public proclamations. One is better off, I think, not using such statements at all in attempts to come to an understanding of Lincoln's faith in God than in relying on them as direct, literal expressions of Lincoln's theology.

There are two ways of approaching the matter. One can follow the path set out by Trueblood, Anderson, et al., and see Lincoln as a prophet who called upon Americans to confess their sins and transform their lives, believing that if they did not do so, God would not effect their salvation; or one can see this call in its proper historical and theological context as first and last an effort to bring the people to acknowledge their own wretchedness in the presence of God's grace.

The first alternative is taken by Robert Benne and Philip Hefner in their book, *Defining America: A Christian Critique of the American Dream* (1974). They say that Lincoln "struggled valiantly to open his contemporaries' eyes to the fact that their woe was in fact a manifestation of wrath"; and then they state what is certainly the logical correlate of that conclusion when examining Lincoln from the perspective of interpreting him as a prophetic figure. Lincoln, they hold, believed that if the people, by working to bring about fundamental human rights, could help establish freedom and equality for all men, "further wrath might be avoided. . . ."[8] The relation between the two interpretations of Lincoln—the one that sees him believing the war to be the true judgment of a wrathful God, the other seeing the judgment averted only after national works of righteousness have begun—is a close and natural one. It is, as so many chroniclers of Lincoln's religion have said, the understanding of history of the great biblical prophets.

An alternative would be to say that Lincoln used this traditional language not because he believed God's working of good to be dependent upon a prior human act but simply because it was an appropriate way to move the people to their first duty of looking to God rather than themselves in moments of crisis. What Lincoln really wanted was for citizens to realize that their salvation came *sola gratia* rather than by their own striving, that they were justified by faith alone, and so should stop looking to themselves and their own righteousness but rather turn to God. I do not know precisely what President Reagan intended when he declared November 22–28, 1981, to be Bible Week and suggested 2 Chronicles 7:14[9] as an appropriate text for the occasion; but I would submit—against Benne, Hefner, Anderson, and Trueblood—that the point of view expressed in that text was not part of Lincoln's deep theological interpretation of the Civil War and say instead that he believed God would heal the land no matter what the people did.

It should be noted that Wolf confined himself to the view that Lincoln believed that the Civil War involved in some way God acting to bring about America's renewal, correction, reformation, and regeneration. In the background of the Gettysburg Address, he argued, lies the image of "baptism" and "biblical regeneration," pointing to the "spiritual rebirth" of America. Wolf did not say that Lincoln believed the existence of the new America to be dependent upon a prior moral revolution in the old America. He did not, in other words, follow the prophetic line of interpretation to the point of saying that Lincoln thought the nation's future could only be secure from the judgments of a wrathful God if it changed its ways and embraced the principle of justice for all.[10]

(1) CRITIQUE OF STANDARD INTERPRETATIONS OF LINCOLN'S FAITH

At this point I want to take up three important elements in the standard approach to Lincoln's faith and offer a critique of them. Lincoln scholars have said that his beliefs changed over a period of time, that he eventually came to see God present in the Civil War punishing the country for allowing slavery to exist for so long, and that he looked forward to a spiritually transformed postwar land.

No hard evidence exists to support the contention that Lincoln's beliefs changed in discernible ways over time. In fact, his central religious affirmations stayed remarkably consistent throughout his life.

One curious feature of this claim that Lincoln's views underwent some kind of transmutation is that, while many writers point to change in his life, each appears to have a different date in mind for this juncture. Thus Raymond Settle asserts that "a change came over" Lincoln in 1839 when he was thirty years of age. Charles Phillips says, though, that "peace came to Lincoln" even earlier than that. A new "conviction" found its way into Abraham's heart on "a certain crucial day in that year 1835." That is just about the time that Ida Tarbell says Lincoln turned his back on Christianity. In a recent article Ronald Rietveld points to a decisive transformation in Lincoln's thinking about himself, God, and the world after a crisis in early 1841. Harlan Horner reports that there was an "unmistakable change in his attitude" in the year of his election to the presidency, 1860. Before that year Lincoln gave "little evidence of being in personal need of God." Ruth Painter Randall, in an article about Lincoln's faith, states that there was a difference "in his religious feeling after Willie's death." Lincoln's son died on February 20, 1862. David Anderson says that the "return of religious faith" on Lincoln's part might have been "initiated by the death of his son Eddie on February 1, 1850." Trueblood draws attention to "remarkable growth" throughout the presidential years and says that it "is especially obvious in Lincoln's spiritual pilgrimage . . . that the theological positions of his early manhood had little in common with those expressed at the end."

One of the latest books about Lincoln's beliefs, *Abraham Lincoln: The Man and His Faith* by G. Frederick Owen (1976, 1981), claims to have evidence that Lincoln became converted to Christianity after his visit to Gettysburg in 1863. He cites three sources in support of this assertion, but all of them depend, as a matter of fact, on one apocryphal quotation. In this spurious saying Lincoln tells "an Illinois clergyman" that he "was not a Christian" when he entered the White House and still was not a Christian during "the severest trial of my life," the burial of his son in 1862. "But when I went to Gettysburg, and saw the graves of thousands of our soldiers, I then and there consecrated myself to Christ. Yes, I *do* love Jesus." Dr. Owen's claim to have evidence of Lincoln's conversion made the *New York Times* a few years ago. As it happens, a little checking will lead one to discover the fact that the only source for this quotation is Osborn H. Oldroyd's *The Lincoln Memorial: Album-Immortelles,* published in 1882.[11] It is a book that is full of inauthentic, undocumented Lincoln utterances. The saying of Lincoln's I have quoted has no further reference than its unhelpful title, "Reply to an Illinois Clergyman." It must be rejected. The evidence cited by the other authors is not appreciably better than Owen's. Lincoln does not mention any change in his beliefs in his writings, and I do not think that any change can be inferred.

The central elements of Lincoln's "mature" religious faith were already present in that of the youthful Lincoln. In 1842 he wrote a letter to his closest friend, Joshua F. Speed, in which he discussed Speed's engagement to be married and stated his belief that "God made me one of the instruments of bringing your Fanny and you together, which union, I have no doubt He had fore-ordained." Here we have clearly expressed a strong belief in God's overruling providence and a conviction that Abraham Lincoln might be employed by God as an "instrument" to bring about the specific good of reconciliation. Both of these would be among the wartime themes of Lincoln's faith. In this same letter he went on to state confidently: "Whatever he [God] designs, he will do for *me* yet. 'Stand *still* and see the salvation of the Lord' is my text just now."[12] This quotation from the fourteenth chapter of Exodus expresses in a nutshell the faith of the Civil War President. He believed God was capable of bringing good out of difficult situations, whether that situation was Egyptian bondage, his own frustrated career, or the sufferings of thousands.

Lincoln's later concern for the whole commonwealth of man was adumbrated in a speech of 1844.[13] His trust in a personal, caring God was expressed in his letter to John D. Johnston in which he commented on his father's fatal illness and asked his stepbrother Johnston to remind Thomas Lincoln "to call upon, and confide in, our great, and good, and merciful Maker; who will not turn away from him in any extremity." God "notes the fall of a sparrow, and numbers the hairs of our heads; and He will not forget the dying man, who puts his trust in Him."[14] In an address eulogizing an early hero, Henry Clay, Lincoln mentioned faith in "the continued care of Divine Providence, trusting that, in future national emergencies, He will not fail to provide us the instruments of safety and security."[15] Thus he saw God as One who is active not only to relieve personal suffering but also to care for the nation.

Wolf points to several periods of spiritual transformation in Lincoln's life,[16] but the one on which I now want to focus is that final year during which Wolf says "Lincoln's gift of mystical intuition led him into a specific explanation of the slavery issue in terms of the Old Testament prophets."[17] According to Wolf Lincoln finally arrived at a clear theological understanding of the war's meaning. The conflict was now perceived as a judgment of God that would eliminate slavery and renew America.[18] Wolf's asseveration of a change in Lincoln's last year leading to a heightened mystical awareness of the divine purposes in the war is an interesting and important one but it is hard to know exactly what he means by it. Since he has already said that Lincoln spoke of the war as a divine punishment in the proclamations of previous years, he cannot mean that the idea itself was a new element in Lincoln's thought. He could mean that not until his final year did Lincoln give "a full and clear answer" to the question of God's involvement in the war.[19] This is a strong possibility because one finds Lincoln making statements subsequent to the issuance of the presidential proclamations in which he affirmed that God's intentions in the war were hidden. Thus while, for instance, the August 12, 1861, Proclamation of a National Fast Day asked the nation "to pray that we may be spared further punishment,"[20] Lincoln wrote a year later the personal statement that is known as his Meditation on the Divine Will. It is a clear acknowledgment on Lincoln's part that he could not claim to know for sure what the purposes of God were in the war.[21] Wolf could mean, then, that only in the last thirteen months or so of his life did Lincoln perceive God's purposes in the war face to face. Whether as the result of "mystical intuition" or some process of divination or through simple prayer, Lincoln grasped as never before the meaning of the awful conflict.

I can find no evidence, however, for this new awareness. In a letter to Eliza P. Gurney of September 4, 1864, Lincoln told her much the same thing he had told her two years before: although "the purposes of the Almighty are perfect," one is bound to say it is hard "to accurately perceive them in advance." The most that one can do is "work earnestly in the best light He gives us, trusting that so working still conduces to the great ends He ordains."[22] When Lincoln told his audience that, in the conflict, "the Almighty has his own purposes," he did not mean for them to suppose that he would then go on to spell out in detail just what those purposes were. That would indeed constitute a remarkable change in Lincoln's understanding of the war and of his own role: he would in fact have become a prophetic figure. What I think Lincoln meant was simply what he had always meant: we may trust that God is powerfully at work in this drama and that his purposes therein are good, but let us not presume to place ourselves in the position of the Almighty; rather, let us do what we can as human beings to relieve distress and to build a just peace.

Finally, let me address the possibility that what Wolf has in mind is that Lincoln came to see the war as a process whose ultimate meaning lay in the fact that by means of this bloodshed, slavery would be excised like a tumor and the nation would be not only punished but reformed and renewed. It seems to me—and I believe I am not alone in this judgment—that Lincoln's understanding of the primary goal of the war never changed. We still hear him in the last year of his life speaking of "the cause of the Union."[23] For Lincoln this one end—Union— subsumed all other goals. The central question to be determined in the course of the war continued throughout the long years of death and destruction to be, as he put it on November 10, 1864—only five months before his death—"whether any government, not *too* strong for the liberties of its people, can be strong *enough* to maintain its own existence in great emergencies."[24] On this essential aim he never wavered.

As to the other point, that Lincoln came to see reformation of the people as one of God's purposes in the war, this conception of national purification or regeneration was not present in Lincoln either in his specific statements or in his general understanding of the period of history in which he was a principal actor. One searches in vain in the Lincoln corpus for any sign that he came to see the war in a new way in the last year of his life. Indeed, his basic theological approach to the conflict was essentially the same as the understanding of God's ways evinced in his letter to Speed written decades earlier in which he informed his friend that a passage from Exodus 14 was the text that spelled out his marching orders for the day.

Another point to be considered in raising the issue of whether or not Wolf and others are correct in their interpretation of Lincoln is one having to do with the singularity of Lincoln's theological understanding of the Civil War: was there really anything special about Lincoln's view? If Wolf and Trueblood and other commentators are correct, then the only honest answer one can give to such a question is No. Let us examine the meaning of this response in more detail.

Wolf states that Lincoln was able to discover God's will through a process that resembled the ways in which the Puritans arrived at knowledge of God's purposes.[25] Wolf has brought us in these comments to the point of some significant insights but he does not develop them. The Lincoln of conventional interpretation would indeed have had a great deal in common with his Puritan predecessors.

A principal means employed by the Puritans to express their understanding of the workings of God in history was the "jeremiad," which was a sermon delivered on major public occasions in which listeners were reminded that God had a hand in all their sufferings, that these afflictions were his chastisements for sin and signs of his continuing love, and that they should give up their wicked ways and hope for God's deliverance. These sermons were both threatening and comforting in their depiction of God's dealings with men.[26] They attest to the drama of the Puritans' theology of history, which in the early eighteenth century saw God punishing New England in the form of droughts, sickness, fire, and other afflictions. The Puritans saw themselves "as a chosen race, entered into specific convenants with God, by the terms of which they would be proportionately punished for their sins." Their sufferings "were divine appointments, not the hazards of natural and impersonal forces."[27]

The theme of patriotic sermons in the 1750s was providential affliction for national sins. These judgments of God were meant to prompt
the people to mend their ways and reform. "If the people would change
their ways, the Lord was always eager to change their fortunes and
prosper them."[28] Americans began to interpret not only their woes as
God's chastisement for sin but also their successes as signs of divine
favor. God was seen to bring about victory in war. The successful
capture of Louisburg from the French in 1745 during King George's
War was attributed ultimately to God.[29] After 1763 patriot spokesmen
identified political liberty as the principal aim of God in history and
believed it to be in accordance with God's will that America resist
British tyranny.[30] "The Revolutionary era carried on the jeremiad tradition: sin was seen . . . as a major cause of political, social, and
economic evils."[31] According to the same logic, the British flight after
the battles of Lexington and Concord was seen to be the vengeance of
the Lord upon them and their tyrannous ways, and it was also believed
that "if America reformed she would, with God's assistance, utterly
defeat the British."[32] In the period after the Revolution, both Federalists and Republicans claimed God for their own side and policies.[33]
"Providential rhetoric . . . permeated both Federalist opposition to,
and Republican support of, the War of 1812."[34] The Federalists,
"working within the jeremiad tradition," depicted the war as divine
punishment for the nation's sins, whereas the Republicans pointed to
the war's outcome as a vindication of their claims respecting the justice
and merits of the war effort.[35]

The standard interpretation of Lincoln fits neatly into the long tradition of the patriotic jeremiad. As this form developed it came to follow
the same basic scheme through hundreds of repetitions, and it is the
same form that many Lincoln commentators claim is present in his
religious thought. Perry Miller, writing about the use of the jeremiad
during the American Revolution, sums up its main points as follows:
"we have sinned, therefore we are afflicted by the tyranny of a corrupt
Britain; we must repent and reform, in order to win the irresistible aid
of Providence"; the consequence of reform will be the ability to beat
the British, and then "we shall enter upon a prosperity and temporal
happiness beyond anything the world has hitherto seen." It was held
that "expulsion of the British would automatically leave America a
pure society."[37]

One student of rhetoric explicitly states in a recent article, which
includes a detailed examination of Lincoln's thought and especially of
the Second Inaugural, that Lincoln's March 4, 1865, address is very
much like a New England preacher's jeremiad. Lincoln demonstrated

in his Second Inaugural that he recognized "the price that a just God will demand for the propitiation of the nation's mighty sin." The real message had to be one of comfort and hope, however, for "the long hard war was the way to salvation. The nation was to purge itself of its sins, including the sin of slavery, by expending its treasure" and the blood of its young men.[38] In his own rhetoric, then, according to this view, Lincoln stepped into the stream of tradition that included the patriotic jeremiad and its particular theology of history. Indeed, Wolf echoes two central themes of this tradition when he writes in his latest book that Lincoln's faith "could see the nation as justly punished . . . if it disobeyed God's covenant with it."[39] One could try to claim, then, that Lincoln's important presidential statements are quite special because they forthrightly stated the case in a manner reminiscent of that displayed in the Election Day sermons of the previous century. This assertion becomes a much narrower and less significant claim, though, if one recognizes that others during the Civil War period shared the interpretation ascribed to Lincoln and is consequently forced to conclude that finally what makes Lincoln estimable is only the fact that he said these things in his capacity as President of the United States.

In our own day when, as the sociologists tell us, God is no longer widely seen to be involved in the course of political and social history but is instead perceived to be present and active only in individual lives here and there as the assuager of private grief and sorrow, it is easy to suppose that the picture that has been handed down to us of Lincoln's faith is one that depicts religious perceptions virtually unique for his own day as well as for ours.[40] But such is not the case. Men and women of Lincoln's time had not yet lost their strong sense of providential activity in contemporary national events. This was true in the South as well as in the North. As James Silver has written in *Confederate Morale and Church Propaganda*, "Every Confederate victory proved that God had shielded his chosen people and every defeat became the merited punishment of the same people for their sins. The war itself was a chastisement. . . ."[41]

This approach to the divine activity, while it transcends that view which automatically identified God's purposes with those of the South, is still somewhat narrower than the interpretations of Bushnell, Schaff, and others. These men saw in the war God's judgment upon the entire nation for the sin of slavery. The war was a way toward rebirth and authentic nationhood. Regeneration meant for Bushnell a new national consciousness consisting of the recognition of God and response to his calling. The Civil War would purge America of its guilt through suffering and bring it to true nationality; out of the tragedy would come cleansing, unity, righteousness, and redemption. For Philip Schaff, the Civil War was a necessary evil designed to humiliate and heal an arrogant nation. It was God's judgment upon the nation for deserting its true vocation, which consisted of the bringing together of many peoples through the promise of freedom. This judgment was merciful, however, and would lead to the new birth not only of the country but also of its true calling of unification. The war was, in Schaff's words and in Bushnell's conception too, a "baptism of blood."[42]

It is important to go on to note that some of these ideas were not the exclusive property of a few insightful religious thinkers. One can even say that the theme of national suffering for sin was a fairly typical response to the war. As Judith Wimmer has shown in her 1980 dissertation, Roman Catholics of the period "spoke of God's lordship over history and His providence exercised in the war as chastisement for national and personal sins." They sometimes expressed hope "that the war and the blood shed would lead to a greater or more perfect national life."[43] American Catholics especially tended to see the war as the consequence of adherence to "the Protestant principles of divisiveness and anti-authoritarianism at work in the nation." The war was seen as proof that "the nation needed Catholic principles, to survive and flourish."[44] American Catholics identified as the sins being punished not rebellion and slavery but pride, greed, materialism, and forgetfulness of God.[45] Some Catholics noted that the United States had prospered and received many blessings. "But the blessings and prosperity had caused the nation to forget God, to become proud."[46] Wimmer also finds in the writings of Roman Catholics of the time "several allusions to a re-birth through blood, or to a baptism of blood" but concludes that this theme was never developed to any appreciable extent.[47]

One can find opinions close to those imputed to Lincoln in other materials from the Civil War period. A writer in the Evansville, Indiana, *Journal* of April 20, 1861, stated his belief that the war could very well be God's means of ridding the country of slavery, an institution for which both North and South were responsible and for which both had to suffer and pay the penalty.[48] Of course all such sentiments could have been influenced by Harriet Beecher Stowe's *Uncle Tom's Cabin* (1852), which concludes that "both North and South have been guilty before God" and that the Union can be saved only "by repentance, justice, and mercy." Stronger than "the eternal law by which the millstone sinks in the ocean" is the "law, by which injustice and cruelty shall bring on nations the wrath of Almighty God!"[49]

Many Protestants of this time reached the same conclusion. Nathan Bangs, a prominent Methodist, said that the war was God's retribution on the whole country for its sin. A Congregationalist paper, *The Inde-pendent,* saw national suffering as the necessary result of allowing oppression to continue.[50] Grosjean states in his recent study of the views of Protestant clergymen of the North that the preachers' primary understanding of the conflict consisted in the belief that the war was the judgment of a wrathful God designed to punish national sin and that the removal of this scourge required thoroughgoing repentance. North-ern ministers saw "a direct correlation between the military and the moral course of the conflict. The preachers were virtually unanimous in pointing out this correlation. . . ." They believed that the course of the North improved in the war after the issue of the Emancipation Proclamation; the North began to be victorious in battle as soon as it demonstrated its moral commitment to freedom.[51]

One cannot say that Lincoln was unusual in that he saw the war not only as a period of judgment but also as a time of regeneration. Protes-tants looked for all sorts of dreams to be fulfilled after the war. They hoped for the dawning of the millennium and the establishment of God's kingdom on earth. They worked for a holy society of righteous men and women, and they sought the completion of a theocratic ideal. They expected cleansing of sin and a new life for all Americans. North-ern evangelical ministers saw the war as a cosmic drama taking place in the center of history; in these apocalyptic events slavery would be conquered and a redeemer nation born. Protestants, then, seeing the nation's history as a period of sacred transformation, looked for varie-ties of salvation of every hue to follow the bloodshed.[53] If a person were to conclude that Lincoln had a vision of the war bringing with it a time of spiritual regeneration, and if that person were able also to describe that religious expectation, then I would suggest that one could find numerous other contemporary examples. And if one could do that, then in what way would Lincoln's vision be exceptional?

More important, though, than questions of change and singularity is the fundamental problem we must now address: Did Lincoln under-stand the war to be God's punishment of the nation for the sin of slavery? Was this his basic theological interpretation of the conflict?

Scholars answering in the affirmative to these questions frequently use the presidential proclamations of days of fasting, humiliation, prayer, and thanksgiving as evidence to support their contentions. Sometimes, though, the Second Inaugural is the complete basis for their positions. The proclamations are difficult to deal with partly be-cause we are not sure Lincoln actually wrote any of them. They are also rather shaky support for the reason that they are fairly conven-tional period pieces wholly characteristic of the times and often out of harmony with what we know of Lincoln's religious beliefs. It is a dangerous matter to press these proclamations because they invariably involve their advocate in making contradictory statements. A proclamation, for example, presented God's deliverance as something that was dependent upon the prior repentance of the people. This understanding of the divine grace is, as we shall see, at variance with Lincoln's personal view.

Not contradictory but certainly odd are some statements Wolf is drawn into making through his reliance on this proclamation form. His theory of religious development would have us believe Lincoln pictured the war as a punishment early on, then changed his mind and had doubts about the ultimate meaning of the whole venture, and finally resolved those doubts in a mystical apprehension of the divine purposes and saw the war (again) as punishment.

Lincoln was usually asked to proclaim these special days by Congress or private citizens. The presidential declarations sometimes included the language of the original request. Then the author of the proclamation continued its theme and stated its purpose in more detail. The Proclamation of a National Fast Day of August 12, 1861, declared that it was proper to recognize God's government in all things and to submit to his chastisements, to confess one's sins, and to pray for pardon. It went on to refer to the affliction of civil war and said "it is peculiarly fit for us to recognize the hand of God in this terrible visitation, and in sorrowful remembrance of our own faults and crimes as a nation and as individuals, to humble ourselves before Him" and to pray for mercy in the hope that "further punishment" might be averted. It proceeded to ask citizens to pray for a blessing upon the nation's arms.[54]

One year later Lincoln wrote out his personal statement, Meditation on the Divine Will, in which he affirmed both that "the will of God prevails" and that it is difficult to know what that will is. It was a simple confession of trust and hope in things not seen.[55] In his Reply to Mrs. Gurney a month and a half after this Meditation, he told her that "we must believe that He permits it [the war] for some wise purpose of his own, mysterious and unknown to us," and even though we "with our limited understandings" may not be able to discern those purposes, "yet we cannot but believe, that he who made the world still governs it."[56] This statement, which Lincoln made on October 26, 1862, was one that he could have made at any date because his point of view never changed.

In Lincoln's proclamations it was typical for him in attempting to bring the nation to a proper attitude of humility and reverence to discuss the possibility of just punishment not in the form of declarative sentences but rather in the form of questions or through the use of conditional clauses. The Proclamation Appointing a National Fast Day written on March 30, 1863, asked, ". . . may we not justly fear that the awful calamity of Civil War . . . may be but a punishment, inflicted upon us, for our presumptuous sins . . . ?" It went on to mention the many gifts from God the nation had received and stated that in the presence of all this richness Providence had been forgotten. "Intoxicated with unbroken success, we have become too self-sufficient to feel the necessity of redeeming and preserving grace, too proud to pray to the God that made us!" It then asked that the people "rest humbly in the hope" that God would hear their prayers and bless the land.[57]

In the Proclamation of Thanksgiving, July 15, 1863, mention was made not of chastisements but simply of the hand of God that was present—and that should be recognized as present—"equally in these triumphs and in these sorrows."[58] An exception to the customary grammatical structure I have pointed out occurred in the Proclamation of Thanksgiving of October 3, 1863. In the middle of this document are the three sentences in which Wolf says "Lincoln provided the theological interpretation of the nation's situation."[59] And in one of these sentences is the statement that God is "dealing with us in anger for our sins"—a clear enunciation once and for all of the war-as-punishment theme. The only difficulty is that Wolf errs in assigning authorship of this paper to Lincoln. The proclamation was not written by the President but by Secretary of State Seward.[60]

One piece of evidence Wolf cites that Lincoln actually did write is the letter of April 4, 1864, to Albert G. Hodges, editor of an influential Kentucky newspaper. This bit of correspondence incorporates a closing statement in which Lincoln appears to have sounded the theme of the war as an instance of divine retribution. It is the only place he did so of which we can be certain outside of the Second Inaugural itself. In the course of this lengthy missive, Lincoln set forth an explanation of his policies on slavery and the war. Emancipation of the slaves was discussed as a requisite means for prevailing in the conflict. Lincoln wrote that in order to preserve the Union and the Constitution, he had had to lay "strong hand upon the colored element." In taking this action, he "was not entirely confident." The fact was, though, that "more than a year of trial shows no loss by it in our foreign relations" or anywhere else. "On the contrary, it shows a gain of quite a hundred and thirty thousand soldiers, seamen, and laborers." The letter was a justification of Lincoln's emancipation policy. In it he was telling the border states that defense of the Union required him to lay hold of more men for support of the armed forces, that that move necessitated liberation of those held by the rebels in bondage, and that, as a matter of fact, the policy had turned out to have altogether positive results.

At this point, Lincoln began his last paragraph. There he explained that "in telling this tale I attempt no compliment to my own sagacity. I claim not to have controlled events, but confess plainly that events have controlled me." The rest of the paragraph was written to express this idea—that to God, not Lincoln, belonged the tribute for any good that might come out of these dealings. "Now, at the end of three years struggle the nation's condition is not what either party, or any man devised, or expected. God alone can claim it." He then expressed in his closing sentence his understanding of the relative positions of God and man in the conflict. God's part was such that he would be victorious in expunging slavery. Man's part was such that he should take no credit for the resultant good, which was God's work alone. Man deserved in return for his efforts through the years not rewards but punishments. "If God now wills the removal of a great wrong, and wills also that we of the North as well as you of the South, shall pay fairly for our complicity in that wrong, impartial history will find therein new cause to attest and revere the justice and goodness of God."[61]

What Lincoln wished to do at the end of this long letter describing the virtues of his own actions was not to develop a theodicy but rather to emphasize in the strongest terms that he did not feel he should be thought of as one deserving of any glory for the success of his programs. The language of this sentence was a way of doing just that—of deflecting the credit from man to God. He used this means of expression not to theorize about God's purposes in the war but to point out in this letter to a Southern editor that before God the North was as guilty as the South, that both sides were, in fact, so guilty that if it were the case that this entire war were but a punishment for corporate transgressions, one would have to acknowledge that the sentence was just and true. The whole country participated in slavery and therefore helped to bring on the war. And so both sections deserved to reap the bitter harvest from the seeds they had sown. Whatever afflictions they might bear could not be said to be more than their fair share. Men were responsible beings whose deeds could cause great injury. When the result of man's misdeeds was suffering and hardship, that was all the more reason to turn to God rather than oneself, to recognize his justice and goodness rather than one's own.

It would be much too facile an interpretation of this passage to say that Lincoln here saw God punishing the nation for its sin. That was not where the emphasis lay at all. The nation was obviously paying for its years of divisiveness and oppression. And those woes had to be attributed ultimately to God, not because anyone could know that he sent them to judge and punish man, but because he is Lord of all things, he is overruling Providence who directs whatever happens in the cosmos. According to Lincoln's strongly predestinarian theology, one had to say that God willed whatever occurred. This was not the same as saying that he wanted to punish the country. God does not want to punish, but neither could it be said that he desires a world in which acts do not have consequences. When the people suffered as a result of these acts one had to acknowledge that they did so within the world God has made, and one must then decide whether or not to go on affirming the goodness of that world. The response Lincoln suggested consisted in affirming that victors should not lord it over vanquished because all were guilty, and that God alone deserved to be exalted because he only is the Author of good.

These same central asseverations recur many times in the last year of Lincoln's life as the war's termination drew closer and closer. The President told a gathering of citizens in May of 1864 that in their rejoicing over victory they should be modest and show gratitude to God.[62] The overriding concern of all these pronouncements was to urge citizens to remember that God was at the center of their nation's life.

Some further comments are in order at this point before turning to Lincoln's Second Inaugural Address. The first is that it is impossible to derive the theological understanding of the war as punishment from the proclamations and other materials I have discussed. The troublesome nature of these documents has been noted. I mentioned the declaration that carried an explicit retribution theme but which happens to be the work of Seward. I would now point out the way in which clashing sentiments were sometimes expressed in these proclamations. Where some might ask Americans if it would not be right to treat the war as a judgment and to acknowledge their transgressions in the face of the same, another might point to virtue, not wrongdoing, as the cause of the war. The Proclamation of Thanksgiving of October 20, 1864, stated clearly that the United States had been plunged into civil war because of its "adherence as a nation to the cause of Freedom and Humanity."[63] At least the biblical prophets and the Puritan preachers of jeremiads were consistent! They would have confined themselves to the simple assertion that their woes were God's punishments for sin, not the consequences of devotion to virtue.

And yet do we not have to say—secondly—that all these proclamations, addresses, letters, and so forth were highly influenced by their immediate contexts? That is, were they not all occasional pieces written with a definite practical end in mind, rather than attempts at abstract theorizing? In this light, the "contradictory" nature of the documents makes more sense. When it was the intention of the author of one of these papers to move his audience to submit themselves humbly to God, to repent of their sins, and to mend their ways, it was certainly logical for him to ask them to agree that what they had done wrong was such that it merited a just penalty, and that, therefore, under the circumstances, was it not proper for them to repent? Certainly these hearers had to confess that slavery and divisiveness had led to conflict. The proclamations of days of humiliation and fasting were designed to confront citizens and let them know why they needed to humble themselves and to fast—namely, because their righteousness was as filthy rags. This situation was brought home to them effectively through questions having to do with their own just deserts under the circumstances. These proclamations asked their hearers to admit that their transgressions were so great that the sufferings of the war would have been a fitting divine response to them. These papers did not identify a wrathful God who visits the sins of the fathers on the children. They rather urged the people to turn to the God of all mercies in the hope that their sins would be forgiven and the nation blessed.

It was in just this manner that Lincoln in his letter to Hodges met the temptation to attribute glory to his own efforts in the war. His response was a strong reaction to the tendency to attribute greatness to oneself rather than to God. The situation the author of the October 20, 1864, Proclamation of Thanksgiving wished to confront was patently different from these other ones. There it is clear that he wanted to call forth a response of gratitude, and so the entire context was more positive; while the war was still seen as an affliction, it was no longer described as the result of sin but was seen rather as a consequence of the nation's dedication to the principles of freedom and equality for all. The document focused on God's many blessings to the country. The point is that in neither of these two types of proclamation was Lincoln or whoever wrote them announcing the details of God's workings in American history. He was, instead, calling upon the people to respond to that God who, one could affirm, was surely at work in the life of the nation. The direct focus in these papers was not on suffering and trying to explain it but rather on the need to turn to God in times of relative health and prosperity and in times of adversity—that is, really, at all times. They had different styles—one negative, the other positive—but the same ultimate goal.

Lincoln was aware of the nation's sins and its virtues. He knew that if it had not been for slavery there would have been no war, and if it had not been for the North's resolve to oppose rebellion and battle for democracy there would have been no fight either. So he could mention either as he saw fit in his efforts to prompt the nation to acknowledge its sins or to confess its debts to Providence. Lincoln would not have said that either explanation of the war's existence was wrong, but neither would he have said that they even approached the ultimate theological reasons for the war. In these documents we do not yet see Lincoln trying to come to terms directly with the suffering entailed in the war.

Thirdly, in none of his statements leading up to the Second Inaugural Address do we see Lincoln proclaiming a new awareness of the war as an instance of divine retribution. In fact, six months before the address (and five months *after* the letter to Hodges), he wrote to his Quaker friend, Eliza P. Gurney, and reiterated themes he had been stating for years. "The purposes of the Almighty," he told her, "are perfect, and must prevail, though we erring mortals may fail to accurately perceive them in advance." God knows what is best for the nation and has determined that the war should not end as soon as we had hoped it would. "We shall yet acknowledge His wisdom and our own error therein." All that people can do while the war goes on is to "work earnestly in the best light God gives us, trusting that so working still conduces to the great ends He ordains." Those purposes of God were not identified and presumably could not be clearly discerned. "Surely He intends some great good to follow this mighty convulsion, which no mortal could make, and no mortal could stay."[64] God was working in the war to achieve "some great good" that "we erring mortals" could not clearly make out. The accomplishment of that good was not dependent upon what men did—despite what may have been suggested in some of the presidential proclamations.

We are now left with only the Second Inaugural Address to consider among those writings adduced as evidence in support of the war-as-punishment idea. It is by far the most important of these documents. More theological interpretations of Lincoln have been based on it than on any other of his statements. But often these studies have failed to take into account the historical context of this address. In his speech Lincoln had to confront a variety of consequential matters, both old and new; no understanding of his remarks can even approach adequacy without first coming to grips with the milieu out of which he spoke.

In a recent essay Donald Capps does make an attempt to appreciate the impact of events surrounding the occasion of the Inaugural and concludes, "Discouraged by the fact that the termination of the war was not yet in sight, Lincoln sought an explanation for God's allowing it to continue."[65] What is particularly astute about this comment is that Capps recognizes that Lincoln was speaking about *future,* not past, events when he stated that "if God wills that it ["this mighty scourge of war"] continue, until all the wealth piled by the bond-man's two hundred and fifty years of unrequited toil shall be sunk, . . . still it must be said 'the judgments of the Lord, are true. . . .' "[66] Capps has read the text carefully and has tried to extrapolate from what is stated therein an indication of the trend of circumstances and of Lincoln's emotional state at the time of writing. He has deduced that Lincoln, discouraged by the protracted nature of the conflict and by the fact that its termination was not at hand, finally came to see the war's prolongation as a means by which God might go on to accomplish his further purposes through the tragedy. Capps's is an intelligent reading of the text, but, unfortunately, it is not one that is true to the actual milieu of the address. The speech cannot be understood today unless we discover more about the situation to which it was addressed in 1865.

As a matter of fact, the end of the war *was* in sight. This point is not a controversial one; most writers would agree with the statement of historian Richard Hofstadter that "Lincoln wrote his Second Inaugural Address . . . after the victory of the Union cause was secure. . . ."[67] As early as October 31, 1864, Lincoln told the Rev. William Nast that he did not believe it was too soon "to rejoice together over the promise of the speedy removal of that blot upon our civilization," referring, of course, to the institution of slavery and its imminent destruction.[68] Even in the Second Inaugural itself it is possible to find evidence that Lincoln and his listeners knew that the war would soon be over. "The progress of our arms," he said in the first paragraph, ". . . is as well known to the public as to myself; and it is, I trust, reasonably satisfactory and encouraging to all." The time of victory was so near that Lincoln wanted to be modest in his references to it: "With high hope for the future, no prediction in regard to it is ventured."[69] The whole speech is, in fact, only properly seen as an effort to describe how to respond to the situation when peace finally came.

In his last few months Lincoln's attention shifted more and more to the problem of rebuilding a torn and bleeding country. In his Last Public Address he informed his joyful audience of the difficult task that lay ahead: "By these recent successes the re-inauguration of the national authority—reconstruction . . . is pressed much more closely upon our attention. . . ."[70] It is no exaggeration to say that Lincoln knew in March of 1865 that how he addressed the issues of recovery and national reunification in the hazardous post-bellum situation could affect the course of the next hundred years.

We need to know something about what the President was up against. There were at the time evangelicals who saw the war as a holy crusade in which the children of light battled the children of darkness in a bloody Armageddon.[71] There were Northerners who preached vindictiveness and who, like Horace Bushnell, called for further retribution on those who had taken up arms against the United States.[72] There were Catholics who blamed the outbreak of hostilities on Protestants.[73] There were clergymen like Henry Ward Beecher who believed that Southerners, as a breed, were uniquely depraved and uncivilized.[74]

One task Lincoln addressed in his speech was that of countering sectional attitudes of overweening pride. The North had no monopoly on this trait. The views of the Rev. Thomas Smyth of Charleston, S.C., were typical of those held by many Southerners. In an 1863 journal article he spoke of the North's "fanaticism" and its people's "mendacity, perfidy, shameless brutality, and . . . unbridled despotism." God was seen to be in the war "executing judgment for the poor and oppressed"—i.e., the South. He it was who had spoken to the South two years earlier, "saying, 'Come out of the Union, my people. From such withdraw thyself. . . .'" The war being carried on by the North "is rebellion against the Lord God omnipotent" and should be seen as "a judgment upon the North, for its persistent, perjured, Abolition fanaticism." God was on the side of the South in this war. "She has His word, and providence, and omnipotent government with her."[75]

As extreme as these statements might appear to modern ears, and as shocking as the alacrity with which their speakers claim God's power for their cause certainly is, such sentiments were not at all unusual. As Martin Marty reminds us, even individuals like Bushnell, Beecher, and Finney were quite "ready to tie the purposes of God to the details of American empire and mission."[76]

In identifying the meaning of the war and the reasons for fighting it, not all men shared with Lincoln a concern for the establishment of the principles of democracy. Many had narrower aims in the conflict. "Certain Unionists [like Charles Sumner] . . . reduced it to an invidious sectionalism. . . . Some praised war itself as a fine, exhilirating thing. . . . Still others lost all sense of balance in sheer vindictiveness. . . ." In this last group were persons "like Parson Brownlow, the Tennessee firebrand, and Thad Stevens, the embittered Pennsylvania congressman."[77] Such were the beliefs and attitudes that in part made up the general climate of public opinion as Lincoln rose to give his speech. As Paul M. Angle has observed, "It would have been but human [at this time "with the end of the slaughter in sight"] to have rejoiced at the prospect of success, while to have called for vengeance on the conquered would at least have been within understanding."[78] Of course Lincoln did not yield to either temptation but instead urged upon his audience a humbler response to circumstances of victory.

That Lincoln must have been acutely sensitive to the mood of the country can scarcely be questioned. All during the war he had had to contend with the difficulties caused by arrogance and factionalism. A little less than one year before the Inaugural Address he wrote to an acquaintance saying that what he "dreaded" in the whole effort to make emancipation a reality was that "jealousies, rivalries, and consequent ill-blood" would cause division and ultimate defeat.[79] Lincoln knew that the war had not always brought out the best in people, and he must have known how hard it would be to establish true peace and justice after it was over. As Sydney Ahlstrom has written, "The vindictive positions of Munger and Dabney lived on in too many war-embittered hearts to give charity much of a chance. And the nation's endemic racism stood squarely athwart the freedman's opportunity for genuine freedom."[80] But Lincoln would do what he could, and he would urge that a start be made by laying aside all vindictiveness and by treating the Southern people leniently. This was the theme of his final Cabinet meeting on April 14, 1865. He is said to have told the members assembled: "Enough lives have been sacrificed; we must extinguish our resentments if we expect harmony and union."[81] The Second Inaugural Address, while it is certainly an exceptional document, was nonetheless still part of this one consistent effort in the final months of the war to rebuild a nation. It must be seen as a *political* act by a master statesman rather than a theological treatise.[82] In it we see Lincoln as leader of the nation trying valiantly to upgrade the ways in which citizens saw themselves, their neighbors, and their responsibilities.

In opposition to those who claimed to know what God's purposes were and who identified those purposes with the aims of the North, the South, or the United States itself, Lincoln said, not that he knew what God's purposes were and that he could see that they were different from those of either side, but simply that "the Almighty has his own purposes," the implication being that no one could—and therefore no one should—say that he knew what God's intentions were. He pointed out how wrong men had been in the past when they thought they could see where events were leading. The war had lasted longer than anyone expected. No one thought slavery would end before the war itself did. Both sides looked for an easier, faster victory; neither expected the war to take the turns it had taken. People are not so wise as they think they are, Lincoln was saying, nor so good.

How Southerners should be treated after the war was not an academic question for the Commander-in-Chief of the armed forces. Charles Sumner relates that when Lincoln was told that he must not let Jefferson Davis " 'escape the law, he must be hanged,' the President replied calmly, . . . 'Judge not, that ye be not judged' . . . ." When informed that "the sight of Libby Prison made it impossible to pardon him, the President repeated twice over the same words."[83] Neither side should claim any particular merit for its efforts. Both deserved punishment for helping to bring about the offense of slavery. Lincoln said that if God were to go so far as to require that the war proceed until the country incurred losses in money and men exactly equal to the amount of blood and treasure given up over many years by slaves, we would have to say we had been meted out a just punishment, so great are our debts.[84] Lincoln's quotation of scripture borrowed a sentence from Psalm 19: "the judgments of the Lord are true and righteous altogether."[85] This psalm, which talks about God's "laws," "statutes," and "commandments," provides a good way to understand the word "judgment" as a kind of legal decision or court verdict. At least in Lincoln's usage, what he seems to have been trying to get his audience to agree to was this: were God to hand down this terrible sentence on us for our "presumptuous sins" (Ps. 19), we would still have to say the Judge's verdict was a fair one. In other words, it would be wrong to try to suppose that any of us is wholly righteous. Lincoln was saying here that people are not as wise or as good as they think they are—but God lacks nothing in either wisdom or goodness.

What Lincoln's audience must have been much more aware of than we are today, indeed what they must have experienced as a palpable fact, was that the war was virtually over. As Capps realized, Lincoln had been speaking of an event—a penalty meted out—that was to take place in the future; but what Capps did not know was that the war looked as though it was about to end, not go on indefinitely. What this means is that Lincoln never expected the punishment he described to be carried out. The judgment he spoke of he knew was a sentence suspended. In his essay on this speech, Bormann speaks of the punishment as something that has already taken place. He says that Lincoln in his Second Inaugural implied that with the war's end, "the sin of slavery would be propitiated and the nation could then go forward, cleansed. . . ."[86] But this was not Lincoln's idea at all, and a recognition that he was speaking of a possible future event would have prevented this kind of mistake.

Actually, what Lincoln was doing in this part of his speech was carrying forward his earlier condemnation against judging. I would insist that Lincoln was not pronouncing judgment in these words on the entire country in behalf of God. He was not saying that the whole nation had paid the price for its sins, or that it was going to have to pay it before the war ended. Lincoln's whole effort was to move the discussion away from talk of human works and the value and efficacy thereof. So he was actually not speaking of punishment in either the past or the future. It was not that we had paid the price, it was rather that the payment we owed would not be demanded of us. Lincoln was not saying anything here that could lead to the foolish supposition that we had covered the cost of our sins, effected propitiation, and cleansed ourselves as a people. There is no hint of the capabilities of human virtue in these words, only a deep and abiding confidence in the mercy and goodness of God. The proper attitude was neither self-congratulation nor fear of the future but rather continuing repentance.

In the Second Inaugural Address Lincoln, far from adhering to the notion of retributive justice, effectively broke that idea apart. From his own comments not long before he wrote his address, it is possible to see that Lincoln had no understanding of God acting in the war to demand retribution of money and blood. In fact, just days before he delivered the speech, Lincoln wrote that God had been gracious to America throughout the war.[87] Only three months before the Second Inaugural Lincoln spoke in his Annual Message to Congress in such a way as to indicate he had no understanding of the war equalling the slaves' expenditures over 250 years. In fact, his words may even surprise us in their expression of equanimity: ". . . it is some relief to know that, compared with the surviving, the fallen have been so few." The thousands of newly-arrived immigrants he saw as "one of the principal replenishing streams which are appointed by Providence to repair the ravages of internal war. . . ."[88] Again, what these remarks suggest is that Lincoln did not feel the burden of the war was nearly as large as it could have been, nor did he see the sufferings it inflicted to be as great as the nation deserved. Lincoln saw Providence in the war continuing to deal graciously with America.

On the one hand, Lincoln declined to label the sufferings of the country punishments of God; and on the other, he refused to give any support to the idea that worldly success was a sign of divine favor, a kind of reward. Unlike James Andrews, I would maintain that in his Second Inaugural Lincoln had *no* desire "to substantiate the purity of northern motives" but wished instead to point up the distorted nature of man's perceptions and the sullied quality of his willings and doings.[89] Victory could not be interpreted as God's approval of the North's conduct. Lincoln emphasized in his address the guilt of both sides. In doing so he was countering the position of men like Henry Ward Beecher who held that God bestowed wealth, victory and rulership upon the North because of its righteousness.[90]

The final paragraph of the address constitutes no sharp break with what has gone before. "With malice toward none; with charity for all; with firmness in the right, as God gives us to see the right, let us strive on to finish the work we are in. . . ." Lincoln recognized the ones who had suffered the most, asking the people "to care for him who shall have borne the battle, and for his widow, and his orphan"; and he urged that true harmony and justice replace animosity, imploring citizens to "do all which may achieve and cherish a just, and a lasting peace, among ourselves, and with all nations."[91] There is continuity here in these phrases with the sentiments expressed in earlier paragraphs. Lincoln throughout the speech was concerned to impress upon his audience the reality of human limitation and the extent of man's presumption. He told Thurlow Weed in a March 15, 1865, letter that the goal of the Inaugural had been to point out the "difference of purpose between the Almighty and [human beings]."[92]

In his final paragraph Lincoln presented an appropriate response to the situation at hand after he had already demonstrated the inappropriateness of other responses such as attitudes of vengeance or smug satisfaction. In opposition to postures of self-sufficiency, this response claimed nothing for itself but simply and straightforwardly moved to meet present needs. Lincoln, after confessing the justice of a harsh divine verdict, effectively walked away from the whole domain of judgment and circumscribed the smaller area within which proper human action lay. He had already suggested that part of what one should do in the midst of trials like war was to acknowledge the presence of one's own hand in the process of establishing the conditions that had led to strife. Now in this last paragraph he asked that Americans gaze no longer upon themselves but rather on their brothers and sisters of the land, who required immediate attention—and that not so much in the form of more words as of concrete acts of love and justice. By this point the speech is well past the whole effort to depict worldly troubles and successes in terms of divine punishments and favors. Lincoln's response to suffering was not a theoretical one, in which suffering was explained from the perspective afforded by a special, supernatural vantage point, but a practical one, to be accomplished in repentance.[93]

The Second Inaugural may be understood as an expression of Lincoln's living faith. From the address's opening sentence to its last we see Lincoln thinking theocentrically. Richard M. Weaver, who in *The Ethics of Rhetoric* calls attention to Lincoln's "self-effacement," which, in the first part of the speech especially, "goes to the extent of impersonal constructions," concludes that, "There have been few men whose processes of mind so well deserve the epithet *sub specie aeternitatis* as Lincoln's."[94] The author of the Second Inaugural trusted in a God whose ends he could not clearly discern, but he assumed there, as he did in his letter six months earlier to Mrs. Gurney, that the Almighty would bring some great good out of the tragedy, greater even than the elimination of slavery (since the war continued after its primary cause had ceased). Throughout the speech, but especially in its final paragraph, we see the loyalty aspect of Lincoln's faith at work: the concern for putting an end to self-aggrandizement and for making a start toward reconciliation. In these words is embodied an altogether realistic faith that did not put its confidence in man's ability, through war, to end conflict. It placed its hopes in God alone, as the task of conversion continued.

My third major criticism of the standard picture of Lincoln's view of the war emerges directly out of what I have written above. Lincoln evinced in his Second Inaugural Address, in his last public statements uttered the following month, and in the concerns expressed in the Cabinet meeting held on the day he was shot, a profound awareness of the problems the country faced in the aftermath of war. There is no hint in any of these remarks that he believed the American people had been renewed or reformed, that their bleeding had effected cleansing and atonement, or that defeat of the South was finally made possible by the repentance of Northerners. These ideas were all completely foreign to Lincoln's outlook. Norman Graebner has written with perspicacity on this matter. "Lincoln saw that the noble purpose of liberation must still be limited by the complexities of the problems that always follow the freeing of peoples." Lincoln had no notion of man's capacity to build the kingdom of God on earth. "He doubted that human society could ever approach utopia, for its maladjustments mirrored the general frailty and depravity of mankind." Lincoln was cognizant of the problems free blacks would face in the South. "Whatever the destruction of the South and its military power, the Southern whites would continue to possess the social, economic, and political power over the Negro whether he were slave or free." Lincoln's understanding of the mission of the United States was different from and, in a way, more modest than the view many had of America as a "redeemer nation." "For Lincoln, America's contribution to human progress would be limited largely to example. The nation would fulfill its obligation to humanity by being true to itself."[95] Simply maintaining its own political integrity was not, however, a minor task for the eighty-nine year old democracy. That preservation of an existing order of principles and values was the perceived end rather than production of a perfect society cannot be taken to imply that Lincoln supposed there was anything easy or insignificant about what the nation had to do.

Throughout the war Lincoln's goal was no more and no less than the preservation of the Union. In his Speech to the One Hundred Sixty-Fourth Ohio Regiment he said that the nation had a "free Government, where every man has a right to be equal with every other man." The outcome of this war, he told them, would determine whether or not the experiment would be allowed to continue. "In this great struggle, this form of Government and every form of human right is endangered if our enemies succeed." Involved in the war was "the question whether your children and my children shall enjoy the privileges we have enjoyed. . . ."[96] In another speech to a regiment of troops Lincoln told the young men the purpose of the war was to guarantee that they would have the same "equal privileges in the race of life" their predecessors enjoyed. The "inestimable jewel" for which they fought was the "birthright" which provided each of them with "an open field and a fair chance."[97] The contest would decide whether or not those rights had to be surrendered.

Lincoln's goal in the war was, then, quite conservative; but he saw the war's outcome as something that would be highly consequential. He went so far as to say, late in 1864, that, "Thoughtful men must feel that the fate of civilization upon this continent is involved in the issue of our contest."[98] Where many religious writers of the time entertained visions of Armageddon and new worlds, the result Lincoln hoped for was different. It had to do not with the erection of a paradise but with the establishment of a principle. The following quotation from one of his letters is not only famous, it is also thoroughly representative of his views: "It will then [when peace comes] have been proved that, among free men, there can be no successful appeal from the ballot to the bullet; and that those who take such appeal are sure to lose their case, and pay the cost."[99] Lincoln believed that such a demonstration would be a tremendous achievement. Looking back on the conclusion of the war, we can now say that Lincoln's somewhat abstract and limited hope betokened a more realistic appraisal of the nature and possibilities of man and society than did the uncontrolled visions of those who hoped for a new heaven and a new earth. Surely Lincoln would have understood better than the dreamers what transpired when, after the war, the old men came out again, made their peace, and called it reconstruction.

Having examined some of the important flaws of the prevailing interpretation, we are now ready to proceed to a new understanding of Lincoln's faith.

(2) LINCOLN'S THEOLOGICAL UNDERSTANDING OF THE CIVIL WAR

We can begin by asserting the converse of what we have denied. It is highly questionable that Lincoln's understanding of the war was transformed in a process whereby it passed through a stretch of doubt to arrive finally at certainty. Lincoln's religious experience of the war did not begin with the disclosure of mystery and end with the discernment of purpose. He did not at the last come to see the conflict in terms of retribution and reformation at all: to him its ultimate theological meaning remained mystery. We have seen expressions of this view in some of the works already discussed: the Meditation on the Divine Will, the 1864 letter to Mrs. Gurney, the Second Inaugural Address. As Bruce Catton has written in *This Hallowed Ground,* the President took "final victory for granted," and he "wanted to give the victory an undying meaning." But he could never quite grasp that meaning conceptually. Even as he tried, "a fog of dust and smoke lay on the land, the horizon was forever ringed in murky flame, and wherever he turned—from the beginning of the war to the end—he kept touching a great mystery."[100]

I tend to agree with the opinion of Daniel Simundson that a difficulty with the Old Testament view of suffering as divine retribution is that it is "presumptuous"; it assumes that a human being can know God's reasons for doing something, but how can he? "It leaves no room for mystery. It shows an insensitivity to others if we interpret their troubles as if we know something that only God knows."[101] By acknowledging, in the phrase of John Hick, the "epistemic distance" that exists between man and God, Lincoln (as far as we can tell) avoided committing the sin of idolatry.[102] He refrained from trying to confine the meaning of God's actions to a man-made picture of them. He did not attempt, as John Bowker puts it, to bring God "within our grasp and ostensive definition."[103] This refusal to make an image of God is only one aspect of Lincoln's appreciation of God's greatness.

To Lincoln God was the all-powerful Determiner of events, who makes use of human beings to accomplish his ends. Victory would come to the North if God so willed. The war's outcome was not dependent upon the prior repentance of the people. God would bring "some great good" out of "this mighty convulsion," a good "which no mortal could make, and no mortal could stay." God's purposes "must prevail."[104]

The same view of Providence was expressed in his letter to Speed written when Lincoln was in his early thirties. There Lincoln stated his strong belief that God would bring to pass whatever he had foreordained, that "whatever he designs, he will do for *me* yet."[105] James F. Wilson, a United States Senator during the Civil War, reported that in 1862 he and a few other men called on the President to discuss the state of the nation and to propose possible remedies. One gentleman urged that slavery be struck down, saying that if the country did not do what was right God would let it go its own way to ruin, but that if it did do what was right and freed the slaves then God would "lead us safely out of this wilderness, crown our arms with victory, and restore our now dissevered Union." As we saw above, just this sort of understanding of Providence has been attributed to Lincoln by a number of commentators. This fact makes Lincoln's answer all the more interesting. He is reported to have replied by stating his belief that God "will compel us to do right in order that He may do these things, not so much because we desire them as that they accord with His plans of dealing with this nation. . . ."[106] Like all *post eventum* accounts of conversations this one must be approached with caution, but it does seem to capture a quality of Lincoln's faith we have noted in other expressions of his thought.

In his Meditation on the Divine Will one is able to see something of this belief in God's power over human thoughts and actions. Lincoln felt he had to conclude that "God wills this contest, and wills that it shall not end yet" because "by his mere quiet power, on the minds of the now contestants, He could have either *saved* or *destroyed* the Union without a human contest. . . . Yet the contest proceeds."[107]

Throughout his life Lincoln held to the following beliefs: that events would transpire as God willed them to happen, that with God's help no man and no nation could fail, that without his support human efforts accomplished nought, that one should rely on "the Supreme Being for the final triumph of the right."[108] Americans did have some reason for confidence because, as he reminded audiences, God had "never forsaken this favored land."[109] Lincoln believed that he himself was "a humble instrument in the hands of our Heavenly Father . . . to work out his great purposes."[110] Lincoln's principal religious response to the war was, then simple trust in the God of power and might, who, Lincoln hoped, would bring to pass some great good for the United States and the world through the instrumentality of himself and the American people.

In his 1862 Annual Message to Congress, Lincoln stated that "while it has not pleased the Almighty to bless us with a return of peace, we can but press on, guided by the best light He gives us, trusting that in His own good time, and wise way, all will yet be well."[111] Lincoln relied on the grace of God but he also tried to respond to that grace by seeking to align himself with God's purposes in the war and, of course, by doing his utmost to pursue a course that would eventually lead to the establishment of a more perfect Union.

In responding in trust to God and in attempting to see clearly the situation in which Providence had placed him, what may we say Lincoln observed in the war? It is hard to believe that he saw, in Wolf's words, that "the human suffering caused by slavery would be equaled by the suffering of those who had maintained the offense against God."[112] Here Wolf has extrapolated too much from Lincoln's statement that all Americans stood guilty before God for tolerating the institution of slavery. In fact, as Thomas Pressly has pointed out, Lincoln really felt that Southerners were *not* responsible for the events that had led to war. Lincoln believed, further, that it was their leaders who had started the war by deluding them and enticing them into rebellion.[113] And Lincoln certainly knew that the Confederate leaders would be among the ones to suffer the *least* in the war, that it would, as always, be precisely those men, women, and children who had not maintained the offense against God who would end up the chief victims of the slaughter.

The spectacles through which Lincoln peered to catch a glimpse of the war's meaning probably could not even have had the tint of retribution. We know that after Lincoln learned that reports of a massacre at Ft. Pillow of Union troops by Confederate soldiers were true, he could have ordered a *quid pro quo* response: the execution of a like number of captured rebel soldiers. This course had in fact been proposed. But Lincoln declared in a letter to the Secretary of War, Edwin Stanton, that "as blood can not restore blood, and government should not act for revenge," no Southern prisoners should be killed.[114] Nor did Lincoln see God himself acting to wreak vengeance (or even punishment) upon human beings. His beliefs concerning the life to come were similar to those of the Universalists: all men are saved; there is no hell.[115]

Perhaps the most poignant, and telling, comments of Lincoln's that reflect his feelings on the relationship (or lack thereof) between earthly sufferings and divine punishments come in a piece of correspondence that is similar in some ways to his much more famous letter to Mrs. Bixby of Boston. The letter to Fanny McCullough was written to a little girl whose father, Lt. Col. McCullough of Bloomington, Illinois, had lost his life in the war. "In this sad world of ours," the President wrote, "sorrow comes to all; and, to the young, it comes with bitterest agony, because it takes them unawares. The older have learned to ever expect it."[116] Lincoln evinced a recognition in these words not only that the innocent in this life may be sent afflictions, but that their sufferings may actually be more acute than those of anyone else.

What we see when we look upon the war with Lincoln's eyes is its terrible cost. Images of suffering dominated the wartime landscape. "By the end of 1862, Mr. Lincoln could scarcely drive or walk in any direction about Washington without passing a hospital. . . ." Even near his summer retreat, Soldiers' Home, "the rolling hillside was dotted with white hospital tents during the entire war."[117] As Catton notes, Lincoln knew that the price of the war included young boys dying of disease and gunshot, disrupted homes "with the goods that were to keep a family through the winter trampled on by grinning hoodlums," the sorrow of those "who had just hoped to get along the best they could, winning a little happiness out of life if their luck was in."[118] We know that Lincoln was repeatedly caught up in the suffering of the war in a most personal way through the deaths of close friends and through the funerals he was required to attend.[119] We also know how deeply he must have been affected by the cost of the war by the fact of his extraordinary concern for the lives of his men. The stories of his seizing upon "extenuating circumstances" at every opportunity to lighten the penalty of convicted soldiers are legion and, for the most part, accurate.[120] The President was a frequent visitor of the wounded in Washington hospitals.[121] He was known to be especially concerned about what would happen to his men when the war ended.[122]

It was the sacrifice of these innocent lives that affected Lincoln most deeply. One of Lincoln's friends, Ward Hill Lamon, is undoubtedly correct when he says that "it was the havoc of the war, the sacrifice of patriotic lives, the flow of human blood, the mangling of precious limbs in the great Union host that shocked him most. . . ." Lamon says that Lincoln was sometimes so disturbed by the sight of this suffering as to be almost unable "to control either his judgment or his feelings."[123] Confronted with these tragic circumstances, what must have both buoyed his hopes and increased his anguish was the knowledge that the God of mercies in whom he trusted was also the One who determined the destinies of all.

Throughout the war Lincoln's highest praise was reserved for the soldiers and for those who cared for them, like the workers of the Sanitary Commission. To him the thousands of enlisted men and draftees were like unblemished lambs being offered up for immolation so that the nation might live more abundantly. Any adequate understanding of Lincoln's religious approach to the war must come to terms with this fact. It is not enough to focus on one or two statements of his in which he mentioned God and the war and establish one's interpretation of his outlook on the basis of those limited references. Lincoln never sat down one day toward the end of the war and thought up a theological explanation for all the strife. Rather, he lived his faith and expressed it week in and week out every year. What Lincoln saw on a daily basis was the undeniable truth that those who were least responsible for what had come to pass were bearing the heaviest burdens. In other words, he saw the suffering of the war in terms of vicarious sacrifice. The relatively innocent were shedding their blood for others, who were usually the greater debtors. And, as a radical monotheist, he had to acknowledge that this, too, must be God's doing.

In all of Lincoln's works, no single type of utterance is more common than that in which the Commander-in-Chief spoke of his regard for the merits of the nation's soldiers and sailors. America should ever be grateful to the ones "who have endured toil, privations and wounds, that the nation might live." It is they who "are endeavoring to purchase with their blood and their lives the future happiness and prosperity of this country." The "toil and blood" of the volunteer soldiers "have been given as much for you as for themselves." They bear "the harder part," offering and often yielding up their lives. To them and their families the world is indebted, gratitude and support ought to be offered, and patronage should be given. Whatever is done for their good cannot fail to be blessed by God.[124]

Illustrating this belief, late in 1864 Lincoln wrote to Mrs. Lydia Bixby, who lost two sons in the war, and mentioned at the close of his letter "the solemn pride that must be yours, to have laid so costly a sacrifice upon the altar of Freedom."[125] Earlier in the war Lincoln responded to Carl Schurz's assertions that the Union effort was failing because the war was being conducted by non-Republicans, who were personally at odds with Lincoln's policies. The names the President mentioned in his sharp reply belonged to men who died in the war. "In sealing their faith with their blood, Baker, an[d] Lyon, and Bohlen, and Richardson, republicans, did all that men could do; but did they any more," Lincoln asked, "than Kearney, and Stevens, and Reno, and Mansfield, none of whom were republicans, and some . . . of whom, have been bitterly, and repeatedly denounced to me as secession sympathizers?"[126] The suggestion of course was that each of these Union officers sealed his faith with his blood. One can easily understand why it was that Lincoln was so moved by Holmes's poem "Lexington" and especially by the stanza that begins with the line, "Green be the graves where her martyrs are lying!"[127] Lincoln believed that in all of their worthy deeds the soldiers were acting "under Providence."[128]

Did Lincoln see the nation—especially through its fighting men—expiating its guilt through suffering, purifying itself of its offenses through a kind of baptism of blood, and thus accomplishing atonement with God and restoration of the human community? Such a view of Lincoln has been held by talented writers, and it is certainly one that sounds reasonable.[129] After all, Lincoln's language appears to lend itself to this kind of interpretation, and, moreover, the approach itself is an understandable religious way of coming to grips with the meaning of innocent suffering in wartime.[130]

We know that the Congregational minister Horace Bushnell understood the war in these terms. If Lincoln also shared this view, we shall have to recognize some congruity of outlook in the two men. For Bushnell the shedding of blood was an altogether glorious and positive experience. The "heroic sacrifice" offered by the war dead of both sides made possible the purchase of "a new great chapter of life" for the nation. Before the war not enough blood had been shed for the United States to become "a proper nation," but as a result of this "righteous bleeding," "our unity is cemented and forever sanctified." This "triumph" could come about in but one way: "It is only when we are rallied by a cause, in that cause receive a great inspiration, in that inspiration give our bodies to the death, that at last, out of many such heroes dead, comes the possibility of great thoughts, fired by sacrifice, and a true public magnanimity." By means of the great sacrifice of money and blood, "we have bought and sanctified consentingly . . . all that is grand in this . . . history." American institutions, having been bathed in blood, are now "hallowed," and "governement" has become "grandly moral" and "sacred," with the "stamp of God's sovereignty" upon it. Bushnell looked for "a new era" bringing "new gifts and powers and holy endowments from on high" to "break forth." The living he thought ought to follow the heroic example of those who sacrificed their lives and should dedicate themselves to thoroughly vanquishing the South.[131] William A. Clebsch summarizes Bushnell's interpretation of the war this way: "As the blood of Christ was shed in vicarious sacrifice for mankind's redemption, so the blood of Americans was shed in vicarious sacrifice for the redemption of the American nation."[132] Bushnell understood the suffering of the soldiers in the Civil War to be analogous to the passion of Christ. In both cases atonement was made possible by bloodshed and the expiation of sin.[133]

Although some surface similarities do exist in the thought of Lincoln and Bushnell, I believe there is not as much overlap in their thinking as one might suppose or as much as some have seen there. The two men clearly had widely diverging attitudes and expectations about the post-bellum period. I have said enough about the views of each on that particular subject not to have to detail those further. Other contrasts just as significant are also present. Indeed, in the end I cannot help thinking of Austin Farrer's comment concerning Job's friends: They are "liars," Farrer says, "and their mendacity is a moral fault, not simply a speculative failure. It is the hardness of a heart which refuses to feel the sorrow it dares to explain."[134] Almost as great a difference exists between Abraham Lincoln and Horace Bushnell as exists between Job and his comforters. I will mention four points of divergence between them.

The first has to do with their personal responses to the war. To Bushnell it was a glorious venture to be met with joy; to Lincoln it was a horror in the face of which one could not but feel anguish even as one tried to find hope. "War, at the best," Lincoln said, "is terrible, and this war of ours, in its magnitude and in its duration, is one of the most terrible."[135] For Bushnell suffering for a righteous cause was something to be embraced, even sought; Lincoln accepted war only when it was thrust upon him and nothing ever inured him to the bloodshed.[136]

The second difference is related to the first. Bushnell presented a picture of combatants marching forward heroically to identify themselves in a fully conscious and selfless manner with the principles for which they fought. Lincoln had a more realistic understanding of Americans, North and South, caught up in a war not of their own making or choosing. Carl Sandburg has noted wisely: "He did not assume that the drafted soldiers, substitutes, and bounty-paid privates had died willingly under Lee's shot and shell, in deliberate consecration of themselves to the Union cause."[137] He knew that those who suffered the most in the conflict were the ones who were least intellectually and emotionally enthusiastic about fighting; he realized few of them had any desire to be heroes or even soldiers.

Third, the two men had different notions of what the war's sacrifices would achieve. Bushnell pointed to expiation, atonement, and redemption. Lincoln stopped short of saying that the war was in any way a dying for sin, a covering of debts, or an atoning for guilt. It was not the case that he understood the war's suffering to equal that of the slaves over many years. Lincoln did see the war as involving the sacrifice of those who were relatively innocent, but he did not claim, or even in his language imply, that any expiation of corporate guilt was thereby effected. Indeed, there would have been something rather out of character for him if he had. Lincoln apparently had a strong belief in the once and for all nature of the atonement made by Christ.[138] At least he never indicated that any further sacrifice for sin was necessary.

Fourth, for Bushnell the good produced by the war effort was something achieved principally by man. The revitalized institutions in the new era were emblems of an authentic nationhood that *we* bought and that *we* sanctified. All of this is in line with his theory of Christ's atonement, which, at least through the period when he wrote *God in Christ* (1849) and *The Vicarious Sacrifice* (1866), was akin to the subjective, moral influence type first set forth by Abelard. Bushnell's theory of the war parallels his thought on the work of Christ. In fact, in both instances "vicarious sacrifice" is a phrase that really means not so much one person suffering in place of another but rather one human being serving as a heroic, loving, and therefore inspiring example for another human being, who should then be motivated to serve others in a similar way. In Lincoln's case, on the other hand, we can be confident that if he ever entertained thoughts concerning the various theories of the atonement he would have favored one of the "objective" types over the humanistic versions. For Lincoln no good ever came into being except it was achieved by God's grace. He did believe that some positive result would follow the mighty convulsion of war but it was a good that no human being could make or stay.

We are led back to saying that Lincoln developed no theory to explain away the terrible suffering brought on by the war. In response to its horrors he did not talk about atonement or redemption but about binding up wounds and caring for combatants' families. He recognized what he could not help seeing—the hardest part being borne by those who had done least to create the burden—and responded to what he saw by asking for words and deeds of true repentance. He did not glorify evil and say it was right, but he did acknowledge in the midst of the mystery and the strife that God works in all things for good.

It would be a mistake to conclude on the basis of the evidence thus far presented, however, that Lincoln had absolutely no notion of God's purposes in the war. In fact he had a good idea. But he did not derive this understanding from the perception of the intentions of God revealed to him in discrete epiphanic moments. No special knowledge was vouchsafed to him. When he wrote in a message to Congress that "we can but press on, guided by the best light He gives us," Lincoln indicated a desire for another kind of illumination, the sort that pertains more to the "active" than the "contemplative" life.[139] Lincoln walked a pilgrim's path, but the signposts he required were those indicating how to apply the Summary of the Law, not the ones pointing the way to mystical experience. In seeking to respond appropriately and practically to the purposes of God in the Civil War, Lincoln, relied on no new vision but rather on an old way of seeing. He trusted in the Father of all humankind and sought with the eyes of faith to learn not the details of the workings of Providence but how best to serve those to whom God is faithful.

A better way of approaching Lincoln's ethical conduct than that of focusing on his dedication to values like freedom and equality is to see him as a man of faith who tried in every action to be loyal to God's cause of universal community. All the rest of the norms can be subsumed under this one insight. Lincoln responded to other human beings in such a way as to express his belief that all were children of God. His outlook and behavior during the war years can thus be understood as being all of a piece with that of his whole adult life. He was constantly working to foster reconciliation, to induce people to see themselves as responsible members of a larger family. As early as 1842 he took an unpopular stand in an address on the reformation of drunkards by saying that non-drinkers had been spared falling victim to the vice more from "absence of appetite" than "mental or moral superiority." He urged a more compassionate and effective, less condescending and denunciatory, approach upon his audience of temperance advocates.[140]

Later, in the Civil War, Lincoln was to distinguish himself from Northern abolitionists by refusing to treat Southerners as evil men and the war as a holy cause. One finds in his masterpiece, the Gettysburg Address, "no accusations, no recriminations, no lash of invective, not even a mild outspoken reproach of the enemy."[141] Herbert Butterfield has written words that can be applied in this context. He reasoned that "we are not justified in expanding a legal verdict into a judgment on a personality. . . . If it is necessary to hang murderers, we must be sure that we are doing it because of a necessity and not out of moral indignation." (This was Lincoln's attitude:) "And when we have done it we shall do well to reflect sadly on the bitterness of the necessity, and say: 'There, but for the grace of God, go I.' "[142]

Lincoln adopted the moral stance he did vis-à-vis the South because of, not in spite of, his position on slavery and human rights. Back of both approaches lay his fundamental conviction that all men are sons and daughters of one God. Lincoln felt that both legally and morally he was entitled to take toward the South only that single governing action which would bring about its restoration to the Union. He did not believe he should sit in judgment upon Southerners. After his election in 1860 he asked that "in our rejoicing let us neither express, nor cherish, any harsh feeling towards any citizen who, by his vote, has differed with us. Let us at all times remember that all Americans are brothers of a common country, and should dwell together in the bonds of fraternal feeling."[143] The subject of Lincoln's last words to the Cabinet and to the nation—overcoming sectional antagonisms, the restoration of national unity—was really the theme of most of his remarks throughout the war.[144]

The universal scope of Lincoln's vision is evident also in his statements concerning the purpose of the conflict. He believed the United States to be engaged in a cause of world-wide applicability. Though he acknowledged that he was capable of error in judgment, he believed this cause to be "good" and "just."[145] He felt that "the past action and influences of the United States were generally regarded as having been beneficent towards mankind," and he hoped that this latest movement would be also.[146] The Declaration of Independence had given "hope to the world for all future time," and now its principles had to be defended. If the United States could "prove to the world" that a democratic system of government was capable of working, that much more secure was "the progress, civilization, and happiness of mankind." That much more likely would it be that "government of the people, by the people, for the people, shall not perish from the earth."[147] For Lincoln it was the fact that the contest had world-wide implications that made it so crucial.

We should note, too, that Lincoln became active in politics again in the 1850s precisely because he detected a lack of universal concern on the part of his fellows. He felt acutely a decline in citizens' regard for the interests of others and decided he had to step in to reawaken Americans' sense of a common responsibility. The spirit embodied in the Kansas-Nebraska Act and Douglas' principle of popular sovereignty, Lincoln realized, was akin to, in Barth's phrase, "that godlessness in action which is truly atheism."[148] It was this mentality that truly threatened to undermine the vitality of free institutions and which had to be countered by an effective leader calling the people back to their ethical obligation to establish justice for all. Slavery he saw more as symptom than cause of the nation's disorder. The people's growing indifference to that institution—as expressed in political compromises allowing its spread—was a result of their selfishness and lack of civic virtue.[149] Lincoln's effort here as elsewhere was to persuade citizens to see themselves as members of a larger body. He knew in 1865 that their failure to do so had led to civil war, and he realized that if they continued in the same way after the war similar problems would arise. This perception is why in his Second Inaugural he tried to prompt the people to move forward on a new basis according to which they would affirm their proper tasks of mutual concern extending to "all nations."[150] He indicated Americans' corporate guilt in that speech only as a step along the way to pointing out their common humanity and universal responsibility.

Abraham Lincoln, whose faith required loving fidelity to the whole commonwealth of man, sought to be loyal to God's cause by doing what he could to establish fundamental human rights for all. His thinking on these matters contained two characteristic, related points of emphasis. The linchpin of each was preservation of the Union. Both were expressed in these two sentences from his 1862 Message to Congress: "In *giving* freedom to the *slave,* we *assure* freedom to the *free*—honorable alike in what we give, and what we preserve. We shall nobly save, or meanly lose, the last, best hope of earth."[151] For Lincoln the purpose of the Union was to safeguard the people's liberties, which are "given to mankind directly by the Maker."[152] Equality to him meant freedom of opportunity. The Declaration of Independence "gave promise that in due time the weights should be lifted from the shoulders of all men, and that *all* should have an equal chance."[153]

The point of putting down the rebellion was to maintain a system whereby "every man has a right to be equal with every other man. In this great struggle, this form of Government and every form of human right is endangered if our enemies succeed." Lincoln believed that involved in the war was "the question whether your children and my children shall enjoy the privileges we have enjoyed"; the purpose of the war was to hold on to the "inestimable jewel" of equality, whereby "each . . . may have through this free government . . . an open field and a fair chance for [their] industry, enterprise and intelligence. . . ."[154] If the Union could not be held on to without denying these rights, then it was not worth preserving.[155]

This contest was indeed the "test" of "whether any government, not *too* strong for the liberties of its people, can be strong *enough* to maintain its own existence. . . ."[156] Lincoln felt that if the nation made it through this test then the perdurability of the republican form of government would have been demonstrated. All would then be able to see proof of the fact that a free nation could survive internal strife with the rights of its people intact. Lincoln believed this result would be a "great consummation," one that "the world will forever applaud, and God must forever bless."[157]

Lincoln's purpose in the war may be seen, then, to have two aspects. On the one hand, he wanted to free the slaves and safeguard the liberties of the people. On the other, he wanted to prove the health of the

American experiment to the world. The one end was more immediate and national, the other more abstract and universal. Both, however, required for their successful achievement that the rebellion be put down and the Union preserved. And in both Lincoln sought to establish more firmly the principle of equality and to broaden its scope.

To Lincoln the Civil War was a test of the people's devotion to this cause. One of the words he used most often as an alternative designation for the conflict was "trial." The full phrase that appears to have suited his purposes the best was "fiery trial." Others used this expression to refer to the war—Charles Sumner, for instance—and of course at the time it may have seemed a virtual cliché.[158] It is more likely than not, however, that Lincoln employed the term with full conscious knowledge of its biblical matrix. It occurs in the Bible only in 1 Peter and there in but one passage: "Beloved, think it not strange concerning the fiery trial which is to try you, as though some strange thing happened unto you: But rejoice, inasmuch as ye are partakers of Christ's sufferings; that, when his glory shall be revealed, ye may be glad also with exceeding joy" (4:12–13, King James Version). The reference here is, of course, to the ordeal of persecution. Did Lincoln derive his phrase from this text? I think that is probable for several reasons: 1) it is not an obscure, little-noticed passage, 2) Lincoln was thoroughly familiar with the Bible,[159] 3) his usage is harmonious with that of the author of 1 Peter, and 4) the religious attitude expressed in the biblical text is consonant with what we know of Lincoln's theological outlook.

The biblical context of "fiery trial" is the experience of martyrdom. Our word "martyr" is a transliteration of the Greek *marturos,* which means witness. As Robert McAfee Brown has written, "A martyr was a witness; he was not trying to draw attention to himself, but to witness to his trust in the power of God even over death."[160] The martyr embodied faith as we have defined it, demonstrating both trust in God and loyalty to his cause. His suffering was understood to be not a punishment for sin, or even a purging or refining by fire; nor was his sacrifice a means of expiation or atonement. It was comprehended to be, rather, a kind of participation in the sufferings of Christ. C. S. Lewis has written that "the sacrifice of Christ is . . . re-echoed among His followers in very varying degrees, from the cruellest martyrdom down to a self-submission of intention. . . ."[161] The witness to God, whether he endures actual religious persecution or not, is in any case one who seeks in all things to do God's will and who trusts in the graciousness of Being rather than in the capacity of any of his own resources.

For Lincoln one way in which the Civil War was like a martyr's trial was that it called for a response of what he termed "sublime Christian heroism." This is the phrase he used to refer to the conduct of the workingmen of Manchester, England, who had sent him a memorial expressing support of the Emancipation Proclamation. He wrote them, saying, "Through the actions of our disloyal citizens the workingmen of Europe have been subjected to a severe trial, for the purpose of forcing their sanction to that attempt." Lincoln praised the Manchester workers for backing the cause of "justice, humanity, and freedom."[162] Frequently when he used the word trial he appears to have had in mind a terribly difficult situation whose successful passage required a submission to the right and a firm resolution to carry that decision through. In the 1862 Message to Congress, in which he told his audience that an opportunity had been presented to them to choose "the way" that is "generous" and "just," he prefaced his closing statement by letting his listeners know that "the fiery trial through which we pass, will light us down, in honor or dishonor, to the latest generation."[163] In many instances throughout the war he simply referred to the whole experience the nation was undergoing as "a great trial" or as "a fiery trial."[164] For the combatants it was more a matter of endurance of sufferings than of conscious choice of right or wrong. There could be a passive quality to the word, then, as when the soldiers were in the midst of the "great trial" of warfare.[165] In those and similar cases Lincoln apparently saw Americans more in the role of patient than actor; indeed, one of his constant points of emphasis throughout the conflict was that the war had not been started in order to preserve the Union but in order to destroy it: one party—the insurgents—*made* war, the other *accepted* it.[166]

(3) KNOWLEDGE OF THE DIVINE WILL

At this point we must pause to enter into discussion of certain controversies concerning Lincoln's faith. It would be one thing for Lincoln to have advocated certain policies and programs because he believed them to be right and another for him to have proclaimed them as God's will. Granted that he admitted to a lack of knowledge of God's ultimate purposes in the war, is there any evidence that Lincoln felt he could grasp the more immediate divine intentions for particular situations? Did he not only *hope* that he was doing the will of God but also, at least on some occasions, suppose he *knew* he was doing it? Reinhold Niebuhr has claimed that Lincoln avoided "the error of identifying providence with the cause to which the agent is committed."[167] It would be impossible to continue making this claim, however, if one were forced to admit that Lincoln believed himself to be privy to a realm of special knowledge. If such was the case, then Lincoln would have tended to identify God's cause with his own. This would have made a difference not only in his religious attitude but also, possibly, in his conduct as a statesman.

Let us examine two fairly recent sets of statements concerning Lincoln's access to special revelation. One occurs in an article in *Church History* by Melvin B. Endy, Jr. The other may be found in the various writings of William J. Wolf. Endy's article contains an attack on the notion that Lincoln relied solely on the Bible, the democratic process, and reasoning to discover God's will for himself and the nation. He argues that Lincoln also relied on direct revelation for guidance in daily affairs and that this "vision of himself" as a "divinely guided instrument" prompted him to identify the Union cause as God's own and possibly also to feel entitled to violate the United States Constitution.[168] Wolf, by insisting on the reliability of a few historical accounts of Lincoln receiving just such divine guidance, unwittingly lends Endy some much needed ammunition.

Endy writes that "as the war progressed and the pressures and anxiety increased, Lincoln manifested more and more a propensity to rely on direct personal revelation of God's will." Lincoln, Endy says, was superstitious and might have relied on dreams and spiritualism as means of revelation. He came to view himself at times as a "latter-day Moses learning God's will on the presidential mountain and bringing it down to the people." After 1862, "Lincoln increasingly expected, and believed that he received, divine guidance in a special manner that bypassed the ways of democracy, including advice, debate, popular will and even, at times, his own reasoning process." Trueblood, Niebuhr, and others have said that "Lincoln . . . did not assume an identity between his cause and God's," but in fact Lincoln sometimes did just that.[169]

The evidence Endy points to in order to support his contentions is weak at best and sometimes nonexistent. He simply refers the reader to Richard N. Current's book, *The Lincoln Nobody Knows,* for example, for reports on Lincoln's dabbling in mysticism, spiritualism, revelation through dreams, etc. But Current's brief (and dated) account is almost wholly made up of apocryphal anecdotes on the one hand and stories of Lincoln's skepticism on matters mystical on the other. Current relates, for instance, the tale about a dream Lincoln supposedly had just shortly before he was assassinated in which he saw a body lying dead on a catafalque and was told by a guard it belonged to the President. A more likely story has Lincoln attending a séance at which a number of spirits deliver contradictory messages. Lincoln wryly said the ghosts sounded like members of his Cabinet. One trustworthy account that Current does relate has to do with a disturbing dream Lincoln had that induced him to telegraph his wife, who was in Philadelphia with their son Tad, asking her to take Tad's pistol away from him. We know that the report is true because the telegraph message is still extant and is included in the *Collected Works*.[170] But that is the *only* report of this kind that we do have, and it should be noted that this dream has nothing to do with a revelation of the will of God for the nation. In fact, all that it means is that Lincoln felt uneasy after "an ugly dream" with respect to his son's having a gun, an experience that could surely happen to any skeptic today. Endy also leans heavily on the account of a conversation Lincoln supposedly had with L. E. Chittenden. This report is, in my view, exceptionally unreliable and is, at any rate, overturned by evidence in statements made by Lincoln that we know are authentic but which Endy does not see fit even to cite in a footnote, such as the Meditation on the Divine Will.[171] In sum, Endy needs more to make his case than he has provided us with in his essay.

Perhaps he receives the help he needs from Wolf, who puts a great deal of stock in a couple of accounts which do indeed suggest that Lincoln received direct personal revelations from God. The first concerns Lincoln's decision on the timing of the issuance of the Emancipation Proclamation. Wolf holds that Lincoln reached his decision after turning to God for the answer. "God was ultimate yet personal reality, and He made Himself accessible to one who sought Him out. For Lincoln, God was the final court of appeal when he was uncertain about the moral aspects of a question." Then Wolf adds in a curious flourish: "God's guidance was sought when Lincoln wanted to pass through the tides of political expediency to stand on bedrock."[172]

As evidence Wolf advances three versions of the statement Lincoln made to his Cabinet on September 22, 1862, concerning his action to free the slaves. One of these is an account of the event given to Francis Carpenter (a painter who lived in the White House for about six months) by Secretary of the Treasury Salmon P. Chase. The other two are diary accounts of the meeting recorded by Chase and Secretary of the Navy Gideon Welles. The Carpenter version is the least significant of the three not only because it is farthest removed from the actual event but also because it adds nothing of interest to the Chase diary account. Carpenter says Chase told him that at the Cabinet meeting, which took place "immediately after the battle of Antietam," Lincoln stated that the time had come for the announcement on emancipation and that he had promised God he would issue it. Chase asked Lincoln to repeat the part about the promise to God, and Lincoln said: "I made a solemn vow before God, that if General Lee was driven back from Pennsylvania, I would crown the result by the declaration of freedom to the slaves."[173] According to the account in Chase's diary for the day of the Cabinet meeting, Lincoln made the following statement:

> When the rebel army was at Frederick, I determined, as soon as it should be driven out of Maryland, to issue a Proclamation of Emancipation such as I thought most likely to be useful. I said nothing to any one; but I made the promise to myself, and (hesitating a little)—to my Maker. The rebel army is now driven out, and I am going to fulfill that promise.[174]

Since this quotation is historically more reliable than the Carpenter account of Chase's statement, and since there are no significant differences between them, we will let the Chase diary supersede the Carpenter account. This is the Welles version of Lincoln's remarks.

> In the course of the discussion . . . he remarked that he had made a vow, a covenant, that if God gave us the victory in the approaching battle, he would consider it an indication of Divine will, and that it was his duty to move forward in the cause of emancipation. It might be thought strange, he said, that he had in this way submitted the disposal of matters when the way was not clear to his mind what he should do. God had decided this question in favor of the slaves. He was satisfied it was right, was confirmed and strengthened in his action by the vow and the results. His mind was fixed, his decision made. . . .[175]

In his article, "Lincoln and the Bible," Wolf notes as part of his discussion of this event that "The taking of vows and covenants is a characteristic feature of Calvinism. This practice was imbedded in Lincoln's Biblical piety and came to him as part of the early religious heritage of the nation."[176] Whether or not that is exactly so I won't venture to say at this point. What is obvious is that Wolf, quite sanguine in the use of these quotations himself, leaves his position open, by drawing the conclusions he does, to just the sorts of charges Endy makes in his criticism of the Moses-like Lincoln. Another serious problem is that the Lincoln of the Welles account reduces faith and prayer to a magical, *do ut des* exercise in trading with a rather finite, wheeler-dealer divinity. The closest parallel to this story in our own day may be

found in Peter Shaffer's drama *Amadeus* where the court composer
Antonio Salieri prays to "the God of Bargains" for ability and fame in
return for the honor of his music.[177]

Upon close inspection one notices that these two diary accounts are
not exactly the same. The Chase version of events does not necessarily
presuppose the type of vow described in the Welles version. In fact, in
the former it would appear that Lincoln had already chosen his course,
and the promise to God was a way of solemnizing, of saying "Amen,"
to that momentous decision. The Welles account, on the other hand,
would lead one to suspect that the President was not quite sure he even
wanted to free the slaves. It makes it appear he used the upcoming
battle like a bettor's coin—"when the way was not clear . . . what he
should do." In Chase the right path *was* clear and Lincoln moved
forward with firm determination, swearing an oath to God along the
way. Wolf, of course, in his own description of these circumstances,
develops the Welles line.

But this approach to the occasion of the issuance of the proclamation
is incongruous with what we know of the historical reality. Lincoln had
written and decided to announce the Emancipation Proclamation long
before the battle of Antietam. He hesitated in making the decision
public for political reasons alone. Seward had advised the President to
delay the proclamation's issue until a Union victory came along. This
strategy was designed to keep the administration from appearing desperate. Lincoln judged this to be sound counsel when it was first offered and history shows that he acceded to it. Lincoln's own version of
these events runs as follows:

> Finally, came the week of the battle of Antietam. I determined to
> wait no longer. The news came, I think, on Wednesday, that the
> advantage was on our side. I was then staying at the Soldiers'
> Home. . . . Here I finished writing the second draft of the prelimi-
> nary proclamation; came up on Saturday; called the Cabinet to-
> gether to hear it, and was published the following Monday.[178]

This account would seem to support the contention that Lincoln had
made his decision long before bloody Antietam. When results from that
battle began to look even a little promising, Lincoln set the machinery
in motion. There was no need for a flip of the coin with a Cosmic
Trader. He had long before come to the conclusion that Union victory
required increased manpower, European neutrality, the elimination of
a major part of the enemy's work force—all the things he hoped to gain
from emancipation.

The Chase rendering of the September 22 Cabinet meeting is consistent with what we know of the history of this brief period. It is also the account cited by John Hope Franklin, author of *The Emancipation Proclamation* and foremost expert on this episode. He does not give the Welles version in his book at all.[179] When asked to render a judgment concerning the reliability of these two accounts Franklin responded by stating that Lincoln's

> decision to issue the Emancipation Proclamation arose from his strong belief that it was absolutely necessary for the survival of the Union. He hoped that God was on his side, but his resolution to issue the Proclamation was I think independent of religious or theological considerations. You can see, therefore, that I come down on the side of Chase rather than Welles.[180]

While I do not think Lincoln's action took place outside a general theological context inclusive of his overall aim to establish the hope of freedom for all men, neither do I believe he reached this specific political conclusion by the sort of process Welles suggests and only after the "immediate awareness of the presence of God" of Wolf's description.[181]

Another story Wolf credits as being the accurate report of a historical event is the one in which Lincoln visits General Sickles in the hospital. After the latter asked the President if he had been anxious concerning the recently fought battle of Gettysburg (at which Sickles had been wounded), Lincoln said that although some members of the Cabinet had been worried he had not been fearful at all. Sickles wanted to know how this was and Lincoln replied by giving this account of his experience:

> In the pinch of the campaign up there, when everybody seemed panic-stricken, and nobody could tell what was going to happen, oppressed by the gravity of our affairs, I went to my room one day, and I locked the door, and got down on my knees before Almighty God, and prayed to Him mightily for victory at Gettysburg. I told Him we couldn't stand another Fredericksburg or Chancellorsville. And I then and there made a solemn vow to Almighty God, that if He would stand by our boys at Gettysburg, I would stand by Him. And He *did* stand by your boys, and I *will* stand by Him. And after that (I don't know how it was, and I can't explain it), soon a sweet comfort crept into my soul that God Almighty had taken the whole business into his own hands and

that things would go all right at Gettysburg. And that is why I had no fears about you.[182]

Wolf assures us that this narrative has "the same authentic ring in the idiom about 'a solemn vow to Almighty God' that had earlier marked his approach to emancipating the slaves."[183] Of course it is in the same category as the Welles account but that is only all the more reason to question its authenticity. The picture of Lincoln conveyed in this story is at odds with the Lincoln of the *Collected Works,* who indicated just the opposite view: that it was impossible to receive ultimate assurances of this kind. Moreover, the story is internally dubious if not downright nonsensical. It has Lincoln suggesting both that God determines the outcome of events and that his purposes can be thwarted, both that Lincoln is anxious to do the will of the Almighty and that Lincoln could conceive of doing something other than "standing by" the Lord in his righteous cause. We have to agree with Sandburg that this account is probably not trustworthy.[184] It is the type of story that chroniclers of Lincoln's religion used to include in their books but which is now rejected by most historians.[185]

Madison Peters, for example, has Lincoln going on to tell Sickles: "I am in a prophetic mood today. You will get well."[186] G. Frederick Owen says Lincoln told his Cabinet after the Union victories of Gettysburg and Vicksburg: "I knew it would come out all right, for God told me so."[187] These tales are on a par with the ones related by William J. Johnson in *Abraham Lincoln: The Christian.* According to these Lincoln decided to free the slaves after hearing "the voice of God, crying, 'Let my people go,'" and realized what action he should take to provide relief to suffering soldiers and sailors after God, in Lincoln's alleged words, "put the Sanitary Commission in my mind, with all its details."[188] As the years have passed, stories of this nature have been increasingly thrown out as solid evidence indicative of Lincoln's true religious beliefs. To a greater and greater extent we are left with the more reserved Lincoln of the *Collected Works.*

In the Fragment on Pro-slavery Theology, for example, Lincoln stated that while "there is no contending against the will of God," he had to admit "there is some difficulty in ascertaining, and applying it, to particular cases." Did God will that the slaves be set free? "The Almighty gives no audable answer to the question, and his revelation—the Bible—gives none—or, at most, none but such as admits of a squabble, as to it's meaning."[189] Later, in his reply to a delegation of churchmen from Chicago, he said that he would try to discover and carry out the will of God, but "these are not . . . the days of miracles, and I suppose it will be granted that I am not to expect a direct revelation." He told them he "must study the plain physical facts of the case, ascertain what is possible and learn what appears to be wise and right."[190] There is a humorous story Carpenter tells in which, after listening to a visiting minister's long anti-slavery tirade composed largely of Old Testament quotations, Lincoln says to him and the group he is with: "Well, gentlemen, it is not often one is favored with a delegation *direct* from the Almighty!"[191]

In his own decisionmaking we see Lincoln relying on no extraordinary procedures. Moral principles, biblical injunctions, practical reasoning—all were brought into play by him in seeking the best course of action. The grounds on which he concluded that slavery was wrong, for example, were various: 1) it was a contradiction of God's laws in that it robbed a man of what was rightfully his and failed to treat him according to the prescriptions of Christian charity and the Golden Rule, 2) it threatened the survival of democracy inasmuch as governments derive their power from the consent of the governed and slaves had given no consent to their condition, 3) it constituted a betrayal of the principles embodied in the Declaration of Independence: equality, liberty, the right of all to rise and better themselves, and 4) it might spread and eventually cover the whole country, thereby forcing white laborers to compete with unpaid black workers.[192]

As this example indicates, Lincoln used a variety of methods in reaching a conclusion. His custom was, as he put it, to study the plain facts of the case, working in the best light God provided. There was a discernible emphasis in his moral reasoning on the role of vision, on first trying to see what the particular facts and requirements of the individual situation at hand actually were before attempting to impose a predetermined principle or policy. A well-known passage from his House Divided Speech contains this characteristic concern of his: "If we could first know *where* we are, and *whither* we are tending, we could then better judge *what* to do, and *how* to do it."[193] David Donald has written about Lincoln's abhorrence of rules and set procedures, his rejection of doctrinaire approaches to problems and issues, and his realistic, practical attitude by depicting him as a representative of the American pragmatic tradition.[194] An equally fair way of describing Lincoln is to characterize him as a practitioner of the Christian virtue of prudence. He was always concerned to make sure his action was appropriate to the particular situation at hand, that it took into account all the richness and density of actuality in the specific time of decision.

So he was anxious to inquire, What is really happening here? How can principles of equality and love be applied here and now? What might God be doing and intending for these persons in this context?[195]

Our discussion began in response to my account of Lincoln's seeing the Union effort as a good and just cause. We paused at that point to consider the question whether he might then have gone too far and in fact have attributed to himself extraordinary capacities to discover the divine will. If he did then it would appear that he not only supported certain political actions but also viewed them as part of a holy effort endorsed by the Lord of hosts. I said that if the sorts of reports mentioned by Wolf and Endy proved to be accurate, one would have to agree that Lincoln saw himself as a person privy to special knowledge and therefore as one who could like a prophet proclaim what he knew to be God's cause. I have tried to show that these reports are unreliable and also incongruous with the picture of Lincoln's methods rendered in the accounts we know to be authentic. In fact, Lincoln did not do any more than forcefully advocate as an imperfect, fallible, limited human being the cause he took to be consonant with God's purposes for mankind, acknowledging all the while that he could be wrong, that no special revelation had been vouchsafed to him, that he wanted to forbear judging while working toward his designated, official ends, and that to God alone belonged the credit for accomplishing good.

An appropriate way to understand Lincoln might be to see him as a witness to God. We have noted how in his various efforts as a statesman he kept in mind his duty before God to build community. He fought growing moral indifference to the plight of black men in the 1850s, worked in the war years to preserve the Union and establish the principle of democracy for all the world to see, and performed his tasks without judging his fellow men, giving them up as wicked, or seeking retribution from them. In all this he served as a witness, calling others to dedicated action on behalf of the universal commonwealth, and thereby expressed the active, imperative side of his faith: fidelity to God and to his cause. In the midst of war he responded and urged others to respond, not merely or even primarily to the deeds of rebellion, but also to the whole experience of national suffering, asking the entire country to acknowledge its corporate sins and unrighteousness, to repent and turn itself around, and to reach out in charity to seek true justice and liberty for all.

Lincoln was not only a witness—to freedom, equality, and so forth—but emphatically a witness to *God*. He could proclaim what he took to be worthy goals. When confronting directly the question whether he knew for certain the content of the divine purposes, he had to answer he did not. He did not know the why of the war, but he believed the world to be governed and ordered by Providence and so trusted that there was a why. He did not, like Bushnell, treat the war's afflictions as something glorious and look for wholly positive results, but neither did he accept the horrors for what they were and reason that God therein was wreaking his vengeance upon the nation. Rather, he took the war for the moral evil it was but hoped at the same time that God would accomplish some good even through the strife. In like manner he did not accept victory as divine ratification of a job well done but turned its circumstances into an occasion for profound *metanoia,* a complete reorientation of heart, mind, and will. In all of this he expressed his abiding confidence in the merciful God of power and might.

We can say, too, that to Lincoln the Civil War was a fiery trial. It was a double test of the nation's faith. He understood the war as a trial of the country's commitment to those principles of justice and charity enjoined by God. Would Americans say, "Thy will be done" and submit themselves in obedience to God's commands or would they continue on their self-centered course? For Lincoln it was a time for practical response to the situation at hand, for doing one's duty, for binding up wounds and freeing captives, not for trying to demonstrate one's own righteousness or the unrighteousness of others. So on the one hand it was a trial of conduct. On the other the conflict was a test of the nation's attitudes. Would Americans in victory, for instance, look to themselves as the authors of all good or would they humbly accept God's sovereignty over all? Would they be self-congratulatory, divisive, and vindictive or would they respond humbly to God's grace and pray, "Not unto us, O Lord, not unto us, but unto thy Name be the praise." For Lincoln, unless Americans reformed their mode of perception and behavior the conflict would not be the nation's last. A movement of repentance was held to be required, a conversion of both action and thought. Lincoln expresses each of these approaches to the war at least implicitly in the Second Inaugural.

The war was a fiery trial in a distinct but related sense. It is significant that Lincoln used this phrase to refer to the nation's tragedy because it fits his approach to the suffering as well as any shorthand description possibly could. There are four ways in which the conflict was like a martyr's death. Lincoln grasped the war according to all four understandings but whether or not he directly associated all of them with the phrase "fiery trial" I cannot say for sure. First, the war involved submission to God's will, the sacrifice of one's personal interests for the sake of the common good. Second, the war had not been sought but had rather been thrust upon the Union by a rebellious minority. In being something accepted instead of something looked for it was like the experience of persecution. Third, the burdens of the strife fell most heavily on the relatively innocent rather than on those whose actions had precipitated the conflict. Fourth, God was relied upon with all one's being to bring good out of torment.

In understanding the war in these ways Lincoln was not making any attempt to explain it theologically. He was simply describing what he saw and felt and hoped. In a sense he could not do anything else. He spoke of the blood of boys shed for the sake of others and prayed that the horror might soon cease. He trusted that God was a beneficent Ruler but could not say what good thing God had in mind to give the world. Perhaps the positive result would have something to do with the establishment of a principle: the demonstration that a nation founded on freedom and equality could survive an attempt at its violent dissolution. All he knew was that God must intend "some great good" to follow this fiery trial and that no human being could create it or prevent it.

It would be surprising if Lincoln had been any more specific than that for he was a believer who trusted in the workings of Providence without claiming to have any special insight into their meaning, responding, rather, in faith to God's actions in every action upon him. He did not interpret his own or his country's afflictions as tokens of divine disfavor but accepted them in an attitude of repentance and looked for God to work in those things also for good. Similarly, he did not interpret his own or his nation's successes as unambiguous signs of God's favor. So we should not wonder that he failed to specify the benefaction God intended in the war—for Lincoln must have realized that that gift had to be greater than and different from any good he could imagine.

PART 2
THE FAITH OF A RADICAL MONOTHEIST

CHAPTER II
PROBLEMATICAL ASPECTS OF LINCOLN'S OUTLOOK

It is not the purpose of this chapter to survey all the questions and possible criticisms that could be raised concerning Lincoln's beliefs. I have discussed various difficulties and have developed some of the practical implications of his views at a number of points throughout this essay. Now I want to examine in greater detail two topics adumbrated to some extent above. One has to do with ends and means: In his quest for union did Lincoln countenance the employment of any and all methods that would serve the restoration of the Republic? The second issue follows from this question: If there were intervening norms—such as democratic principles—that he followed and that forestalled the assumption on his part of dictatorial powers, to what degree, if any, did they function as, not merely highest values, but as centers of value, that is, as gods? Specifically, was Lincoln's faith actually a *henotheism* in which "the people" were regarded as the true and the ultimate object of trust and loyalty?

In the first chapter we have seen that Melvin Endy considered the possibility of a connection between Lincoln's vision of himself as a supernaturally instructed instrument of the Almighty and his willingness to grasp as much presidential power as he could and to violate the United States Constitution.[196] Reasons were set forth for dismissing the first part of Endy's claim while acknowledging that Lincoln did indeed see himself as an instrument and witness of God. Now we turn to the second half of Endy's statement, realizing that if Lincoln did feel free to break the nation's laws with impunity he may have arrogated to himself this supposed authority in the context of thinking of himself as a special agent of Providence.

M. E. Bradford, one of the sixteenth President's harshest critics, has written that Lincoln's worst habit was his practice of clothing his political policies in language borrowed from the Bible, thereby "concealing within the Trojan Horse of his gasconade and moral superiority an agenda that would never have been approved if presented in any other form." By using the language of Scripture, according to this view, Lincoln was able to point to his programs as righteous causes; it did not matter what means were employed as long as they served the worthy goal. Lincoln delved into the realm of the sacred whenever he needed to come up with rationales for enlarging the national government or when he required justifications for the use of severe, coercive tactics. In the process he managed to transform the nature of the Union, making it and the Constitution vulnerable to the latest moods and whims of the President and the masses. He initiated the development of a view of executive prerogative according to which the President might, as the people's representative, consider himself competent to judge what was in their best interest and then go on to do whatever he decided was right for the nation without regard for the law; indeed, in this interpretation one's private vision of the good replaces all legal requirements. Lincoln believed that serving the just end of saving the Union entitled him to do anything he wished. including expanding the powers of the presidency to an unprecedented degree.

According to critics, this belief led to gross misconduct and abuse of office. His "tenure as a dictator" began in the spring of his first year as President when he spent public funds without legal warrant, enlarged the regular army beyond its statutory limits, proclaimed a blockade of Southern ports, defied the Supreme Court and various laws of the land, and more. Later he would go far beyond the provisions of the Constitution by creating governmental units hitherto unknown; he would seize property and make mass political arrests, confining his enemies in prison without affording them their right to a trial; he would shut down newspapers that criticized his policies; he would create a state out of the western counties of Virginia in violation, again, of the U.S. Constitution; and he would commit other transgressions, some of them even more serious than these.[197]

If Bradford's interpretation is correct, then even a comparison of Lincoln with the most tyrannical twentieth century political leader would not be as outlandish as it might first appear. One could then note on the basis of this account that both men saw themselves as instruments of God and voices of the people and explained their actions in just these terms; both disregarded legal and moral boundaries in pursuance of their sacred projects.[198] Indeed, while Edmund Wilson does not compare Lincoln to Hitler, he does link him to Bismarck and Lenin and state that all were idealists "who put their ideals before everything else"; each, he says, "became an uncompromising dictator."[199]

As extreme as these judgments are it is necessary that we give their authors the credit due to them for not shying away from a difficult and troubling issue. T. Harry Williams has remarked that one important aspect of Lincoln's leadership that many have refused to recognize was his willingness to use political power. Interestingly enough, in his own discussion of this matter Williams agrees with Bradford on many of the facts having to do with Lincoln's conduct of the war and his treatment of the Constitution. But he interprets Lincoln's acts differently and so reaches a conclusion that is opposite to Bradford's at more than one point. Men like Lincoln, he says,

> men who love power, have done much evil in the world. They have also done great good. It has been the fortune of the democracies that in threatening crises such men have appeared to lead. Nobody can explain why they appear or why democracies have the wisdom to accept them and place them at the head of affairs. All we can do is to be thankful that they come.[200]

Clearly to Williams Lincoln was a good leader in large part because he was an effective President; he knew how to obtain and employ efficacious means, the implements of political power. In the hands of many another person this unusually augmented power might not have been used so wisely or so well; indeed, catastrophe might have resulted if the President himself had not been a decent man, dutiful and self-effacing, and if his goal had not been a noble and limited one.

But here the Christian tradition notes that even if a man possesses all these attributes he still has to admit that the shadow of his selfishness invariably continues to fall across all his perspectives; and while he may plan and act according to the illumination provided by his highest efforts of moral reasoning, still it is true that the best light he has is but as darkness. Bradford's most telling criticisms are not met by an approach like that of Williams (nor, in fairness to the latter, are they meant to be), for his objections really do not have to do with the possibility that Lincoln lacked various positive personal qualities so much as they decry an attitude according to which he was eager to substitute his own convictions and perceptions of the right for the rule of law. Something of what Bradford means can be discovered in the positions of other actors in the Civil War. The abolitionists appealed from the Constitution and the positive law to their own interpretations of the "higher law" embodied in the principles of the Declaration of Independence. In this way they justified revolt and the abrogation of the legal rights of other Americans. Slave owners came up with rationales for their peculiar institution by pointing not to the Declaration but to human history and the nature of man. Slavery was viewed to have been decreed by God as a necessary instrument in the development of civilization. John C. Calhoun simply held that no difference existed between the natural law and the positive law—e.g., the Fugitive Slave law or the statutes of South Carolina—of particular states; he matter-of-factly identified man's natural state with whatever state the individual happened to find himself in at any moment of history; if the African was a bond-servant then that was his natural condition, in accordance with God's law.[201]

More recent history provides equally interesting examples. A couple of generations ago in Louisiana Huey Long justified what he did to the laws of the nation by arguing that he had only done what was necessary in order to deliver his package of social goods to the citizens of his state. Like Calhoun he viewed all law as positive law and saw it as subject to revision to suit the changing needs of society. Robert Penn Warren compares men like Long to Spenser's "iron groom," Talus, who is servant to the Knight of Justice, Artegall. The "iron groom" administered the punishments ordered by Artegall; he always did whatever was necessary to serve the end laid down by his master. Warren's Jeremiah Beaumont, in *World Enough and Time,* has a highly developed moral sense and so might be more like the abolitionists than like Long; but in his case as well the quest for an ideal, justice, involves callous disregard for the rights of others. He sees himself as a knight serving the "great Purpose"; all else is made subservient to his solitary end: to obtain his own pure goal he will use the dark and sullied ways of the world, to purchase truth he will use the currency of lies.[202] Something of what Bradford is accusing Lincoln of may be seen, then, in these quite different examples. To him Lincoln is like the member of the British intelligence staff named Meinertzhagen described by Colonel Lawrence: this man "was logical, an idealist of the deepest, and so possessed by his convictions that he was willing to harness evil to the chariot of good."[203] But is Bradford correct in his assessment of Lincoln on this score?

No one can question the fact that Lincoln did not govern according to the letter of the United States Constitution. There was a measure of truth in even the hostile criticisms of contemporaries like Supreme Court Chief Justice Roger B. Taney, who accused Lincoln of failing to execute faithfully the laws by his action of imprisoning persons without legal due process.[204] It is not true, however, that Lincoln ever allowed the pursuit of a transcendent goal to override all concern he might have had for legal propriety. We know, for example, that while he held up the principles of the Declaration of Independence as ideals to be striven for, he never joined with those radicals who called these natural rights a higher law that justified revolution.[205] And in the conduct of the Civil War itself he repeatedly urged that certain civilities and acts of discretion be observed and carried out by both sides.[206] He was also a constitutionalist in seeking congressional approval for acts of executive power taken to meet urgent needs, as in raising an army. Further, the war itself was waged for the sole purpose of preserving the Union, but clearly that goal did not nullify all other concerns because for Lincoln the Union itself was only a means to a greater end: the establishment of the liberties of the people. "So long, then, as it is possible that the prosperities and the liberties of the people can be preserved in the Union, it shall be my purpose at all times to preserve it." Lincoln said that he would rather give up his own life than surrender the principle of equality in order to save the Union. He told a group of well-wishers after the election of 1864 that if the rebellion forced the United States to dispense with the vote there would be no point in going on, the nation would therewith already have been "conquered and ruined."[207]

It is important to remember that all of Lincoln's extensions of the powers of the presidency were related to action taken in pursuance of wartime objectives and that even in this area he did not take some measures that might have seemed appropriate. He made no move to censor the Northern press, for example, even though Robert E. Lee and other Confederate generals derived much valuable information about Union troop movements from Yankee newspapers. He deferred to Congress on matters like patronage and almost never used the veto. He was not a strong legislative leader but simply let members of Congress originate and effect passage of the important legislation that came out of the Civil War period. Nor did he exert tight control over his Cabinet. In many ways he governed as a Whig, that is, as a participant in a political tradition that had customarily been opposed to strong executive leadership. Many of his actions had no later impact at all; no permanent increase in the power of the executive over the legislative or judicial branches resulted from this period, although, of course, a number of subsequent Chief Executives have pointed to the precedent of Lincoln while attempting to augment their own authority. Far from seeking to grasp as much power as he could, Lincoln actually had to rebuff congressional attempts to thrust more power upon him than he cared to use.[208] It should be emphasized that Lincoln was attempting to govern in circumstances that called for extraordinary but not irreversible actions.[14] Indeed it is possible that if he had not been President during a period of war his conduct as Chief Executive would have been fairly mild and subdued.[210]

The picture painted by Edmund Wilson and others of a Lincoln who put one or two ideals ahead of everything else does not seem to square with the facts of his tenure. Unlike young Jeremiah Beaumont, who loses his taste for the actual and finally fails wretchedly to work his way perfectly in a disappointingly real, recalcitrant world, Lincoln did not steer his course by celestial lights alone, heedless of the many quirks of his immediate environment. In fact he tended to reject ideological labels and doctrinaire solutions to problems, preferring to face reality as it came, to change with events and to compromise when necessary. He was able to keep in mind his limited, official duty and not give in to the temptation of indulging his personal preferences. When two of his generals issued emancipation orders, their Commander-in-Chief countermanded them even though he too wanted to see slavery expunged.[211] Lincoln thoroughly understood the problematical and often tragic nature of the decisionmaking process, knowing how one ideal never really stands out clearly as the logical end and choice above all others; he knew that political norms often come into conflict with one another and that a decision for this value for these people in a particular set of circumstances here was likely to cut out the rightful entitlements of another group over there. Generally speaking, Lincoln sought the ideal best but recognized that he invariably had to settle for the possible good; he did not wear blinders that prevented his making out the texture of everyday experience but was instead a conscientious practitioner of the virtue of prudence.[212]

Of course these remarks could suggest that Lincoln was a shrewd, practical-minded dictator. I think, though, that a look at Lincoln's actual decisions and the effects of his actions as President and a glance at his conception of the difficult matter of political choosing reveal that he was no monomaniac, divinely guided or otherwise, intent upon leading a crusade founded on his own private intuition of the good but rather a careful statesman sincerely and humbly seeking to do what was best for the country, to choose the most fitting course, and to abide by his oft-repeated promise to safeguard the rights of the people.

From the beginning of his presidency to the end Lincoln expressed his confidence in the ultimate justice of the people's decisions and spoke of his desire to obey their will above all else. The "masses," he said, "under any circumstances will not fail." Their choices were the ones he would follow even if that meant abandoning efforts to hold the Union together. He declared in his First Inaugural that he would perform his duty of executing the nation's laws "unless my rightful masters, the American people, shall withhold the requisite means, or, in some authoritative manner, direct the contrary." He said roughly the same thing over three years later when, shortly before the November elections when his own political future did not look bright, he told a group of citizens who had come to serenade him that, contrary to some recent speculation, he did not intend to "ruin the government" if he lost. He would not, he said, try to seize control of the ship of state in order to prevent the loss of the country but would instead work with his successor so that that person might have the best chance possible to save the Union. Why? Because carrying out the mandate of the people was a higher norm than even that of preventing the country's violent dissolution. "Their will, constitutionally expressed, is the ultimate law for all. If they should deliberately resolve to have immediate peace even at the loss of their country, and their liberty, I have not the power or the right to resist them."[213]

The questions that arise at this point are: Was the will of the people taken by Lincoln to be an absolute? Was the voice of the people understood to be the voice of God? Was their word—or the majority's—the first and last that he regarded, at least when the subject turned to politics? Was Lincoln's faith then idolatrous, making of the people a god?

Such conclusions might certainly be inferred from some of his statements but I think the answers are still no. As in the case of the ends/means issue examined above, it is hard to say, but in both instances one can discern as present in his thought a form of the "Protestant principle"; one finds an at least implicit protest against absolute claims being made by and for finite realities and a confession of faith in the transcendent One who alone is truly Lord above all. Lincoln had a great deal of confidence in the American people, and he often expressed his faith that God would support and influence them; but he did not attempt to say *vox populi, vox Dei*. He knew too well the tendency of humans to try to stifle the Spirit and to take God's word and twist its meaning into something better suited to their own self-centered designs. He was especially concerned in the 1850s to oppose Douglas's popular sovereignty notion, insisting that the people did not have a right to whatever they wanted and calling upon them to serve values above their own narrow interests.[215] He recognized that if some of the voices that rose in their midst went unchallenged, Americans could succeed in taking away the rights not only of black men but eventually of many whites as well. He had always been aware of the fact that the voice of the mob was not to be trusted, that it had to be opposed by reason and law, but it may have been while he was an Illinois legislator that he was first struck by the awareness of how wrong men could be even in their attempts at exercising the franchise in a responsible manner. He came to see how mistaken citizens were when they overwhelmingly backed costly internal improvement projects in 1836–37 and thereby helped to create a huge public debt. Later, as a member of Congress during the Mexican War, he opposed American involvement in that conflict and also the popular will of his own constituents.[216]

Further, while Lincoln was assuredly a man of the people, he did not lead the nation by trying to follow the flow of popular opinion. He was more inclined to search for God's will in the pages of Scripture than in the results of electoral canvasses. He was a radical monotheist, who expressed his faith by being loyal to all beings as creatures of the One who abides when temporal realities pass away. As H. Richard Niebuhr has written,

> the democratic process may be carried on within the context of monotheistic faith. Then no relative power, be it that of the nation or its people as well as that of tyrants, can claim absolute sovereignty or total loyalty. . . . Relying on the ultimate source of being and the ultimate power that conserves beings, men will accept the relativity of all their judgments and continue in their striving to make political decisions that express their universal faith.[217]

This it seems to me Lincoln made an effort to do. He fought with all his might for ideals while remaining ever mindful of his duty to the people, and he served the nation without forgetting the sovereignty of God.

Lincoln's humility and restraint appear also in his understanding of America's role in the world community. His commitment to democratic principles, to the ideals of self-government and majority rule, did not lead him to adopt an aggressive posture vis-à-vis other nations. For him America could best serve the world by being true to itself, by demonstrating the success of republican government. He was neither a territorial nor an ideological imperialist. He did not understand the American mission to be the imposition of Western democratic ideals on the rest of the world.[208] "I think it was John Quincy Adams," writes Hans Morgenthau, "who made the point forcefully that it was not for the United States to impose its own principles of government upon the rest of mankind, but, rather, to attract the rest of mankind through the example of the United States."[219] Of course this statement expresses Lincoln's point of view also. For him the United States was a nation with a calling, not a perfect society but a pilgrim people, which stood under God's judgment and which was always in need of reformation.

It is important to remember that Lincoln's political ethics were grounded in his faith. To state this is to say more than that he derived his fundamental political attitudes to such issues as slavery from the understandings of man and labor and corporate responsibility contained within the pages of the biblical canon. It is to affirm that his actions as a statesman and his thinking about his duties as a leader were consistently carried out within the vistas opened up by an overall theological outlook. It is to point out that Lincoln's ethics were theocentric, God-centered; it is to note that his political ethics are incapable of being grasped apart from his theology.

For Lincoln, God was the almighty ruler over nature and history, the governor of space and time who uses all things as his instruments and who surrenders his sovereignty to none. God is active within the historical process to judge and to redeem, to save and to bring forth life; there is no room in his cosmos for self-appointed avengers and messiahs. This theological understanding was part of Lincoln's outlook and is why he approached the actions of human beings in the war as he did. In a recent book on the sixteenth President, Dwight G. Anderson speaks of Lincoln's having interpreted the Civil War as the means by which the nation could atone for its past sins, achieve collective redemption, and go forward cleansed and regenerated, with the Northern side rewarded with victory as a divine favor for its virtue.[220] Of course Lincoln held no such views as these at all. What worked against his adopting an attitude of self-righteous self-justification was his belief that God, not man, works in all things for good, that God's values are greater than our own, and that his goodness is powerful in a way that ours repeatedly fails to be: God had worked within historical conditions to compel the elimination of a repulsive American institution that citizens' best social and political intentions had been unable to remove.

The charge that is levelled at Lincoln at this point is that his theological understanding of Providence, while it prevented his turning the war into an abolitionist's crusade for righteousness, reinforced a tendency on his part toward passivity in his approach to the matter of extending rights to black men. Thus writers like George M. Frederickson and Melvin Endy have said that Lincoln held conservative positions on social reform precisely because he was confident that God's will would prevail and slavery would disappear in the Lord's own good time and way.[221] It was true in the nineteenth century that certain theories concerning the divine control of the social and economic order led to a thoroughly conservative explanation of financial crises, poverty, and even disease. According to the pattern of ideas often referred to as "clerical laissez faire," the socio-economic order, which was perceived to be God-ordained, functioned to punish sinners with poverty and pestilence and to reward the pious with riches. This system of thought, liberals contended, encouraged individual piety while absolving Americans of their social responsibility.[222]

For Lincoln, though, the divine action in history was not so much perceived to provide backing for the status quo and to underscore human norms as it was seen to work in such a way as to transform temporal institutions according to divine values and purposes that transcended and possibly even contradicted finite ends and values. The answering human movement involved trust first and last but it also included making an attempt to conform one's own intentions with the divine purposes in history. This did not necessarily mean passivity in the face of injustice but could well demand aggressive, stalwart opposition to prevailing practices and forms of thought.

In Lincoln's theocentric ethics man is the creature who is responsible to God for his neighbor. The self and the community of which it is a part are properly oriented toward the action of God—not the Bible or religious experience or creed or church—and seek to serve those to whom God is faithful. Human endeavor in the political realm ought to express loyalty to the divine cause of universal community; it should be concerned to cooperate with and carry forward the work of the one Lord whose dominion extends over both the public and the private realms. Lincoln's conduct was a hopeful response to the redemptive power and intent in historical events. As such it was an attempt by him to deal in love and charity with his neighbor, both near and distant. He worked for freedom and equality and for an end to injustice and hatred. He labored to dilute the poison of vindictiveness and for a recognition of others as citizens of a common country and as brother creatures of one Father.

The most appropriate way to characterize Lincoln's ethics is to refer to them as an ethics of response—response to the divine action and to one's neighbor in the light of that action. This label is more suitable to

Lincoln's political ethics than either "teleological" (concerned with ends) or "deontological" (concerned with laws) is because it takes into account both attention to the details of the concrete situation and the need to see the event within the context of larger patterns. Ends and laws still come into play but there is room as well for reflection on the shadings and dynamics of the particular occasion.

In Lincoln's case response to the divine purposes in history never meant what it did for Presidents like William McKinley, who after several nights of prayer to God for "light and guidance" received the clear perception that "There was nothing left for us to do but to take them all and to educate the Filipinos and uplift and civilize and Christianize them. . . ."[223] McKinley's view is closest to an act-deontological understanding of moral conduct, in which the requirements for a given situation are commanded directly by God.

Lincoln knew well that actualizing the moral life in relation to the problem of constitutional governance was not so easy as receiving a specific divine order and translating it without remainder into practice. Nor did he feel that ethical leadership could be simply a matter of attempting to put into effect a set of formal principles. Lincoln was concerned rather to introduce concrete values within given situations according to the tenets of what might be termed a descriptive ethics that always began with the question, "What is the fitting response to what is going on?" He knew, in Kenneth Thompson's words, that "broad moral princiles seldom if ever can be said to furnish a direct, precise, and unambiguous guide to action" and also that principles can come into conflict with each other as competing action-guides. Moral choice would be simpler "if the leader could select one value as his guiding principle and look upon all the rest as secondary or instrumental." This procedure is impossible, however, because "in every human community . . . the choice between right and wrong is endlessly fraught with complexity and grounded in deep moral pathos. There is an inescapably tragic character to moral choice."[224] Politics requires, therefore, "compromise, the adjustment of divergent interests, and the reconciliation of rival moral claims."[225]

Lincoln sought through moral reasoning or prudence the reconciliation of what was morally desirable with what was politically possible.[226] His ethics of response, which might also be called a practical morality, was one that was capable of remaining close to the actual requirements of the people, the stringent demands of the ethical-religious life, and the political situation at hand.[227] But something else is clear as well. Lincoln's was also an ethical outlook that recognized the pervasiveness of sin and the limitations of the human condition; it was acquainted, to paraphrase Pascal, with both man's misery and his grandeur. As such it was an ethics imbued with Christian realism. This deep awareness of the extent of human selfishness worked against Lincoln's adopting an overly confident attitude toward the capacity of individuals to discern and put into practice the divine will. It limited, in other words, any inclination he might have had to transform the conflict into a holy war or crusade, and it caused him to be wary of all attempts by temporal beings to make absolute claims for themselves or for other finite realities.

This awareness of the depths of human selfishness also made Lincoln a realist in his thinking on the subject of American prospects in the post-bellum period. He had no illusions in this regard, knowing as he did how men were wont to use the freedom entrusted to them. The hallmark of Lincoln's ethical outlook was a salient characteristic of his religious stance as well; this feature of his ethics and his theology that was so significant in his career as a statesman was his humility—not intellectual diffidence, but a realistic acceptance of the boundaries of his own capacities, coupled with an abiding trust in God.

CHAPTER III
CONCLUSION

More than a century after his death, Lincoln remains a compelling figure. He does so in part because he was a man like other men, a representative of the common people who in extraordinary and tragic times rose to impressive heights of leadership and courage. He did not become a superman or demi-god; any foresight and clarity of vision he possessed was more like that which derived from simple prudence and realism than that which partook of the wisdom of Olympus. He was great *as* a man of the people, as one who knew how to employ words and deeds to interpret the nation's calling to his fellow countrymen and to enact its meaning for them and for the world.

What strikes us is that Lincoln achieved what he achieved, not by becoming divine, but by becoming more fully human. To the degree that we embellish the accounts of his life with depictions of him as one who finally attained to supernatural insights, to just that extent does he—this fabricated Lincoln overlaid with the encrustations of myth— tend to slip away from us as an exemplary character. The image of Lincoln as a prophet who arrived in the last year of his life at an understanding of the divine intentions in the war through a process that involved "mystical intuition" is interesting but unreal: not only in the sense that it fails to portray the Lincoln of history, but also because it is a view of him that does not fit into our understanding of the way things are or could be for us. He is transformed into a personage who is no longer like other men; he becomes quaint and irrelevant; he becomes one whom we can touch but not one who can reach out and arrest us. This problem arises, however, only when we make Lincoln say what he did not say, in fact what he carefully avoided saying. Too often in approaching Lincoln we have tried to insert words and meanings where there were none instead of taking into account the significance of the silences that occur in his writings alongside the famous utterances. His prose has frequently been called poetry, and in a way maybe it is; but if so then we should go on to admit that we have paid too little attention to the eloquent caesuras that appear within his lines of stately verse. When we confront this more modest figure we find that he is not so easily dismissed, that he challenges us still.

Lincoln told Mrs. Eliza Gurney that God permitted the Civil War to take place "for some wise purpose of his own, mysterious and unknown to us."[228] Like Calvin he believed that man was incapable of discovering God's intentions by analyzing the events of history. What God seeks to bring about in concrete circumstances is likely to be different from the ends human beings pursue; his values are different from our own. Any insights we may gain into the operations of Providence are taught by God through his biblical message. The God in whom Lincoln trusted was One whose purposes did not change, who was the same yesterday, today, and forever. He was not the Cosmic Trader depicted in some accounts of the episodes leading to the issue of the Emancipation Proclamation, One who ordained events and revealed his will in the context of bargains struck with human partners. Lincoln did not suppose he received divine guidance as the result of vows he made, dreams he had, spiritualistic mediums he consulted, or mystical intuitions. Calling himself an "instrument of the Almighty" was a humble acknowledgment on his part of onerous responsibility rather than a proclamation of prophetic status.

Not in his final year, not ever, did Lincoln's thinking on these matters undergo any significant transmutation. He told Thurlow Weed only a month before the assassination of the "difference of purpose" between God and men.[229] In the Second Inaugural, we find Lincoln pointing up the limitations of man's goodness and wisdom and opposing human efforts to associate victory with divine approbation of Northern motives. He spoke in that address of the righteousness of a divine judgment that would have entailed much more suffering for both sides were it ever handed down. He knew that it was not going to be imposed, however, and so implicitly suggested that the proper Union response was not vindictiveness or self-congratulation but repentance and gratitude. In addressing the suffering of others we discover him to have been chary of theorizing about the intentions of God therein, preferring instead to confront affliction in the practical terms of providing relief and comfort. When he did examine the topic directly he was likely to say something close to what he told little Fanny McCullough, namely that "sorrow comes to all" and to the innocent and the young does it come "with bitterest agony."[230] He had a Calvinistic reluctance to interpret human weal and woe in terms of a neatly proportional system of divine favors and punishments. We are reminded here of the transvaluation of values that the Reformed tradition speaks of as being involved when the revelation of God takes place: "He forces us to take our sorrows as a gift from him and to suspect our joys lest they be purchased by the anguish of his son incarnate again in every neighbor. He ministers indeed to all our good but all our good is other than we thought."[231] These words come close to expressing what apparently was Lincoln's attitude. The tone of the Second Inaugural is remarkably subdued. Lincoln wanted Americans to "suspect their joys" and all their emotions and actions in the time of celebration lest they bring further anguish to those who never ceased to be brothers and who now had to be restored to the status of fellow citizens.

Throughout the Civil War, too, he trusted that God was working in the strife to bring about "some great good."[232] He knew, though, that the nature of this benefaction could not be designated with any precision. What turns out to be good for us is bound to be "other than we thought." In a sermon published in 1962 in which he spoke of the trial of the Cold War, H. Richard Niebuhr, answering his own question concerning what lay in the future, said, "Since it is in God's hands, who can say." But like Lincoln he could at least affirm that "We sense that great things may be in the making but also that we cannot make them, that we are all only instruments in the hands of the inscrutable power . . . , which has greater things in mind than we can have with our intentions toward our limited goods and evils. . . ."[233] Unquestionably Lincoln hoped that God's purposes in the war were in line with his own desires to root the principle of freedom more firmly in the soil of human political endeavor; but he was deeply aware of the boundaries of his own capacities, both to know and to do: "Surely He intends some great good to follow this mighty convulsion, which no mortal could make and no mortal could stay."[234]

To say that Lincoln was skeptical, though, is not to say that he was a skeptic and a non-believer. The duty to shun idols follows from the confession of the sovereignty of one Lord. To Lincoln, God was in all history effecting his holy purposes, the Determiner of the destiny of every existent, whose power was used for good and whose goodness was powerful. The divine kingship was seen to be present in all that happened, in the rain that fell on the just and the unjust, on child and adult; in the sun that shone on evil and good, freeman and bond-servant and slaver; in the maelstrom of war that caught up zealous politicians and unwilling heroes. To what extent was this outlook a fatalistic one? For Jesus, Niebuhr tells us, "every alteraction" was seen to be "included in, or . . . taken up by, the action of God." But this view "was neither fatalistic nor mechanical" because he did not suppose "that all acts of finite agents had been predesigned, as though God were the author of a play in which each actor played a predestined role." The action of the One whom Jesus called Father "is more like that of the great wise leader who uses even the meannesses of his subjects to promote the public welfare."[235] For Lincoln also, God's activity was not limited to supernatural occurrences but was, rather, present in all events, natural and historical.

In some of his statements Lincoln appears to have affirmed belief in a Power that determines what will happen to men and women by foreordained by Providence to bring together his friend Speed and last detail. Thus he wrote of himself in an early letter as an instrument fore-ordained by Providence to bring together his friend Speed and Speed's wife-to-be. In fact he even went so far as to say that he "was drawn" to the relief of his friend's difficulty "as by fate; if I would I could not have done less than I did."[236] Similarly, in the Second Inaugural, he spoke of the institution of slavery as something established by God's decree that did not fall until its divinely "appointed time" had come to a close.[237]

However we may attempt to explain away these remarks by drawing attention to the contexts in which they were uttered, we still must recognize the presence of a fatalistic note that was occasionally sounded in Lincoln's writings. At the same time, however, when the context is taken into account and when these statements are viewed in relation to the rest of his utterances it is easier to see that the God to whom he prayed resembled neither *tyche* nor *moira,* nor any kind of latter-day puppet-master, but was instead more like the Almighty Father whom Niebuhr says Jesus addressed. His God was not an absolute despot who issues arbitrary decrees but a Ruler who has bound himself to his creatures by promises and who calls them to responsible action in behalf of his kingdom.[238] Lincoln clearly did not hold that human beings were merely playing out the parts written for them in a divinely-authored script. When he spoke of God's ordination of events what he apparently wished to affirm was his confidence in God's love and strength, and the hopeless nature of man's condition apart from God. This Lord, he wanted to say, was the One to whom praise should be given, the One to whom we are indebted for every good thing. He it is who reconciles strangers, who removes shackles, and who breaks the bow and causes wars to cease.

Lincoln's was a *beliefful* understanding of the Civil War. He did not merely react to the events of secession by seeking to quash the rebellion but sought also to respond to the actions and intentions of God in the conflict. He did this because he believed God to be active in nature and history, in war as well as in peace; consequently he responded to all actions upon him as actions in which God was acting. In doing so he adopted a point of view like that of the prophets, the apostles, and Jesus himself, for whom all events were expressive of the rule of God.[239]

Lincoln was careful, like them, not to confuse divine and human motives: God works to save at the same time that finite powers conspire to do evil. This was one of the important points made by P. D. Gurley in his sermon, "Man's Projects and God's Results," in which he noted that God's aim in the crucifixion of Christ was different from the intentions of those who put Jesus to death. (Gurley probably derived this theme directly from John Calvin.) Lincoln's interpretation of the Civil War was in this respect similar to Isaiah's response to the Assyrian invasion of Israel. Isaiah held that this event was to be understood not only in military and political terms but also as an act of God; indeed God was seen to be accomplishing his will in and through the evil intentions of Assyria. The correct response to the invasion took into account the nature of this divine action. Israel was to be defended against the destructive designs of Assyria at the same time that it worked by means of internal reformation to make a fitting response to the divine intention as manifested in the experience of chastisement.[240] Throughout the period of the Civil War Lincoln asked what the purposes of the Lord were in the conflict, believing that the North and the South were instruments of God's sovereign will in the same way that Pilate and Assyria had been. The military and political courses that he followed were themselves pursued within a context of action that included attempts on his part to respond in a faithful way to what he believed were the divine intentions in the war.

To Lincoln the Civil War was a "fiery trial." He used these words in a number of different ways, but in one he meant to convey the idea that it was a test of the nation's values, its commitments, its fundamental attitudes. He responded to the divine action in the war first of all by witnessing to *God,* by indicating that Americans should give up their prideful self-understanding and confess their manifold sins. He confronted the experience of war in an attitude of repentance, acknowledging the presence of the hand of man in all that had led to this time of sorrow and the justice of that governing action of God which dealt with the self-assertion of political communities that had transgressed their proper limits and failed to do what they ought to have done. In the face of suffering he confessed the country's trespasses and stated that the judgment was not undeserved, not unfair. As he told Albert Hodges in 1864, "If God . . . now . . . wills that we of the North as well as you of the South, shall pay fairly for our complicity in that wrong [slavery], impartial history will find therein new cause to attest and revere the justice and goodness of God."[241] Lincoln knew that human deeds and misdeeds had led to war, that armed conflict was the result of other forms of hostility that had prevailed and increased over many years: moral indifference, political repression, economic exploitation, inter-sectional hatred—and accepted the war as that condition which must result when such acts occur. In the midst of war he acknowledged the justice of that divine rule which allows human beings to fall into bloody conflict if their sins of omission and commission lead them to that point. There is a form of "retributive" justice that does appear in the order of creation. "There is an order or a rule of divine action which the desires of man cannot change. No matter how much they may wish to escape the suffering and destruction of war, they cannot do the things which lead to war and then evade the consequence."[242] Part of Lincoln's response to the action of God in the war was that he accepted this order in a spirit of self-denial, using the occasion to remember the unrighteousness that had led inevitably to bloodshed.

For Lincoln the Civil War was a trial of conduct as well as of attitudes, a test of whether Americans would dedicate, or re-dedicate, themselves to the mission of increasing justice among men. Mainly from his study of Scripture Lincoln knew that the oppression of human beings could not be in accord with the will of God. Indeed he supposed that one of God's purposes in the war might be to effect the obliteration of slavery.[243] What he hoped was that Americans would conform themselves in their actions to these divine intentions in history. At Gettysburg he said that it was the task of "the living . . . to be dedicated here to the unfinished work which they who fought here have thus far so nobly advanced"; the cause to be striven for was "that this nation, under God, shall have a new birth of freedom—and that government of the people, by the people, for the people, shall not perish from the earth."[244]

Lincoln knew that God was accomplishing his will in history in a process that entailed the suffering of innocents for the wrongs of others, many of whom were long dead. He understood that in this life sorrow comes to all and that the relatively innocent commonly have to bear the sins of the wicked. He did not think of the universe as a moral order in which goodness is automatically rewarded and evil punished but as a world that requires of its best men and women patient endurance, cross-bearing, vicarious sacrifice, "Christian heroism." The Civil War to him was a fiery trial in which those who served were like martyrs, offering their wills and their lives to a cause greater than themselves or their own narrow interests. He did not interpret the suffering of those whose lot it was to carry "the harder part" of the burden as an indication of God's wrath and desire to punish but instead responded to the strife by pointing to the graciousness of all of God's acts on behalf of America. He held that the "mighty convulsion" of war was used by God to bring about some larger benefaction for human beings, one that was ultimately not dependent upon their own efforts.

For Christians, at least for Calvin, Gurley, the author of 1 Peter, and possibly for Lincoln too, the clue for interpreting the meaning of our experience in the world is the life, death, and resurrection of Jesus Christ. So Calvin speaks of the Christian life in terms of self-denial and cross-bearing, so Gurley associates the bleeding of Christ with the rent fabric of national life and preaches hope in the midst of chaos, so the author of 1 Peter recalls the passion of Jesus when he writes of the fiery trial of persecution endured by Christian martyrs, so St. Paul and John Bunyan and many others understood that God's action in the world always takes on a Christic shape. H. Richard Neibuhr has written in *The Meaning of Revelation* of the "life and death of Christ as a parable and an analogy" Christians use to interpret their situation. "We see through the use of the great parable how bodies are now being broken for our sake and how for the remission of our sins the blood of innocents is being shed." The cross enables us to discern a pattern in the chaos: "by great travail of men and God, a work of redemption goes on which is like the work of Christ." It is "the story of Jesus, and particularly of his passion, . . . that enables us to say, 'What we are now doing and suffering is like this.' "[245]

This story of the passion was used by Niebuhr to interpret the meaning of the divine action in World War II. His approach parallels Lincoln's understanding at several significant points. He rejects attempts to see the war as an effort on God's part to execute vengeance, "as an event in a universe in which the laws of retribution hold sway." He recognizes with Lincoln "the fact that in war the burden of suffering does not fall on the guilty, even when guilt is relatively determinable, but on the innocent." Those who suffer for the sins of Hitler and the Nazi Party are "Russian and German soliders, . . . the children of Cologne and Coventry, . . . the Finns and the French." "Wars are crucifixions"; in them it is not the leaders of nations who suffer most "but the humble, little people" who have not had much "to do with the framing of great policies." The "pacifists in jail have little reason to think of themselves as the martyrs of war when they reflect on all the children, wives and mothers, humble obedient soliders, peasants on the land, who in the tragedy of war are made an offering for sin." War involves "vicarious suffering," "moving" sacrifices.[246]

As Lincoln knew, these sacrifices were not usually made by men and women enthusiastically embracing a righteous cause but were more typically offered by conscripts who would just as soon have been somewhere else, by mothers and children who could see no reason for the war at all. As Niebuhr points out, if "suffering in order to be vicarious must be consciously so . . . we shall need to come to [this] conclusion: there is little actual vicarious suffering." But he says that if we want to reconcile the fact that simple peasants "who want only to be left in peace do suffer and are killed for no apparent fault of their own" with "our faith that the world is not an accident and a whirl of atoms, but a meaningful process, then we are required to use the idea of vicariousness in order to understand the peasant's crucifixion." In order to make sense of their suffering in terms of our faith, "we need to say, because we see it to be true, that whether they do so willingly or unwillingly, the innocent suffer for our sins. . . ." We should respond to tragedy "as those who turn away with loathing from their own sin and who try to strike off the shackles they have laid on the victims before and while they deal with the chains that other evil men placed on the sufferers."[247] Lincoln responded to the war in just this fashion, attempting in an attitude of repentance to correct internal injustices at the same time that he sought to reassert federal control over the South.

His faith expressed itself in loyalty (*fidelitas*) to God's cause of universal community. "When I respond to the One creative power," Niebuhr writes, "I place my companions, human and subhuman and superhuman, in the one universal society which has its center neither in me nor in any finite cause but in the Transcendent One."[248] Not only in the period of the Civil War but throughout his adult life we see Lincoln emphsizing the bonds that link human beings together; we find him working, in Calvin's terms, for the common good and practicing self-denial, trusting that in so doing his actions conduced to the great aims of God in history. His experience of the sovereignty of God did not lead to complacency but gave him a powerful sense of moral responsibility; to him the indicative, "You are free," always carried with it an imperative, "Therefore, use your freedom properly as a faithful steward of God's kingdom to build up human fellowship, to increase the rights and to remove the unjust burdens of others." His concern in the 1850s was that beginning to prevail in the land was a growing indifference to the moral evil of slavery: freedom was grasped without its concomitant of responsibility, as merely the power to do whatever

176

one wished to do. For Lincoln, Americans were "brothers of a common country."[249] The Civil War and Reconstruction presented to them a challenge and an opportunity; within these events promises were being offered not only for America but for the whole world. What was necessary to effect their realization was putting an end to divisiveness and self-absorption and the acceptance of concern for the good for each and the good of all.

Lincoln's affirmation of God's sovereignty also carried with it a deep understanding of the proper limits of finite powers. The President in his conduct of the war manifested striking capacities for prudence and restraint. He did not allow his private vision of the right to overwhelm the sense he had of his duty to preserve the Union and safeguard the liberties of the people. He was a realist who doubted faithfully that men were capable of creating a heaven on earth.[250] He recognized the terrible problems that would appear as soon as the war was over. Lincoln as President brought no new word concerning the intentions of God in history but relied, rather, on an old way of seeing that required trying to live according to the impossible demands of the Summary of the Law. He did not fight the Civil War as a holy cause for righteousness; he did not treat Southerners as evil men. His word was "Judge not."[251] Throughout the war he worked for the spiritual as well as the political reunion of the country, treating citizens of the Confederacy without malice or vindictiveness. He limited his own conduct toward the South to that single governing movement that would bring about its restoration to the Union. He met the action of Southerners with hope for their recovery, not anger for their misdeeds.

Abraham Lincoln, who stated that his policy consisted in the absence of policy, would be horrified or, more probably, amused at any attempt on our part today to transform the welter of his sayings, beliefs, directives into a coherent system of dogmas and moral action-guides valid for all people everywhere and always. Lincoln's was an ethics of responsibility that applied rules and recalled ideals as they were appropriate within the particular situation in which he found himself. He knew that each set of circumstances had its own unique texture of interwoven promises and problems. He was a realist who sought, not the establishment of righteousness through force of arms, but the achievement of only those goals which limited power could attain. It would be a mistake to try to convert his beliefs and practices into an ideology and a static framework of norms binding upon us in our responses to the actions of God within the strife-ridden history of our own time. But there are some things the Christian faith might want to go on to say and it can properly have Lincoln in mind, serving as a kind of witness, when it does so. These are not all things that Lincoln would have said and yet they are not lacking in harmony with what he said either.

For Christians the cross reveals that the righteousness of God is not the righteousness of the law; it demonstrates the righteousness of man to be itself unrighteous. It shows that the order of the universe is not one of retributive justice but rather one of divine graciousness in which life-giving rain descends on just and unjust, Lord and malefactor alike. If man tries to live in this world on the assumption that sorrows are always merited and joys are divine rewards, he will come into conflict with the real nature of things. His task is not to judge others, it is not to assess relative guilt and innocence, but rather to respond with gratitude to God's grace.

> The cross does not so much reveal that God judges by other standards than men do, but that he does not judge; it does not demonstrate that men judge by the wrong standards but that their wrongness lies in trying to judge each other, instead of beginning where they can begin—with the acceptance of graciousness and response to it.[25]

Lincoln always began this way: he responded to the fiery trial of war not by standing in judgment over others—not the South, not even the whole nation—but by calling for repentance, for a revolution in thinking and willing and doing, and by asking for increased justice and charity for all, that is, for active concern without regard to the worth of the recipient or the nature of his past offense. In his work and in ours there was and can be an effort to forget about self and to concentrate on the practical needs of the neighbor.

In the recognition of wars as crucifixions or as fiery trials in which vicarious suffering is the order of the day we can see that there ought not to be any effort to make a case for the fact of one's own righteousness because one may be somewhat less of a sinner than others. In his Second Inaugural, after confessing his trust in God's righteousness, Lincoln turned his back on the whole domain of fixing blame and indicating virtue and pointed to the demands of the present, to Americans' concrete responsibilities toward all existents, especially the weak and the long-estranged. In his conduct of the war he never gave up the enemy as lost but looked always for his complete restoration in community, and he made conditions for them as lenient as possible; there was never any desire for vengeance on his part. Christians today will act in war and in periods of hostility that resemble war as Lincoln did if they trust in God and rely on his grace rather than on any merit of their own, if they limit their war efforts to the single restraining action necessary to effect a just peace and forget about crusades for righteousness, if they respond to the presence of grace in the midst of their ungraciousness by serving the divine cause of universal community, and if they hope for Providence to bring some good even out of the tragic convulsion of conflict.

APPENDIX A

Four Key Statements by Lincoln
Letters to Mrs. Gurney, Gettysburg Address
and Second Inaugural Address

Reply to Eliza P. Gurney[1]

October 26, 1862

I am glad of this interview, and glad to know that I have your sympathy and prayers. We are indeed going through a great trial—a fiery trial. In the very responsible position in which I happen to be placed, being a humble instrument in the hands of our Heavenly Father, as I am, and as we all are, to work out his great purposes, I have desired that all my works and acts may be according to his will, and that it might be so, I have sought his aid—but if after endeavoring to do my best in the light which he affords me, I find my efforts fail, I must believe that for some purpose unknown to me, He wills it otherwise. If I had my way, this war would never have been commenced; If I had been allowed my way this war would have been ended before this, but we find it still continues; and we must believe that He permits it for some wise purpose of his own, mysterious and unknown to us; and though with our limited understandings we may not be able to comprehend it, yet we cannot but believe, that he who made the world still governs it.

[1] Copy, DLC-RTL. The copy of the interview preserved in the Lincoln Papers, Vol. 5 is an unknown handwriting and bears the date 1862, "Sept (28?)" having been inserted in a different handwriting. Under this date Lincoln's reply is printed in the *Complete Works* (VIII, 50–51). The New York *Tribune,* October 28, 1862, however, gives an account of the interview as occurring on October 27, but Lincoln's letter to Mrs. Gurney, September 4, 1864, *infra,* specifies Sunday, September 26. Mrs. Gurney was the widow and third wife of Joseph J. Gurney, English Quaker, philanthropist and religious writer. Her address to the president as reproduced in the copy of the interview in the Lincoln Papers

is in effect a sermon, at the conclusion of which Mrs. Gurney knelt "and uttered a short but most beautiful, eloquent, and comprehensive prayer that light and wisdom might be shed down from on high, to guide our President . . . After a brief pause the President replied." No newspaper which gives a verbatim report similar to the copy in the Lincoln Papers has been found.

Gettysburg Address

GEORGE BANCROFT COPY[31]

Four score and seven years ago our father brought forth, on[32] this continent, a new nation, conceived in Liberty, and dedicated to the proposition that all men are created equal.

Now we are engaged in a great civil war, testing whether that nation, or any nation so conceived, and so dedicated, can long endure. We are met on a great battle-field of that war. We have come to dedicate a portion of that field, as a final resting-place for those who here gave their lives, that that nation might live. It is altogether fitting and proper that we should do this.

But, in a larger sense, we can not dedicate—we can not consecrate—we can not hallow—this ground. The brave men, living and dead, who struggled here, have consecrated it far above our poor power to add or detract. The world will little note, nor long remember what we say here, but it can never forget what they did here. It is for us the living, rather, to be dedicated here to the unfinished work which they who fought here have thus far so nobly advanced. It is rather for us to be here dedicated to the great task remaining before us—that from these honored dead we take increased devotion to that cause for which they here gave the last full measure of devotion—that we here highly resolve that these dead shall not have died in vain—that this nation, under God, shall have a new birth of freedom—and that government of the people, by the people, for the people, shall not perish from the earth.

FINAL TEXT[33]

Address delivered at the dedication of the Cemetery at Gettysburg.

[31] AD, NIC. This copy was prepared upon request of George Bancroft for reproduction in facsimile in *Autograph Leaves of Our Country's Authors* (1864), a volume to be sold by the Baltimore Sanitary Fair. For particulars see Lincoln's letter to Bancroft, February 29, 1864, *infra*. This text is notable chiefly for Lincoln's change of "upon this continent" to "on this continent." Written on both sides of a single sheet of paper, the manuscript was not suitable for reproduction, and hence Lincoln prepared the final copy, *infra*.

[32] "On" replaced "upon" of the earlier versions.

[33] ADS, owned by Oscar Cintas, Havana, Cuba. Generally known as the "Bliss Copy"

from its long possession by the family of Alexander Bliss, a member of the committee which obtained the volume of original autographs to provide facsimiles for *Autograph Leaves of Our Country's Authors,* this was Lincoln's final text. Only one change in wording, as noted, was made in this copy from the Bancroft copy. The exact date that Lincoln prepared this final manuscript is not known, but was sometime later than March 4, 1864, when John P. Kennedy wrote on behalf of the Baltimore Sanitary Fair to explain that the Bancroft copy would not do because it could not be fitted to the pages of the proposed volume.

Four score and seven years ago our fathers brought forth on this continent, a new nation, conceived in Liberty, and dedicated to the proposition that all men are created equal.

Now we are engaged in a great civil war, testing whether that nation, or any nation so conceived and so dedicated, can long endure. We are met on a great battle-field of that war. We have come to dedicate a portion of that field, as a final resting place for those who here gave their lives that that nation might live. It is altogether fitting and proper that we should do this.

But, in a larger sense, we can not dedicate—we can not consecrate—we can not hallow—this ground. The brave men, living and dead, who struggled here, have consecrated it, far above our poor power to add or detract. The world will little note, nor long remember what we say here, but it can never forget what they did here. *It is for us the living, rather, to be dedicated here to the unfinished work which they who fought here have thus far so nobly advanced. It is rather for us to be here dedicated to the great task remaining before us—that from these honored dead we take increased devotion to that cause for which they*[34] *gave the last full measure of devotion—that we here highly resolve that these dead shall not have died in vain—that this nation, under God, shall have a new birth of freedom*—and that government of the people, by the people, for the people, shall not perish from the earth.

November 19, 1863.   ABRAHAM LINCOLN.

[34]"Here" is omitted from the phrase "they here gave," which appears in preceding versions.

To Eliza P. Gurney[1]

Eliza P. Gurney.

                                                Executive Mansion,
My esteemed friend.   Washington, September 4. 1864.

I have not forgotten—probably never shall forget—the very impressive occasion when yourself and friends visited me on a Sabbath forenoon two years ago. Nor has your kind letter, written nearly a year later, ever been forgotten. In all, it has been your purpose to strengthen my reliance on God. I am much indebted to the good christian people of the country for their constant prayers and consolations; and to no one of them, more than to yourself. The purposes of the Almighty are prefect, and must prevail, though we erring mortals may fail to accurately perceive them in advance. We hoped for a happy termination of this terrible war long before this; but God knows best, and has ruled otherwise. We shall yet acknowledge His wisdom and our own error therein. Meanwhile we must work earnestly in the best light He gives us, trusting that so working still conduces to the great ends He ordains. Surely He intends some great good to follow this mighty convulsion, which no mortal could make, and no mortal could stay.

Your people—the Friends—have had, and are having, a very great trial. On principle, and faith, opposed to both war and oppression, they can only practically oppose oppression by war. In this hard dilemma, some have chosen one horn and some the other. For those appealing to me on conscientious grounds, I have done, and shall do, the best I could and can, in my own conscience, under my oath to the law. That you believe this I doubt not; and believing it, I shall still receive, for our country and myself, your earnest prayers to our Father in Heaven. Your sincere friend

A. LINCOLN.

¹ALS, PHi; ADfS, DLC-RTL. See Lincoln's reply to Mrs. Gurney, October 26, 1862, *supra*. On August 8, 1863, Mrs. Gurney wrote Lincoln from Earlham

Second Inaugural Address¹

[Fellow Countrymen:]   March 4, 1865

At this second appearing to take the oath of the presidential office, there is less occasion for an extended address than there was at the first. Then a statement, somewhat in detail, of a course to be pursued, seemed fitting and proper. Now, at the expiration of four years, during which public declarations have been constantly called forth on every point and phase of the great contest which still absorbs the attention, and engrosses the enerergies [*sic*] of the nation, little that is new could be presented. The progress of our arms, upon which all else chiefly depends, is as well known to the public as to myself; and it is, I trust, reasonably satisfactory and encouraging to all. With high hope for the future, no prediction in regard to it is ventured.

On the occasion corresponding to this four years ago, all thoughts were anxiously directed to an impending civil-war. All dreaded it—all sought to avert it. While the inaugeral address was being delivered from this place, devoted altogether to *saving* the Union without war, insurgent agents were in the city seeking to *destroy* it without war—seeking to dissol[v]e the Union, and divide effects, by negotiation. Both parties deprecated war; but one of them would *make* war rather than let the nation survive; and the other would *accept* war rather than let it perish. And the war came.

One eighth of the whole population were colored slaves, not distributed generally over the Union, but localized in the Southern part[2] of it. These slaves constituted a peculiar and powerful interest. All knew that this interest was, somehow, the cause of the war. To strengthen, perpetuate, and extend this interest was the object for which the insurgents would rend the Union, even by war; while the government claimed no right to do more than to restrict the territorial enlargement of it. Neither party expected for the war, the magnitude, or the duration, which it has already attained. Neither anticipated that the *cause* of the conflict might cease with, or even before, the conflict itself should cease. Each looked for an easier triumph, and a result less fundamental and astounding. Both read the same Bible, and pray to the same God; and each invokes His aid against the other. It may seem strange that any men should dare to ask a just God's assistance in wringing their bread from the sweat of other men's faces; but let us judge not that we be not judged. The prayers of both could not be answered; that of neither has been answered fully. The Almighty has His own purposes. "Woe unto the world because of offences! for it must needs be that offences come; but woe to that man by whom the offence cometh!" If we shall suppose that American Slavery is one of those offences, which, in the providence of God, must needs come, but which, having continued through His appointed time, He now wills to remove, and that He gives to both North and South, this terrible war, as the woe due to those by whom the offence came, shall we discern therein any departure from those divine attributes which the believers in a Living God always ascribe to Him? Fondly do we hope—fervently do we pray—that this mighty scourge of war may speedily pass away. Yet, if God wills that it continue, until all the wealth piled by the bondman's two hundred and fifty years of unrequited toil shall be sunk, and until every drop of blood drawn with the lash, shall be paid by another drawn with the sword, as was said three[3] thousand years ago, so still it must be said "the judgments of the Lord, are true and righteous altogether"

With malice toward none; with charity for all; with firmness in the right, as God gives us to see the right, let us strive on to finish the work we are in; to bind up the nation's wounds; to care for him who shall have borne the battle, and for his widow, and his orphan—to do all which may achieve and cherish a just, and a lasting peace, among ourselves, and with all nations.[4]

[Endorsement]

Original manuscript of second Inaugeral presented to Major John Hay.   A. LINCOLN
   April 10. 1865

[1] AD, DLC. The salutation is not in Lincoln's handwriting. An autograph copy of the final paragraph, written by Lincoln at the request of Mrs. John P. Usher, is now owned by Arthur Wendell, Rahway, New Jersey.
[2] Lincoln deleted "half" and inserted "part."
[3] Lincoln first wrote "four," erased it and substituted "three."
[4] Lincoln deleted "the world" and inserted "all nations."

NOTES

PART ONE

Chapter II.

1. Roy P. Bassler, Editor, *The Collected Works of Abraham Lincoln* (New Brunswick, New Jersey: Rutgers University Press, 1953), Vol. I, 78.
2. Vol. I, 320.
3. *Ibid.*
4. Vol. I, 382.
5. Vol. II, 10.
6. Vol. II, 96.
7. Vol. II, 96.
8. Letter to Albert G. Hodges, editor of the Frankfort, Kentucky *Commonwealth* Vol. VII, 282.
9. Vol. V, 26.
10. Vol. V, 26.
11. Vol. V, 419, 420.
12. Vol. V, 403, 404.
13. Vol. VIII, 333.
14. Vol. III, 204, 205.
15. Vol. VIII, 155. This account has an interesting history which illustrates Lincoln's character as well as the importance he attributes to the account. Noah Brooks, a newspaperman, records the circumstances under which it was written: ". . . Upon another occasion, hearing that I was in the parlor, he sent for me to come up into the library, where I found him writing on a piece of common stiff boxboard with a pencil. Said he, after he had finished, 'Here is one speech of mine which has never been printed, and I think it worth printing. Just see what you think.' He then read the following which is copied *verbatim* from the familiar handwriting before me: (text as above)
"To this the President signed his name at my request, by way of joke, and added for a caption, 'The President's Last, Shortest, and Best Speech,' under which title it was duly published in one of the Washington newspapers. . . ." ("Personal Recollections of Abraham Lincoln," *Harper's New Monthly Magazine,* July, 1865, p. 230).
16. Vol. VI, 244, 245.
17. Vol. VIII, 333.
18. Ibid.

19. Vol. VI. 535, 536. (A second version of this speech is different only in phraseology.)
20. Vol. V, 478.
21. Vol. VII, 535.
22. Vol. V, 404.
23. Vol. VII, 282.
24. Vol. VIII, 367 (See also page 17).
25. J. G. Randall, *Lincoln the President,* (New York: Dodd, Mead & Co., 1945), Vol. II, 314.
26. Benjamin P. Thomas, *Abraham Lincoln,* (New York: Alfred A. Knopf, 1954), 426.

Chapter III

27. Vol. I, 229, 230.
28. Vol. VIII, 191, 192.
29. Vol. VI, 392.
30. Vol. VI, 559.
31. As a footnote to this episode which caused such ridicule, I want to call attention to the touching letter Lincoln wrote to a magazine editor on May 2, 1860: "It is wonderful that you should have seen and known a sister of Robert Burns. You must tell me something about her when we meet again." (Vol. IV, 48).
32. Vol. I, 391.
33. Vol. IV, 45.
34. Vol. IV, 247.
35. Vol. V, 297.
36. Vol. VII, 301, 302.
37. Quoted from Richard Hofstadter, *The American Political Tradition,* 129.
38. Vol. VII, 213.
39. *Thomas, loc, cit.,* 492.
40. Vol. VI, 502–4.
41. Vol. I, 446–7.
42. Vol. I, 457.
43. Vol. I, 473.
44. Vol. I, 473.
45. Vol. VI, 554–5.
46. Vol. VI, 139.
47. Vol. V, 358–9.
48. Vol. V, 509–10.
49. Vol. IV, 261.
50. Vol. III, 511.
51. Vol. III, 511.
52. Vol. IV, 127.
53. Vol. VIII, 98.
54. *Ibid.*
55. Vol. V, 108.
56. Vol. IV, 209.
57. *loc. cit.,* 218.
58. See *loc. cit.* 219,, 223, 224, 227, 228, 233, 238, 242,

59. *loc. cit.,* 228.
60. *loc. cit.,* 243; see also 81, 232–3, 238.
61. *loc. cit.,* 246.
62. Vol. III, 253, 254.
63. *loc. cit.,* 509.
64. Vol. IV, 40.
65. *loc. cit.,* 441.
66. Vol. VII, 384.
67. Vol. VII, 197–8. (For the identical argument see Vol. VIII, 394).
68. Vol. III, 377.
69. *loc. cit.,* 395.
70. Vol. IV, 36.
71. Vol. IV, 51.
72. loc. cit., 194.
73. loc. cit., 197.
74. loc. cit., 207.
75. Vol. V, 306.
76. Vol. VI, 282.
77. *loc. cit.,* 281.
78. *loc. cit.,* 518.
79. *Thomas, loc. cit.,* 289.
80. Vol. VIII, 223.
81. Vol. V, 208.
82. Vol. VI, 466.
82. Vol. VII, 324.
84. Vol. IV, 211.
85. loc. cit., 212.
86. Vol. VII, 132.
87. *Ibid.*
88. Vol. I, 8.
89. Vol. III, 473.
90. Vol. IV, 350.
91. Vol. IV, 326.
92. Vol. VII, 89–90.
93. *loc. cit.,* 488.
94. *loc. cit.,* 93.
95. Vol. VIII, 255–6.
96. Vol. I, 9.
97. Vol. II, 46.
98. Vol. III, 339.
99. Richard Hofstadter, *The American Political Tradition,* 130.
100. Vol. VI, 450.
101. Thomas, loc. cit., 403.
102. Vol. VII, 483.
103. Vol. VI, 129.
104. Vol. I, 484.
105. Vol. V, 347.
106. Vol. V, 474.
107. See above page 19–20.
108. Vol. IV, 35.

109. Vol. I, 423.
110. See above page 19.
111. Vol. IV, 242.
112. Vol. I, 31.
113. Thomas, *loc. cit.,* 423.
114. Id., 465.
115. Vol. VII, 487.
116. Vol. VII, 208.
117. Thomas, *loc. cit.,* 463.
118. Vol. VI, 335.
119. Thomas, *loc. cit.,* 517.
120. Vol. VI, 167–8.
121. Vol. VIII, 189.
122. Vol. VIII, 224.
123. Vol. VII, 111.
124. vol. VIII, 116.
125. Vol. VI, 140.
126. Vol VI, 67.
127. Vol. VII, 217.
128. Vol. VIII, 373.
129. Vol. V.
130. Vol. VI, 538.
131. Vol. VIII, 116–7.
132. Vol. VI, 16–7.
133. Vol. V, 288.
134. Vol. VI, 33.
135. Vol. V, 493.
136. Vol. V, 537–8.
137. Vol. V, 551.
138. Vol. VI, 60.
139. Vol. VI, 55.
140. Vol. Vi, 542.
141. Vol. VIII, 228–9.
142. Vol. VI, 33–4.
143. Vol. IV, 372.
144. Vol. VI, 501.
145. Vol. IV 428–9.
146. Id, 429–31.
147. Vol. VII, 169.
148. Vol. VI, 557.
149. Vol. VI, 492.
150. Id.
151. Vol. VII, 254–7.
152. Thompson, *loc. cit.,* 452.
153. *Ibid.*
154. Vol. VII, 338.
155. Vol. V, 47.
156. Vol. V, 128.
157. Vol. VI, 414.
158. Vol. VI, 505.

159. Vol. VI, 522.
160. Vol. III, 474.
161. *Loc. cit.,* 475.
162. Vol. VI, 438.
163. Vol. VII, 462.
164. Vol. VI, 237.
165. Id, 266–7.
166. Id, 302–3.
167. Vol. II, 15.
168. id., p. 15–6.
169. Id., p. 111.
170. Id., p. 112.
171. Id., p. 96–7.
172. See above page 7.

Chapter IV.

173. Vol. I, 165–7.
174. Vol. II, 82.
175. Vol. VI, 234.
176. Vol. I., 180.
177. *Id.,* 202–3.
178. Id., 523.
179. Vol. V, 160.
180. Vol. VII, 185.
181. Vol. I, 484–5.
182. Thompson, *Loc.cit.,* 494.
183. Vol. I, 148.
184. Vol. III, 390–1.
185. Vol. VII, 489.
186. *Id,* 490.
187. *Id.,* 494.
188. See for this episode Thompson, *op. cit.,* 352.
189. Vol. V, 98.
190. Vol. VI, 164–5.
191. Id, 257.
192. Vol. IV, 545–5.
193. Vol. V, 291–2.
194. Vol. IV, 541.
195. Vol. V, 484.
196. Vol. V, 304.
197. Vol. VI, 321–2.
198. Vol. V, 118–9.
199. *Id.,* 185.
200. Id., 460–1.
201. Vol. II, 437.
202. Vol. III, 357.
203. Id, 358.
204. Id, 361.
205. Vol. IV, 192.

206. Vol. I, 93.
207. Vol. II, 32ff.
208. Vol. V, 365.
209. Vol. VI, 272.
210. Id., 270.
211. Vol. VII, 43–4.
212. Vol. VII, 118.
213. Id, 209.
214. Vol. VI, 163.
215. Vol. VI, 448, 485; Vol. VII, 510; Vol. VIII, 3.

Chapter V.

216. Vol. II, 220–1; see also 221–2.
217. Vol. II, 532.
218. Vol. VIII, 552.
219. Vol. IV, 267.
220. "Fragment," circa August 26, 1863. Vol. VI, 410.
221. First Inaugural Address—Final Text. March 4, 1861. Vol. IV, 270.
222. Speech at Kalamazoo of October 27, 1856. Vol. II, 366.
223. Response to a Serenade, November 10, 1864, Vol. VIII, 100.
224. Vol. IV, 438.
225. September 17, 1859 (?), Vol. III, 462.
226. Id., 468–9.
227. Vol. III, 478. Cf. "Annual Message to Congress," December 3, 1861, Vol. V, 52–3.
228. Vol. IV, 161.
229. Vol. IV, 168–9.
230. Vol. II, 499–500.
231. Vol. VII, 40.
232. Vol. VII, 38–39.
233. Vol. III, 380.
234. Vol. IV, 24–25.
235. Vol. II, 124.
236. Vol. IV, 437.
237. Vol. VII, 512.
238. Speech to the 189th New York Volunteers, October 24, 1864. Vol. VIII, 75.
239. "Address before the Young Men's Lyceum of Springfield, Illinois." January 27, 1838. Vol. I, 108. Illegible portions of the text are bracketed as given by Nicolay and Hay.
240. Vol. V, 388; cf. also the letter to Major General John A. McClernand of January 8, 1863, Vol. VI, 48, and the Annual Message to Congress of December 3, 1861, Vol. V, 49.
241. "Reply to the Frontier Guard," April 26, 1861. Vol. IV, 345.
242. Vol. II, 355; cf. "Speech at Leavenworth, Kansas," December 3, 1859, Vol. III, 502.
243. Vol. VII, 514.
244. Thomas, *loc. cit.*
245. Vol. VII, 395.

246. Vol. VIII, 1.
247. Vol. VII, 435.
248. Vol. VII, 517.
249. Letter to Charles Francis Adams, United States Ambassador in London, of February 7, 1865. Vol. VIII, 286–87.
250. Vol. VIII, 386.
251. Vol. I, 109.
252. *Ibid.,* 110–12.
253. *Ibid.,* 112.
254. *Ibid.,* 113.
255. *Ibid.,* 113–114.
256. *Ibid.,* 114.
257. *Ibid.,* 115.
258. *Ibid.,* 451–52.
259. Vol. II, 126.
260. Vol. IV, 237.
261. Randall, *op. cit.,* Vol. 2, 318.
262. Vol. IV, 426.
263. Vol. IV, 439.
264. Vol. V, 212.
265. Vol. VII, 23.
266. Vol. VIII, 100.
267. Vol. VIII, 101. CF. also Vol. V, 319; Vol. VI, 319; Vol. VIII, 184.
268. Vol. VIII, 101.
269. Ibid.
270. Vol. VIII, 333.

PART TWO

Introduction

 i. T. E., Lawrence, *Seven Pillars of Wisdom* (Great Britain, 1935; rpt. N.Y.: Penguin, 1978); 22–23. See Roland N. Stromberg, *Redemption by War: The Intellectuals and 1914* (Lawrence: Regents Press of Kansas, 1982).
 ii. H. Richard Niebuhr, *The Kingdom of God in America* (N.Y.: Harper and Row, 1959), 121–22.
 iii. This definition of faith is derived in large part from the work of H. Richard Niebuhr. Niebuhr himself was indebted to the American philosopher Josiah Royce for the "loyalty" feature of this approach to faith.
 iv. Herbert Butterfield, "Morality and Historical Process in International Affairs," unpublished manuscript for June 12, 1956, meeting of Columbia University Seminar on Theory of International Politics, p. 1, as quoted in Kenneth W. Thompson, *Christian Ethics and the Dilemmas of Foreign Policy,* The Lilly Endowment Research Program in Christianity and Politics (Durham, N.C.: Duke Univ. Press, 1959), 98–99.
 v. Waldo Beach, "The Pattern of Providence," *Theology Today,* 18 (1959), 234; H. Richard Niebuhr, *The Responsible Self,* p. 173; Langdon Gilkey, *Reaping the Whirlwind: A Christian Interpretation of History* (N.Y.: Seabury, 1976), 178.

Chapter I.

1. William J. Wolf, "Abraham Lincoln and Calvinism," in *Calvinism and the Political Order,* ed. George L. Hunt (Phila: Westminister, 1965), 152–53.
2. Stephen B. Oates, *With Malice Toward None: The Life of Abraham Lincoln* (N.Y.: Mentor-New American Library, 1977), 446.
3. J. G. Randall and Richard N. Current, *Lincoln the President: Last Full Measure* (N.Y.: Dodd, Mead, 1955), 371; Timothy L. Smith, *Revivalism and Social Reform: American Protestantism on the Eve of the Civil War* (Gloucester, Mass.: Peter Smith, 1976), 200–1; Conrad Cherry, ed., *God's New Israel: Religious Interpretations of American Destiny* (Englewood Cliffs, N.J.: Prentice-Hall, 1971), 159; Ronald Marstin, *Beyond Our Tribal Gods; The Maturing of Faith* (Maryknoll, N.Y.: Orbis, 1979), 82; John Updike, *Buchanan Dying: A Play* (N.Y.: Knopf, 1974), 253; Richard Hofstadter, ed., *Great Issues in American History From the Revolution to the Civil War, 1765–1865* (N.Y.: Vintage, 1958), 385; Ernest G. Bormann, "Fetching Good Out of Evil: A Rhetorical Use of Calamity," *Quarterly Journal of Speech,* 63 (1977), 137; John Wesley Hill, *Abraham Lincoln: Man of God,* 2nd ed. (N.Y.: Putnam's, 1922), 356; George B. Forgie, *Patricide in the House Divided* (N.Y.: Norton, 1979), 289; Geoffrey C. Ward, *Lincoln and His Legend* (Springfield: Sangamon State Univ., 1978), 25–26; Richard S. Emrich, *Lincoln and God: A Meditation on the Life of Abraham Lincoln* (Cincinnati: Forward Movement, n.d.), 8–9; Ida M. Tarbell, *The Life of Abraham Lincoln* (N.Y.: Lincoln Memorial Association, 1900), II, 221.
4. Elton Trueblood, *Abraham Lincoln: Theologian of American Anguish* (N.Y.: Harper and Row, 1973), 121.
5. 1 Cor. 13:12 (NEB).
6. Trueblood, 88.
7. David D. Anderson, *Abraham Lincoln* (N.Y.: Twayne, 1970), 162.
8. Robert Benne and Philip Hefner, *Defining America: A Christian Critique of the American Dream* (Phila.: Fortress, 1974), 126.
9. The passage suggested by Reagan says that "if my people who are called by my name humble themselves, and pray and seek my face, and turn from their wicked ways, then I will hear from heaven, and will forgive their sins and heal their land" (2 Chron. 7:14, RSV). See the entire passage including the divine admonition, 7:11–12.
10. William J. Wolf, *Lincoln's Religion* (Phila.: Pilgrim, 1970), 120.
11. Raymond W. Settle, "Abraham Lincoln's Faith," *Christianity Today,* Feb. 3, 1958, 7; Charles Phillips, "Abraham Lincoln," *The Catholic World,* Feb. 1929, 513; Tarbell, II, 90; Ronald D. Rietveld, "Lincoln and the Politics of Morality," *J. of the Ill. State Historical Society,* 68 (1975), 33; Harlan Hoyt Horner, *The Growth of Lincoln's Faith* (N.Y.: Abingdon, 1939), 126–28; Ruth Painter Randall, "Lincoln's Faith Was Born of Anguish," *New York Times Magazine,* Feb. 7, 1954, 26; Anderson, 105; Trueblood, 7, 9, 10, 26–27, 89; G. Frederick Owen, *Abraham Lincoln: The Man and His Faith* (Wheaton, Ill.: Tyndale, 1981), 163–64; Osborn H. Oldroyd, *The Lincoln Memorial: Album-Immortelles* (N.Y.: Carleton, 1882), 366.
12. *The Collected Works of Abraham Lincoln,* ed. Roy P. Basler (New

Brunswick, N.J.: Rutgers Univ. Press, 1953), I, 289. Lincoln quotes Ex. 14:13. All references to *The Collected Works* will be cited henceforth as CW.

13. CW, I, 338.
14. CW, II, 97. Professor Robert V. Bruce of Boston Univ. stated in a lecture recently that Lincoln's words in this letter were probably a "harmless lie" designed merely to comfort a dying man. *Lincoln and the Riddle of Death*, The Fourth Annual R. Gerald McMurtry Lecture (Fort Wayne, Ind.: Louis A. Warren Lincoln Library and Museum, 1981), 13–14. The evidence he adduces to support his interpretation is meager at best. I am grateful to Dr. Mark E.Neely, Jr., director of the Warren Library and Museum, for making a copy of this lecture available to me.
15. CW, II, 132.
16. Wolf, *Lincoln's Religion*, 65–66, 115.
17. Wolf, *Lincoln's Religion*, 184.
18. Wolf, *Lincoln's Religion*, 185.
19. Wolf, *Lincoln's Religion*, 120.
20. CW, IV, 482.
21. CW, V, 403–4.
22. CW, VII, 535–36.
23. CW, VII, 396.
24. CW, VIII, 100.
25. Wolf, *Lincoln's Religion*, 148–50.
26. John F. Berens, *Providence and Patriotism in Early America 1640–1815* (Charlottesville: Univ. Press of Virginia, 1978), 22; Giles Gunn, *New World Metaphysics and the Religious Interpretation of American Writing*, The University Lecture in Religion (Tempe, Ariz.; Arizona State Univ., 1980), 7–8; Thomas A. Schafer, rev. of *The American Jeremiad*, by Sacvan Bercovitch, *J. of Religion*, 60 (1980), 345; Perry Miller, "From the Covenant to the Revival," in *The Shaping of American Religion*, ed. James Ward Smith and A. Leland Jamison, Religion in American Life, I (Princeton: Princeton Univ. Press, 1961), 327.
27. Miller, 325.
28. Berens, 34–35.
29. Berens, 44–45.
30. Berens, 4, 50–54.
31. Berens, 58.
32. Berens, 65, 87.
33. Berens, ch. 6.
34. Berens, 156.
35. Berens, 150, 163.
37. Miller, 346.
38. Bormann, 137, 138.
39. William J. Wolf, *Freedom's Holy Light* (Wakefield, MA: Parameter, 1977), 57. Cf. Miller, 359–60.
40. Donald E. Miller, "Sectarianism and Secularization: The Work of Bryan Wilson," *Religious Studies Review*, 5 (1979), 169.
41. James W. Silver, *Confederate Morale and Church Propaganda*, 2nd ed. (1957; rpt. N.Y.: Norton, 1967), 31.
42. Daniel D. Williams, "Tradition and Experience in American Theology,"

in *The Shaping of American Religion,* 488–91; William Anthony Clebsch, "Baptism of Blood: A Study of Christian Contributions to the Interpretation of the Civil War in American History," Diss. Union Theol. Sem. in N.Y. 1957, 69, 75, 76, 81, 83, 90–92, 122, 127, 134, 215; William A. Clebsch, *From Sacred to Profane America: The Role of Religion in American History* (N.Y.: Harper and Row, 1968), 194–96.

43. Judith Conrad Wimmer, "American Catholic Interpretations of the Civil War," Diss. Drew Univ. 1980, 239–40.
44. Wimmer, 11. See also 240.
45. Wimmer, 242.
46. Wimmer, 244. See also 276–77.
47. Wimmer, 277.
48. Evansville *Journal,* April 20, 1861, as quoted in *The Causes of the Civil War,* ed. Kenneth M. Stamp, rev. ed. (Englewood Cliffs, N.J.: Prentice-Hall, 1974), 108.
49. Harriet Beecher Stowe, *Uncle Tom's Cabin: Or, Life Among the Lowly* (Boston: Osgood, 1873), 322.
50. Smith, 200, 209.
51. Paul Eugene Grosjean, "The Concept of American Nationhood: Theological Interpretation as Reflected by the Northern Mainline Protestant Preachers in the Late Civil War Period," Diss. Drew Univ. 1977, 68.
52. Grosjean, 168.
53. Smith, ch. 13; Stephen A. Marini, rev. of *American Apocalypse: Yankee Protestants and the Civil War 1860–1869,* by James H. Moorhead, *J. of the American Academy of Religion,* 47 (1979), 675; Donald G. Matthews, rev. of, among other works, *American Apocalypse,* by Moorhead, and *The Sacred Cause of Liberty: Republican Thought and the Millennium in Revolutionary New England,* by Nathan Orr Hatch, *Religious Studies Review,* 5 (1979), 15–21.
54. CW, IV, 482.
55. CW, V, 403–4.
56. CW, V, 478.
57. CW, VI, 155–56.
58. CW, VI, 332.
59. Wolf, *Lincoln's Religion,* 168.
60. CW, VI, 497; Lincoln National Life Insurance Company, *Lincoln Proclaims Thanksgiving Day* (Fort Wayne, Ind.: Lincoln National Life, [1976]; Trueblood, p. 91; and see Carl Sandburg, *Abraham Lincoln: The War Years* (N.Y.: Harcourt, 1939), II, 359; III, 375.
61. CW, VII, 281–83.
62. CW, VII, 334.
63. CW, VIII, 55.
64. CW, VII, 535.
65. Donald Capps, "The Death of Father Abraham: The Assassination of Lincoln and Its Effect on Frontier Mythology," in *Religious Encounters With Death: Insights from the History and Anthropology of Religions,* ed. Frank E. Reynolds and Earle H. Waugh (Univ. Park: Penn. State Univ. Press, 1977), 243.
66. CW, VIII, 333.
67. Hofstadter, p. 385; *Literary History of the United States,* ed. Robert E.

Spiller et al., rev. ed. (N.Y.: Macmillan, 1957), 509; James R. Andrews, *A Choice of Worlds: The Practice and Criticism of Public Discourse* (N.Y.: Harper and Row, 1973), 43; Paul M. Angle, "Lincoln's Power with Words," in *Papers of the Abraham Lincoln Association,* III, ed. Kathryn Wrigley (Springfield: Abraham Lincoln Assn., 1981), 26.

68. CW, VIII, 83.
69. CW, VIII, 332.
70. CW, VIII, 399–400.
71. George M. Fredrickson, "The Search for Order and Community," in *The Public and the Private Lincoln,* ed. Cullom Davis, et. al. (Carbondale: Southern Ill. Univ. Press, 1979), ch. 6.
72. Ernest Lee Tuveson, *Redeemer Nation: The Idea of America's Millennial Role* (Chicago: Univ. of Chicago Press, 1968), 206–7; see also Sydney E. Ahlstrom, *A Religious History of the American People* (Garden City, N.Y.: Image-Doubleday, 1975), II, 137.
73. Wimmer.
74. Chester Forrester Dunham, *The Attitudes of the Northern Clergy Toward the South, 1860–65,* United States Pamphlets, 19 (Chicago: Univ. of Chicago Libraries, 1942), 82–86; see also Cherry, pt. 4.
75. Thomas Smyth, "The War of the South Vindicated," *The Southern Presbyterian Review,* 15 (1863), 480, 482, 483, 497, 498.
76. Martin E. Marty, *Righteous Empire: The Protestant Experience in America* (N.Y.: Dial, 1970), 120.
77. *Literary History of the U.S.,* 508.
78. Angle, 26–27.
79. CW, VII, 226.
80. Ahlstrom, II, 137.
81. A. Lincoln to Cabinet, April 14, 1865, as quoted in *The Lincoln Reader,* ed. Paul M. Angle (New Brunswick, N.J.: Rutgers Univ. Press, 1947), 520; J. G. Randall, "Abraham Lincoln," *Dictionary of American Biography,* ed. Dumas Malone (N.Y.: Scribner's, 1933), VI, 257.
82. William Lee Miller, "Lincoln's Second Inaugural: The Zenith of Statecraft," *Center Magazine,* July/August 1980, 62.
83. Charles Sumner, "Promises of the Declaration of Independence, and Abraham Lincoln," Eulogy on Abraham Lincoln, before the Municipal Authorities of the City of Boston, June 1, 1865, in *Charles Sumner His Complete Works* (1900; rpt. N.Y.: Negro Universities Press, 1969), XII, 284. See Carl Sandburg, Introd., *Lincoln's Devotional* (Great Neck, N.Y.: Channel, 1957), ix. Sandburg says that Senator Sumner was the man who addressed Lincoln.
84. CW, VIII, 332–33.
85. Ps. 19:9 (KJV).
86. Bormann, 138.
87. CW, VIII, 326.
88. CW, VIII, 152, 141.
89. Andrews, 42. See also 43.
90. Sidney E. Mead, *The Lively Experiment* (N.Y.: Harper and Row, 1963), 143–44.
91. CW, VIII, 333.
92. CW, VIII, 356.

93. Although in their approaches to the problem of evil significant differences exist between them, I think an important feature of Lincoln's view is expressed in Austin Farrer's statement that "The Christian sufferer goes on quietly with his duties, and embraces his opportunities of well-doing, sustained by the general belief that through these things God will make suffered evils fruitful of good. He needs a faith in the working of particular providence, not a detection of it." *Love Almighty and Ills Unlimited* (London: Fontana-Collins, 1962) 172.

94. Richard M. Weaver, *The Ethics of Rhetoric* (Chicago: Regnery, 1953), 110.

95. Norman Graebner, "Abraham Lincoln: Conservative Statesman," in *The Enduring Lincoln,* ed. Norman Graebner (Urbana: Univ. of Ill. Press, 1959), 80, 81, 84, 87; see also T. Harry Williams, "Abraham Lincoln: Pragmatic Democrat," in *The Enduring Lincoln,* 33.

96. CW, VII, 504–5.

97. CW, VII, 512.

98. CW, VIII, 184.

99. CW, VI, 410.

100. Bruce Catton, *This Hallowed Ground* (N.Y.: Pocket, 1960), 487.

101. Daniel J. Simundson, *Faith Under Fire: Biblical Interpretations of Suffering* (Minneapolis: Augsburg, 1980), 38–39.

102. John Hick, *Evil and the God of Love,* rev. ed. (San Francisco: Harper and Row, 1978), 281.

103. John Bowker, *The Sense of God* (Oxford: Oxford Univ. Press, 1973), 113. Two other writers on this subject who have impressed and influenced me are Walter L. Michel, "Job's Real Friend: Elihu," sermon preached at Rockefeller Chapel, Univ. of Chicago, July 19, 1981, unpublished manuscript, esp. pp. 3–8; and David L. Bartlett, "The Word Is Near," *Criterion,* 20, No. 2 (1981), 20–21, a sermon on Rom. 10:1–13, preached at Bond Chapel, Univ. of Chicago. Lincoln, like Job in the end, is able to trust in God without knowing the divine reasons for everything. The Book of Job might, in fact, have provided some comfort to the afflicted President. Mrs. Lincoln's servant, Elizabeth Keckley, tells a story in her autobiography about a dejected Lincoln receiving hope from the pages of Job in 1863. See *Behind the Scenes or, Thirty Years a Slave, and Four Years in the White House* (N.Y.: Carleton, 1868), 118–20. Bartlett develops the Pauline passage in such a way as to caution all of us against trying in our speculations and other intellectual and academic endeavors, to "bring Christ down."

104. CW, VII, 535.

105. CW, I, 289.

106. James F. Wilson, "Some Memories of Lincoln," *The North American Review,* Dec. 1896, 667–69.

107. CW, V, 404.

108. CW, VI, 114; see also CW, IV, 190, 234; V, 212–13; VI, 244–45, 531; VII, 333. See Wolf-Dieter Marsch, *Christlicher Glaube und Demokratisches Ethos* (Hamburg: Furche-Verlag, 1958), 83.

109. CW, IV, 220–21; see also IV, 199, 204.

110. CW, V, 478; see also IV, 236; I, 289. It was much more common in Lincoln's day than our own for people to see themselves as instruments

of the Almighty. Gen. George McClellan, for example, told his wife that God had chosen him to save the Union. Stefan Lorant, *Lincoln: A Picture Story of His Life*, rev. ed. (N.Y.: Bonanza, 1975), pp. 141, 160. These claims to be God's instrument can indicate either pride or humility in a person. In McClellan's case I am afraid it was more the former. But for others, like Lincoln, the claim pointed away from any kind of arrogant self-assertion. Mother Teresa of Calcutta is another one who demonstrates how in an individual there can be this sense of both vocation and lowliness when she states, "I'm only a little instrument in God's hands, that's all, a little pencil." Mimeographed transcript of *Prime Time Sunday* television program, Dec. 9, 1979, p. 10; see also 14.

111. CW, V, 518.
112. Wolf, *Freedom's Holy Light*, 19.
113. Thomas J. Pressly, *Americans Interpret Their Civil War* (N.Y.: Free Press, 1965), 34–35.
114. CW, VII, 346.
115. Randall and Current, 374. Professor Bruce (see n. 14) argues that Lincoln gave no indication at all of any belief in an afterlife—a dubious contention.
116. CW, VI, 16–17.
117. Tarbell, II, 158.
118. Catton, 52.
119. J. G. Randall, *Lincoln the President: Midstream* (N.Y.: Dodd, Mead, 1952), 16.
120. Francis B. Carpenter, *Six Months at the White House* (N.Y.: Hurd and Houghton, 1866), 32, 170–78, 284–85, 297–98. Lincoln's personal secretary John Hay reports in his diary account for July 18, 1863, that that day he joined the President and another gentleman in "deciding on Court Martials. . . . I was amused at the eagerness with which the President caught at any fact which would justify him in saving the life of a condemned soldier. . . . Cases of cowardice he was specially averse to punishing with death. He said it would frighten the poor devils too terribly to shoot them." *Letters of John Hay and Extracts from Diary* (Washington: n.p., 1908), I, 88.
121. Sandburg, *The War Years*, II, 85; IV, 171.
122. Sandburg, *The War Years*, II, 91; see also III, 470–81.
123. Ward Hill Lamon, *Recollections of Abraham Lincoln 1847–1865*, ed. Dorothy Lamon Teillard (Washington: The editor, 1911), 103–4.
124. CW, VI, 375–76; V, 438–39; VI, 447; VII, 398; VIII, 399–400; VII, 253–54; VI, 13, 314, 346; VII, 53, 528, 334, 395; VIII, 332–33; VI, 114.
125. CW, VIII, 117.
126. CW, V, 510.
127. Noah Brooks, *Washington, D.C., in Lincoln's Time*, ed. Herbert Mitgang (N.Y.: Collier, 1962), pp. 80–81. The poem "Lexington" is about Revolutionary War soldiers courageously fighting and dying for their country. *The Complete Poetical Works of Oliver Wendell Holmes* (Boston: Houghton Mifflin, 1923), 28–29. See also the story Carpenter tells of a meeting between Lincoln and Pennsylvania Governor Curtin during which the subject of the respect due the volunteer soldier was brought up. Carpenter, 82.

128. CW, V, 213.
129. See, among others, Paul C. Nagel, *This Sacred Trust: American Nationality 1798–1898* (N.Y.: Oxford Univ. Press, 1971), 157–58; Catton, 488; Harry V. Jaffa, *Crisis of the House Divided: An Interpretation of the Issues in the Lincoln-Douglas Debates* (Garden City, N.Y.: Doubleday, 1959), 190.
130. Just such an approach is taken in an early sermon by Albert Schweitzer. See "Sacrifice of Others," in *Reverence for Life*, trans. Reginald H. Fuller (Munich, 1966; rpt. N.Y.: Pilgrim, 1969), 101–7.
131. Horace Bushnell, "Our Obligations to the Dead," in *Building Eras in Religion* (N.Y.: Scribner's, 1881), 319–55.
132. Clebsch, "Baptism of Blood," 92.
133. Ahlstrom, II, 135.
134. Farrer, p. 15. See Roger L. Shinn, *Beyond This Darkness* (N.Y.: Association, 1946), 35.
135. CW, VII, 394.
136. "Unlike some presidents, Lincoln was unimpressed by military show. He saw no glory in bloodshed." Ward, *Lincoln and His Legend,* 21.
137. Sandburg, *The War Years,* II, 476.
138. Mentor Graham recalled that Lincoln defended the idea of universal salvation: he "took the passage, 'As in Adam all die, even so in Christ shall all be made alive,' and followed up with the proposition that whatever the breach or injury of Adam's transgressions to the human race was, which no doubt was very great, was made just and right by the atonement of Christ. . . ." According to Isaac Cogdal, Lincoln "added [to a statement made in conversation against the notion of eternal punishment for sinners] that all that was lost by the transgression of Adam was made good by the atonement: all that was lost by the fall was made good by the sacrifice. . . ." Wolf, *Lincoln's Religion,* 46–47, 104.
139. CW, V, 518.
140. CW, I, 271–79. See R. P. Randall, "Lincoln's Faith Was Born of Anguish," 27.
141. *Literary History of the U.S.,* 779.
142. Herbert Butterfield, *History and Human Relations* (London: Collins, 1951), 109–110. Cf. the attitude toward the enemy expressed in Mark Twain's War Prayer. Mark Twain, "The War Prayer," in *Europe and Elsewhere* (N.Y.: Harper, 1923), 394–98.
143. CW, IV, 142–43.
144. See Allan Nevins, *The Statesmanship of the Civil War,* Univ. of Virginia Page-Barbour Lectures, 1951 (N.Y.: Macmillan, 1953), 74–76.
145. CW, IV, 208–209; VIII, 241.
146. CW, VI, 64.
147. CW, IV, 240; V, 198; VII, 23.
148. Karl Barth, "Letter to a Pastor in the German Democratic Republic," in *How to Serve God in a Marxist Land* (N.Y.: Association, 1959), 50.
149. See Charles Kesler, "A Special Meaning of the Declaration of Independence: A Tribute to Harry V. Jaffa," *National Review,* July 6, 1979, p. 854; Robert Kelley, *The Cultural Pattern in American Politics* (N.Y.: Knopf, 1979), 216; Jaffa, 186, 224, 269, 322–23, 348–60, 408–409.
150. CW, VIII, 333.

151. CW, V, 537.
152. *The Collected Works of Abraham Lincoln Supplement 1832–1865,* ed. Roy P. Basler (Westport Ct.: Greenwood, 1974), 45. Cited hereafter as Supp.
153. CW, IV, 240.
154. CW, VII, 504–5, 512.
155. CW, IV, 233, 240.
156. CW, VI, 88–89; VIII, 100.
157. CW, VI, 410; V, 537.
158. See David Donald, *Lincoln Reconsidered,* 2nd ed. (N.Y.: Vintage, 1961), 122.
159. "No President has ever had the detailed knowledge of the Bible that Lincoln had." Wolf, *Lincoln's Religion,* 131.
160. Robert McAfee Brown, *The Spirit of Protestantism* (London: Oxford Univ. Press, 1961), 250 n. 16.
161. C. S. Lewis, *The Problem Of Pain* (N.Y.: Macmillan, 1962), 104.
162. CW, VI, 64.
163. CW, V, 537.
164. CW, V, 478; VII, 50; VII, 350; VIII, 151. See also uses of the word to refer to a severe test within more particular circumstances, VI, 28; VII, 535; VIII, 100.
165. CW, VII, 374, 388.
166. CW, VIII, 1, 332.
167. Reinhold Niebuhr, "The Religion of Abraham Lincoln," in *Lincoln and the Gettysburg Address,* ed. Allan Nevins (Urbana: Univ. of Ill. Press, 1964), 75.
168. Melvin B. Endy, Jr., "Abraham Lincoln and American Civil Religion: A Reinterpretation," *Church History,* 44 (1975), 229–41.
169. Endy, 231, 232, 240.
170. Richard N. Current, *The Lincoln Nobody Knows* (N.Y.: McGraw-Hill, 1958), 66–71. Sandburg comments on the story of Lincoln meeting his own corpse in a dream, *The War Years,* IV, 245. See CW, VI, 256, for the telegraph message concerning Tad's pistol.
171. Chittenden transmits a three-page, word-by-word account of a conversation he supposedly had with Lincoln. The President not only told Chittenden that "when the Almighty wants me to do or not to do a particular thing, he finds a way of letting me know it," but also assured him that the Almighty "is on our side [in the Civil War], and so is the Bible . . ." and that "all we have to do [to be protected "against any fatal defeat"] is to trust the Almighty and keep right on obeying his orders and executing his will." All three of these assertions are at odds both in tone and in substance with what we know to be the lineaments of Lincoln's theological outlook. *Recollections of President Lincoln and His Administration* (N.Y.: Harper and Bros., 1891), 448–50.
172. Wolf, *Lincon's Religion,* 19–20.
173. Carpenter, 89–90.
174. *Diary and Correspondence of Salmon P. Chase* (N.Y.: Da Capo Press, 1971), 88.
175. *Diary of Gideon Welles,* 1861–March 30, 1864 (Boston: Houghton-Mifflin, 1911), I, 143.

176. William J. Wolf, "Lincoln and the Bible," *Presbyterian Life,* July 1, 1964, 9.
177. Peter Shaffer, *Amadeus* (N.Y.: Harper and Row, 1980), 8. See also 40, 47, 67, 88.
178. Carpenter, 22–23.
179. John Hope Franklin, *The Emancipation Proclamation* (Garden City, N.Y.: Anchor, 1965).
180. Letter received from John Hope Franklin, Feb. 5, 1982. Used by permission.
181. Wolf, *Lincoln's Religion,* 19.
182. James F. Rusling, *Men and Things I Saw in Civil War Days,* 15, as quoted in Wolf, *Lincoln's Religion,* 125.
183. Wolf, *Lincoln's Religion,* 124.
184. Sandburg, *The War Years,* III, 378.
185. Different versions of the Sickles story may be found in Orrin Henry Pennell, *Religious Views of Abraham Lincoln* (North Benton, Ohio: O. H. Pennell, 1899), 32; Madison C. Peters, *Abraham Lincoln's Religion* (Boston: Badger, 1909), 37; Owen, 154.
186. Peters, 37.
187. Owen, 154.
188. William J. Johnson, *Abraham Lincoln: The Christian* (1913; rpt. Milford, Mich.: Mott Media, 1976), 106, 166.
189. CW, III, 204.
190. CW, V, 420.
191. Carpenter, 239.
192. Geoffrey C. Ward, *Lincoln Slavery and Civil Rights* (Springfield: Sangamon State Univ., 1978), 21; CW, VII, 368; VII, 542; Supp., 43–45.
193. CW, II, 461.
194. Donald, ch. 7.
195. David Baily Harned, *Faith and Virtue* (Phila.: Pilgrim, 1973), ch. 9 ("Prudence and God"); H. Richard Niebuhr, *The Responsible Self.*

Chapter II.

196. Endy, 232–33.
197. M. E. Bradford, "The Lincoln Legacy: A Long View," *Modern Age,* 24 (1980), 358–62.
198. Adolf Hitler, *Mein Kampf* (N.Y.: Reynal and Hitchcock, 1940), 116 n. 5, 600–601.
199. Edmund Wilson, *Patriotic Gore* (N.Y.: Oxford Univ. Press, 1962), xvii, xviii.
200. T. Harry Williams, *Two War Leaders: Lincoln and Davis* (Springfield, Ill.: Abraham Lincoln Assn., 1972), 20.
201. Carl Becker, *The Declaration of Independence: A Study in the History of Political Ideas* (N.Y.: Knopf, 1942), 242, 246–48, 254–55.
202. Robert Penn Warren, "In the Time of 'All the King's Men,'" *The New York Times Book Review,* May 31, 1981, pp. 9, 39–40; *World Enough and Time* (N.Y.: Vintage-Random House, 1979), 218, 117, 150, 153, 276, 286–87, 463, 293.

203. Lawrence, 393. Earlier Lawrence states regarding himself and the Arabs that "we had surrendered, not body alone, but soul to the overmastering greed of victory," 27.

204. Lorant, 238.

205. Becker, 243 n. 4.

206. William S. McFeely, *Grant: A Biography* (N.Y.: Norton, 1981), 183.

207. CW, IV, 233; IV, 246; VIII, 101. See the comment on this point in Mortimer J. Adler and William Gorman, "Reflections: The Gettysburg Address," *The New Yorker,* September 8, 1975, p. 48: "Despite the reiteration, 'saving the Union,' taken by itself, quite evidently did not yield the moral justification for the Civil War. Saving the Union was of such awesome importance only because the preservation of the Union was indispensable to this nation's promotion of 'that something,' struggled for in the War of Independence, which 'held out a great promise to all the people of the world [for] all time to come.'"

208. These statements are based on Michael F. Holt, "The Civl War and Presidential Leadership," lecture delivered at the University of Virginia, March 2, 1981.

209. For a good description of an analogous situation during World War II see Garry Wills, "The Kennedy Imprisonment," *The Atlantic Monthly,* Jan. 1982, 38.

210. Don E. Fehrenbacher, "Lincoln and the Constitution," in *The Public and the Private Lincoln,* 128.

211. David Donald, *Lincoln Reconsidered,* ch. 7.

212. Trueblood, pp. 4, 54; Kenneth W. Thompson, "Survival Imperiled: The Threat of Illusion and Despair," *The Virginia Quarterly Review,* 55 (1979), 418, 420–21; Kenneth W. Thompson, *The Moral Issue in State-craft* (Baton Rouge: Louisiana State Univ. Press, 1966), 50. See T. Harry Williams, "Lincoln and the Pragmatic Tradition," in *Ideas in Action: Documentary and Interpretive Readings in American History,* ed. Leland D. Baldwin (N.Y.: American, 1968), I, 504–510; Dumas Malone, "Jefferson and Lincoln," *The Abraham Lincoln Quarterly,* 5 (1949), 347.

213. CW, IV, 243; IV, 265, VIII; 52; see Fehrenbacher, 133–36. Lincoln's trust in the eventually-expressed sagacity of the American people may be contrasted with the attitude of many elected officials in our own day who apparently lack confidence in the capacity of citizens to elect men and women who will truly be good for the country; see *The Connecticut Mutual Life Report on American Values in the '80s: The Impact of Belief* (Hartford: Conn. Mutual Life Ins. Co., 1981), p. 26: "Not only does the public lack confidence in its leaders, fully half the surveyed leaders (50%) believe that the public cannot be relied upon to select the sort of leaders the nation needs."

214. H. Richard Niebuhr, *Radical Monotheism and Western Culture, With Supplementary Essays* (N.Y.: Harper and Row, 1960), 77.

215. Jaffa, 224, 269.

216. Paul Simon, *Lincoln's Preparation for Greatness: The Illinois Legislative Years* (Urbana: Univ. of Ill. Press, 1971).

217. Niebuhr, *Radical Monotheism,* 77; also, 122, 126. Cf. the views of Donald, 142–43; Wolf, *Lincoln's Religion,* 116–18, 150–53; Mead, *The*

Lively Experiment, 81, 86, 88–89; and James H. Moorhead, *American Apocalypse: Yankee Protestants and the Civil War 1860–1869* (New Haven: Yale Univ. Press, 1978), 175.

218. Cf. Frances Fitzgerald, *Fire in the Lake: The Vietnamese and the Americans in Vietnam* (N.Y.: Vintage-Random House, 1973), 115–16, 251, 439–40. For a good account of Lincoln's restrained conduct in foreign relations see Norman A. Graebner, "Abraham Lincoln: Conservative Statesman," 86–91, 94.

219. Hans J. Morgenthau, "Human Rights and Foreign Policy," in *Herbert Butterfield: The Ethics of History and Politics,* ed. Kenneth W. Thompson (Washington, D.C.: Univ. Press of America, 1980), 103.

220. Dwight G. Anderson, *Abraham Lincoln: The Quest for Immortality* (N.Y.: Knopf, 1982), 16, 137, 158, 168, 169, 177–78, 189, and *passim.*

221. Endy, 233, 238; George M. Fredrickson, "A Man but Not a Brother: Abraham Lincoln and Racial Equality," *J. of Southern History,* 41 (1975), 44.

222. Charles D. Cashdollar, "The Social Implications of the Doctrine of Divine Providence: A Nineteenth-Century Debate in American Theology," *Harvard Theological Review,* 71 (1978), 273–77.

223. Ahlstrom, II, 361.

224. Kenneth W. Thompson, *Political Realism and the Crisis of World Politics: An American Approach to Foreign Policy* (Washington, D.C.: Univ. Press of America, 1982), 160; Kenneth W. Thompson, *Morality and Foreign Policy* (Baton Rouge and London: LSU Press, 1980), 52, 53, 76.

225. Thompson, *Political Realism and the Crisis of World Politics,* 14.

226. Thompson, *Morality and Foreign Policy,* 28.

227. Thompson, *Morality and Foreign Policy,* 183.

Chapter III.

228. CW, V, 478.

229. CW, VIII, 356.

230. CW, VI, 16–17.

231. H. Richard Niebuhr, *The Meaning of Revelation* (N.Y.: Macmillan, 1960), 139.

232. CW, VII, 535.

233. H. Richard Niebuhr, "The Illusions of Power," *The Pulpit,* April 1962, 7.

234. CW, VII, 535.

235. H. Richard Niebuhr, "The Idea of Covenant and American Democracy," *Church History,* 23 (1954), 131; "Illusions," 4; *Kingdom,* 55; *Responsible Self,* 164–65, 170–73.

236. CW, I, 289.

237. CW, VIII, 333.

238. H. Richard Niebuhr, "The Idea of Covenant," 131; *Responsible Self,* 173.

239. These are, of course, Niebuhr's themes; e.g., *Responsible Self,* 123–26, 170; "Illusions," 4.

240. *Responsible Self,* p. 169; see James W. Fowler, *To See the Kingdom: The Theological Vision of H. Richard Niebuhr* (Nashville: Abingdon, 1974), 195–97.

241. CW, VII, 282; James M. Gustafson, Introd., *Responsible Self,* 34–35.

242. H. Richard Niebuhr, "A Christian Interpretation of War," unpub. mimeographed ms., 4. I am grateful to Mrs. Florence M. Niebuhr and to her son, Richard R. Niebuhr, for making this essay available to me along with some other materials.

243. CW, VII, 282; VIII, 333.

244. CW, VII, 23.

245. H. Richard Niebuhr, *Meaning*, 90–91.

246. H. Richard Niebuhr, "War as Crucifixion," *The Christian Century*, 60 (1943); 513, 514; "War as the Judgment of God," *The Christian Century*, 59 (1942), 631. In another article, "Illusions," p. 5, in which he discusses Is. 10, Niebuhr writes: "We need to forget in the light of the gospel of Jesus Christ, all those notes and overtones of divine anger and human punishment which are present in Isaiah's formulation of God's word. . . . We are dealing with the Holy One; with holy love that is not envious of man, that needs no vengeance, that does not desire the pain or destruction of his creatures, yet does insist on their healing, on their being made whole, on their becoming truly what they are in possibility."

247. H. Richard Niebuhr, "Is God in the War", *The Christian Century*, 59 (1942), 954.

248. H. Richard Niebuhr, *Responsible Self*, 123–24.

249. CW, IV, 142–43.

250. See Graebner, pp. 77–78, 80–81.

251. See Graebner, pp. 70–71, 72, 82.

252. H. Richard Niebuhr, "War as Crucifixion," 515. Readers should consult this article and also "War as the Judgment of God," esp. 632–33, for a fuller treatment of these themes. I rely closely on each throughout this paragraph.